Victoria Buddhist Dharma Society

TIBETAN YOGA

By the same author:

THE OCCULT ARTS OF ANCIENT EGYPT
IN TUNE WITH YOUR DESTINY

PADMASAMBHAVA (LOTUS-BORN)

Founder of Tibetan yoga (8th Cent. A.D.) seated in lotus posture. *Right hand* holds vajra (thunderbolt), *left* (in lap) holds patra (begging bowl), and *pressed to left side* khatvanga (magic stick).

The image contains grain (symbol of fertility) and a square stick of wood bearing a mana (inscribed prayer).

TIBETAN YOGA

by

BERNARD BROMAGE, M.A.

SAMUEL WEISER INC.
734 Broadway, New York N.Y. 10003

First published 1952
Second Impression 1959
Third Impression June 1971

ISBN 0 87728 040 1

Reproduced and printed in Great Britain by
Latimer Trend & Co. Ltd., Whitstable

TO THE MEMORY
OF
VIOLETTA JULIA CROWLEY

CONTENTS

ILLUSTRATIONS

*The illustrations are from the
collections of the Author and of
Frank Eatwell, Esq.
(Photographed by Leslie Howard).*

CHAPTER I

PHILOSOPHY AND HISTORY OF THE SUBJECT.

IT IS NOT DIFFICULT to awaken interest in Tibet. This land of legend and romance carries in its very name all that is meant by the phrase "the sense of distance," and a great deal more besides. It is also fairly easy to touch people's minds to some realisation of the truth involved in the conceptions behind the science of Yoga. It is not so easy to convince the majority of mankind that these two names are for ever linked by something stronger than the unity of romantic sentiment.

It is attempted here to show that the religion of Tibet, in all its multifarious variety, is a logical outcome of those processes of mental and spiritual development which go under the generic name of Yoga. In this land of monasteries and snows are to be found the completed realisation of all that is implied in meditation, ritual and piety. It is natural that in a country consecrated, for ages past, to religious and psychical research there should be found the finished article rather than the first beginnings of regeneration. Where saints and men have practised for thousands of years the gymnastics of the soul, we may legitimately expect something approaching an authoritative knowledge regarding the powers, actual and potential, which exist within the mind of man.

There is a danger which may confront the reader at the start. We have films, plays and poems about Tibet; Tibet, in fact, is in the news. But the popularity of the theme may have done more harm than good. What is wanted is not a panorama of miracles and marvels, but a sense of continuity and relationship. Those lonely lamas and peripatetic Buddhists are flesh of our flesh and bone of our bone. They have reached the summits of those peaks to which we, in our best moments, aspire. They are, indeed, the elder brothers of the human race, who show us the way to our goal.

The books of many travellers err on the side of sensationalism. For instance, the otherwise admirable accounts of Mde. Alexandra David-Neel and Mr. Theodore Illion contain far too much material which is perhaps inclined to make our flesh creep, and not enough to make us realise the organic nature of the rites and customs they describe. Although there is much information to be

I

found in these volumes they will be of limited use to the reader who is considering the strictly psychological basis of religious systems different from his own. Stories of flying *Dugpas* and levitating ascetics are good enough for the Grand Guignol manner, but are secondary in the serious study of liturgy and ritual.

The greatest care must be taken not to import into our estimate of the value of the religion of Tibet, prejudices culled from our own Western conventions. It is not to be expected that understanding of these things will come until we have cleared our minds, not only of cant, but also of any false conceptions of our own superiority. Major Yeats-Brown tells us in his *Bengal Lancer* that he was put off further researches in Yoga by a *guru*, who told him that he would not be ready for the realisation of these studies until he had rid himself of certain cramping habits of the flesh, smoking, drinking, eating meat, and the rest. It may not be impertinent to suggest that these were only the outward and visible sign of a spiritual hesitancy and intransigeance which betoken the novice rather than the adept. When knowledge is attained then an occasional cigarette or glass of wine may not be so very injurious !

It may clear the ground to point out what is implied in the word "yoga." To many persons it conveys little more than an extremely uncomfortable series of bodily postures which would excite either mirth or disapproval if performed in the sight of friends. To others it conjures up pictures of remote oriental figures consecrating to the contemplation of their navel, what is no longer acceptable to man. The truth is rather more than this. "Yoga" is a generic expression for a process of religious meditation and worship which has its roots in a tried and tested apperception of the laws behind the mechanism of this and all other worlds.

Yoga means simply Union—union with the heart of the world and with all that makes for evolutionary progress. It comprises many aspects of the religious consciousness and many recipes for mental and bodily control. In the Kingdom of Yoga as in the Kingdom of Heaven there are many mansions. It is no stereotyped *vade-mecum* to any smug and superior paradise, but a "way" that includes the best in all other "ways." No human being could ever come out of a system of yogic training without an appreciable enhancement of his faculties and a consolidation of the powers of his will.

The actual founder of Yoga doctrine seems to have been Yajnavalkya, a very learned sage who lived in pre-Mahabarata times and who is credited with the authorship of the White Yajur Veda. To him is attributed the ancient fragments which recommend retirement into the solitude of the forest and concentration of the faculties in contemplation, if peace and knowledge are to be obtained. Professor Max Müller indeed points out that the exhortations of this scholar and seer made a great impression on the mind of Gautama Buddha, who made them the basis of his own message.

But, for all practical purposes, it is Patanjali who stands out in history as the codifier and philosopher exponent of the principles of Yoga. This thinker has given to the world in his *Yoga Aphorisms* a compendium of the basic ideas under all subsequent superstructures erected on the parent foundation. Here are a few of these rules of conduct. "By the establishment of continence energy is gained." "When the cause of bondage has been loosened, the yogi, by his knowledge of manifestation through the organs, enters another's body." "Success is speedy for the extremely energetic." "Each soul is potentially divine."

The inculcation of chastity is a constant through all these aphorisms. Without the dismissal from the mind of all lustful and disruptive thoughts any advance is impossible. The laws of Yoga, without being puritanic in our bad Western sense, demand, at least to start with, a very high degree of self-discipline in the devotee.

The science is generally divided into eight stages of development. First, *Yama*, which involves the excision from our daily life of any sin or idiosyncrasy which involves the "expense of spirit." (2) *Niyama* : Here the concentration is on rites, prayers and solemn dedication. (3) *Asana* : This stage introduces the practice of postures of the body and an expert control of the breath. It is obvious that, in a system which asserts body and spirit to be one, the knowledge of physiological processes is of paramount importance. It is taught that, in certain positions, the body is allowed fuller scope as a medium for mental and spiritual activity than in others. (4) *Pranayama* : An extension of the technique described in the preceding, particularly as regards the mapping-out of the main channels of force of the system. (5) *Pratyahara* : At this juncture, it is sought to withdraw the mind from the least conceivable distraction from objects in the outside world. (6) *Dharana* : Now we reinforce by all means in our power

3

the mental detachment and the spiritual release that we should have attained to by a diligent practice of the previous stages. *Dhyana* and *Samadhi*, the last two steps, lead us to the final object of Yoga — the rapt contemplation of the Absolute, and the perception of the unity in all things. It is this single-pointedness which gives not only the happiness but the knowledge which passes understanding.

There are also several schools of Yoga named according to the aspects of development with which they deal. The chief of these are Hatha, Raja, Gnana and Bhakti corresponding to bodily, occult, knowledge and devotional training respectively. We are not so far away from these concepts as we may think. There is much of Hatha Yoga in the best methods of modern physical training and even military formations and strategy : there is much of Bhakti Yoga in works such as the Spiritual Exercises of St. Ignatius Loyola and the *Meditations* of Molinos.

But many Westerners will find themselves faced with difficulties when they endeavour to emulate the methods of meditation practised in the East. Unless he has a remarkable suppleness of body the occidental student will find it impossible to reproduce the Plough postures and Fish postures which are included for his delectation in a hundred manuals on the subject. *Unless he can discover a master, accomplished in these matters, he will do well to forego any over-zealous attempt to force his body into positions for which it is not adapted. Otherwise he will end, not as an adept, but as a chronic neuropath!*

There are, in fact, many persons who practise a kind of Yoga without realising the fact in their conscious minds. If one leads a pure and virtuous life ; if the mind is free from jarring and disintegrating thoughts : then, as if automatically, the breathing processes function in balance and harmony. There are people who, by force of an inward moral strength, have succeeded in placing themselves "at the centre." In most cases, it would be unwise for them to go further. Except, possibly as mere students of a path which is not for their treading.

For Tibetan Yoga is to the more normal forms as is a painting of Veronese or Titian to steel-engraving or a study in black and white. One can, to some extent, speak in geographical metaphor. The further one goes, north of Bombay, across those rich and rolling plains, the more intensely-laden and intricately designed do religious rites become. It is to a large extent an affair

4

of concentration : the religious sense is hampered by the proximity of commerce and "civilisation." By the time we come into Sikkim and Bhutan "the noise of the world sounds from far off" in Kipling's phrase, and we are approaching a region where religion is a full-time occupation.

As everyone is aware, the Tibetans are none too friendlily disposed to the incursion of foreigners. There are cases galore of strange disappearances and apparently unprovoked assaults. This is not so arbitrary as it may sound. In a land where a large proportion of the population are monks, and contemplatives at that, the irruption of "practical" ideas and cheap sensation-seeking personalities much more anxious to lose than to find themselves, would do little to consolidate faith and fortify devotion. Besides, it is a truism of psychic research that a promiscuous immigration of unsuitable, or even unfriendly vibrations into an environment purified from most forms of taint, is a serious and upsetting factor. And the Tibetans know something of psychic research !

For a comprehension of Tibetan Yoga it is necessary to give some information on the various species of religious and philosophic belief which have influenced what may be termed the more superficial side of the national religious structure. These have coalesced to form the state system of Lamaism, or sacerdotal rule by Lamas who are, as it were, pontiffs of the hierarchy.

The chief of these, the *Dalai Lama* dwells in Lhasa, the capital ; he is regarded as the reincarnation of Avalokitesvara and is pre-eminent in all temporal matters. With him reigns the *Tashi Lama*, to whom the Tibetans have recourse in all spiritual decisions ; but actually this ruler has less power, and Tibetan history contains many records of his comparative subservience to the former. On the death of either of these dignitaries, his spirit is supposed to pass into the body of a newly-born male child, and by a process of divination and casting of lots it is decided who has inherited the honour of succession.

Next in the hierarchy come the *Chutuktus* who correspond to the Cardinals of the Roman Catholic Church. They help to decide on all matters relating to policy and sit on intimate councils with the higher dignitaries. Under these come the *Chubil Khans,* or priests who are responsible for the lower orders of the clergy.

Lamaism is divided into two main branches—the Red Caps and the Yellow Caps. It is the former to whom have been attributed such prowess in sorcery and the less respectable forms of devotion. The sect was formed by a priest named Lobon Padma Chungne. Vastly expert in ritual and trained in every aspect of Buddhism he belonged to that type of mystic who holds no brief for theories of development which involve the forsaking of the body. On the contrary, he taught that true enlightenment only comes when every impulse of the physical vehicle is heightened and refined to its furthest capacity.

Great care must be taken here not to fall into a vulgar error. It is common in certain quarters to assert that every species of "Red Cap" worship savours of black magic, and that these rites represent a degradation of the powers of human nature. Such is certainly not the case. There are, of course, instances of serious abuse in connection with this, as with all other systems. There will always be those who wantonly renounce the aim of all religion, which is an ecstatic union with the Absolute, in whom resides all wisdom and virtue, in favour of a mere gratification of the baser senses. Such aberrations must not be taken as representative of a sect which has cultivated the ramifications of the spirit for many centuries.

The drinking of wine, the eating of fish, meat, and the rest of it, are, in the last resort only the symbols of the most profound of all truths—namely, that the whole of created matter is miraculous, and that one only worships properly when full realisation is attained of the rapture that comes from essential contact with the homeliest and commonest things. The pleasures of eating and drinking are the first step in the progression towards a quintessential sublimation in which these things assume their proper place as the rudiments of a sacrificial concept which ends in complete and unalloyed detachment from all that is not God.

The metaphysical background of Tibetan Yoga has, as its central pillar the theory that the world was created out of matter. There are grosser and finer manifestations of this substance ; but, all phenomena, it is held, are reducible to concrete and ultimately, tactile forms.

The importance of this conception lies in the fact of its ethical corollary. If all inanimate as well as animate nature is part of a continuum with different degrees of development, then all manifested objects are deserving of some measure of lovingly meticulous reverence and observation. Also, the defect of many systems of idealistic philosophy—the tendency to isolate the areas of "mind" and "body" is here obviated. We are in a region of thought where the landscape is all of one piece.

It is no far cry from this conviction to an "ordnance survey" delineation of the human body, involving the most exact correlation between mental impulses and physical results. Here Tibetan "magic" is at one with the latest findings of empirical medicine and science. It is idle nowadays to deny that the wheel of human knowledge is coming full circle and that the hand of the leaders of the higher reaches of religion is helping scientists over certain muddy places into a common meeting ground, where the same language is spoken with a different phrasing.

Science has its superstitions no less than religion. A good percentage of our prevalent misconceptions arise from our apparently innate reverence for high-sounding (and usually misleading) words. When we realise that the language of the symbology of the gods is at one with the accents of verifiable, logical truth, then our mental and spiritual air will clear, and the salutary grace of reverence will be installed once more in the heart of all men of goodwill.

For the purposes of concentration the Tibetans regard the physical body as the lowest of the three vehicles which act as the power-station of the soul. Within this, and retaining some of its lineaments is the "subtle" body, or *Charya Linga*, in Sanscrit terminology. This "astral" entity is the medium through which the subtlest sensations and pleasures manifest themselves. It is only when we can emancipate our emotions from the fell clutch of the gross physical organism and "sublimate" them, in psycho-analytical language, into a realm in which they can be enjoyed in peace and security, that the personality can be said to be truly resolved.

The *Paradeha*, or Casual Body, functions as a remote and informative influence above all the interchange of joy and intellect which represents Lila, the loving intercourse of the Creative Energy with its own shadow. To attain to realisation in this dimension is to know God face to face and to cease for ever from any lust for variety and change. For here all questions are answered ; and the proof of arrival is found in the unalloyed uncritical bliss of an experience which transcends all terms of description. It is probable that all great mystics have at times undergone the transformation of personality involved in this "rapport" with the higher self. One recalls, for instance, a remark of St. Thomas Aquinas a few days

7

before his death : he came into his monastery as one caught up in a dream. On being questioned he confided to his associates that he had "seen" something which had made all his writings and studies appear "as grass." Unfortunately, mystics, particularly of the emotional sort, have not always known the technique by which they could keep continuously on this level of consciousness.

According to the Tibetans, this three-storied temple of spiritual development is found as a constant in many worlds and many planets. The intensely-schooled adept can transport himself at will to any of these regions of the imaginative spirit ; but, for the beginner, it is enough that he recognises the steps by which he can ascend to the *Pisgah*-sight of his own nature. Without a plan there can be no victorious advance.

The *Chakras* or centres of psychic force in the human body are not to be found in any medical manual (though a perceptive student can see in the contemporary fervour for glandular diathesis a return to a very old scheme of physiology). They exist in the "subtle" body above described and have, practically speaking, to be taken on trust. But, in the laws of Yoga, there is as much verification as in the laws of ordinary morals, and devotion to the significance of these etheric junctions is to be judged by its fruits. Anyone who knows anything of the methodology behind the purer kinds of hypnotism, will admit that, without a control of the currents and cross-currents which break and divide on the steadfast rocks of the "chakras" there could be no effective direction of the dominant will.

These centres vary in number according to the subtlety and the psychic scholarship of the observer and mediator. It is one of the distinguishing features of Tibetan Yoga that its pundits present a much more elaborate systematisation of the "subtle" bodily-design than do the more ascetic codifiers of central and southern India. It should also be pointed out that in some Tibetan manuals of higher magic, there is to be found an arrangement of the reticulation of the psychic system which seems to belie the more accepted divisions of the subject. For instance, in a rite to produce transference of consciousness, we find twenty-one centres mentioned, and these not spaced after the usual manner. They are arranged along the length of the spinal column, corresponding roughly to intercalary insertions among the thirty-four spinal vertebræ.

There is no need to detain the reader here with arguments concerning the relative merits of the different modes of grouping. Nor will much good purpose be served by dwelling on the function of what we regard for the present as the minor centres.

From time immemorial the old Tibetan physicians of the soul have postulated *seven* focal " ganglia " in the subtle body of the human being—and, incidentally, in the world at large; for, the physical system of the individual is but a replica of the macrocosm, or Great World which subsumes the former as the greater includes the less.

Also, the conception of *Kundalini*, or the Serpent Power, is as important a feature in Tibetan as in general Oriental Yoga. Inside the perineum, it is taught, there is coiled a snake, representing unmeasured psychic potentiality, which it is the business of the skilled Yogi to awaken. This power comes to life and activity along a line of trajectory of which the " chakras " are the focal centres. Passing through each centre in turn it animates them into a throbbing ecstasy and power, so that all things can be accomplished if the will is pure. At last, making its way through the " aperture of Brahma " at the top of the skull, the Power goes to join the ultimate source of all things.

The positions of the seven accepted *chakras* are as follows: (1) The *Muladhara*, or Earth Centre, situated at the base of the perineum; (2) the *Svaddisthana* at the back of the genital organs; (3) the *Manipura*, in the region of the solar plexus; (4) the *Anahata*, roughly corresponding to the position of the heart; (5) the *Visuddhi* at the top of the spine; (6) the *Ajna*, between the eyes, at the position of the pineal gland; and (7) the *Sahasrara* at the summit of the skull, and the seat of the thousand-petalled lotus.

Sanscrit terms are here used, because they are in rather more general circulation than the more recondite Tibetan nomenclature; also, because the connection of Tibetan doctrine with the more esoteric side of Buddhism is too significant to be ignored.

In the seventh century of our era a number of translations from the Sanscrit were made by Tibetan scholars. These volumes are an invaluable guide to those secret " mysteries " or evocatory rites which had been considered too liable to misconstruction to be disseminated among an undiscerning laity. They embody a lavish and glowing exposition of a technique of adoration which is the richest and most elaborate that the world

9

has ever seen. They are apt commentary on the widespread Western delusion that Buddhism is, in any way, a creed of pessimistic disillusion. On the other hand, these volumes clearly show that the essence of the Buddhist belief is no nihilistic contempt for life, but a constant plea for its enhancement. Without a knowledge of the selective capacity which can be induced by the concentration on religious symbols, the soul is swamped in undisciplined experiment, and progress is inhibited by an ignorance of the laws of form.

If it had not been for the Tibetan translators most of us might still be weltering in misconception regarding the essential nature of the most formidable religious creed in the world. The Sanscrit originals of these texts have, for the most part vanished, and there would have been little hope of explaining the deeper principles of ritual without the commentaries and interpretations put upon these patterns by members of a race already highly trained in investigation of the geography and geology of the psyche.

Among the most valuable extensions added by the Tibetans to this higher Yoga is that of the *after-death state*. The Tibetan *Bardo Thodöl* or *Book of the Dead* can be said to supersede the famous Egyptian production of the same name, in that it contains the most meticulous instructions on how to avoid the pangs of decay and how to project one's self at will into the body of one as yet unborn.

It is not necessary here to go into the various schools of Buddhism which have been either incorporated into or rejected from the Tibetan canon. It is sufficient to point out that it is the tone of the Mahayana (Greater Vehicle) rather than the Hinayana (Lesser Vehicle) School which has coloured the mentalities of the great Tibetan mystics. Or, in other words, it is the more daring and lavish conceptions of the philosophy which have stirred to such fine religious issues the organisers of the Tibetan methods of meditation.

Some influx of ancient Chinese influence there is, too, in the inculcation of certain very intricate processes of mental recollection and in the insistence on the curative aspect of yogic practices. It should never be forgotten that it is to the priests of Bhutan, Sikkim and Southern Tibet that we owe the discovery of medicines of metallic origin. This fact should act as a reminder to those materialistic sceptics who refuse any respect to Yoga because of its lack of connection with " reality."

But, in the last resort, if we seek to find influences behind " Red Cap " beliefs, it is to Brahmanism that we must turn. For the religion of the Brahmins arose and developed out of one fundamental all-important theory of life. This idea the great Buddha himself, in his worst days of doubt, conflict and tortured sympathy, never thought of questioning. During those first weeks under the Bo-tree he was undecided about many things ; but he clung without any wavering to the corner-stone of any vital religious structure—the conviction of reincarnation.

To approach the subject of Tibetan Yoga without a similar trust in this central premiss is to miss the whole track in a whirl of glittering and apparently irrelevant detail. All real religion involves the finding of a road ; and Tibetan religion in particular the re-finding of something which may very easily have been lost. There is the jubilation of an immense victory of logic within the camp of true Yoga. The only manner by which the multifarious accidents and experiments of life can be resolved into a convincing pattern is by recourse to the doctrine of rebirth, and the slow " tacking " into port of the soul which has learnt truth by much trial and error.

It is necessary then, to train the mental and psychic powers in both the forward and the backward-looking direction before we can observe our true destiny. For, if our soul is built up piece by piece out of the sweat and blood of our past, then it is helpful sometimes to look back, maybe with some relief, on the thorny road we once have trod.

Tibetan Yoga is especially rich in the technique of recollection by which we recognise the landmarks of the landscape through which we have passed in previous lives. Nothing is more calculated to inspire in us a sense of the divinity that shapes our ends than to spread out before the clairvoyant eyes of the spirit the slow fashioning of will and mind on the grindstone of necessity. In this way we are fortified against some of the worst trials of our present existence ; for " we only meet at crossroads," and shall realise that the people who come into our lives, however jarringly, the episodes which may seem to us so overcharged with pain, are the inevitable tests imposed on us by our own reactions. " As we sow so shall we reap " : only here there is not the slightest chance of our avoiding the results of our actions. The only judgment-bar we have to face is that set up from within ourselves ; if we act according to the deepest laws of our conscience, we shall experience that inward harmony which will at least assure us that we are guiding our life along constructive paths and incidentally preparing for ourselves the only sure reward of virtue—the certainty that we are a little nearer to our ultimate goal.

The Tibetans, like all Buddhists, believe in the conception of the *Boddhisatva*, or the individual of redeemed and saintly life who voluntarily elects to come back to earth so that he can help weaker beings on their way. Indeed, some Tibetan moralists have gone so far as to suggest that such individuals occasionally commit sin deliberately in order that they may be permitted to come back and point out the path to others. Avalokitesvara, who gazes down at us in such divine compassion from the walls of the Cave of the Thousand Buddhas is perhaps the most celebrated of these blessed ones.

In Tibet there undoubtedly exist a number of beings of enormous wisdom and almost incredible expertise in the practical psychic sciences who are of immense benefit to civilisation as repositories of a mediating sanity. In a world so full of strife and misunderstanding as ours, it can quite feasibly be assumed that such powerful mentalities can work untold good to our less sure-footed systems of thought and government, by projecting "wish-waves" and thought-influences which may cause us to avoid the more glaring man-traps of inefficiency and the more soggy marshes of cloud cuckoo-land.

How these things are done is only to be revealed to those already fully initiate in the delicate engineering of the dynamos of the higher will. But that they can be done is proved by a thousand witnesses in all parts of the world. One has only to follow the inspired life-course of Helena Petrovna Blavatsky, with her unflinching trust in her Tibetan "Masters," to see that the waves of inspiration which floated her schemes to their appointed end were the manifestation of the working through her consciousness of "something not herself working for righteousness." Her life is a standing example of the efficacy of *receptiveness*. If we can learn to leave our minds open to a virtuous guidance from without ourselves, we shall experience not only a great contentment, but also the feeling that we are chosen to do good to our fellow-men. If the world would only listen there is always a divine radio-station ready to transmit its messages to the humble seeker after truth. And this radio-station can only work free and uncensored in a region in which the ether has been sterilised from any taint of egotism or illusion. Such a region is provided by Tibet, and such a weapon is forged by the art of Tibetan Yoga.

It now remains to say something of the " Yellow Caps " or New Sect, which was founded by Pandit Atisha, a priest from India in the eleventh century and was much later given a discipline by Je Tsong-kha-pa.

This order of monks varies in many particulars from the Red Caps. The most important divergence lies in its dislike of images as a medium of communication with the higher Powers. If a comparison is required, we can take this sect as representing the " protestant " side of Tibetan Yoga. The analogy is not quite exact ; for there is nothing approaching the pietistic conscience in Tibet. But, for all practical purposes it can be argued that the Yellow Caps employ a more obvious and a more primitive ascetism in their yoga than do the Red Caps. They wish, not so much for fullness of life as for that detachment from life which comes when the soul feels itself "alone with the Alone." All is *Maya* (Illusion) : therefore the forms created by our own thoughts and desires are equally illusory.

The beginner will encounter a certain difficulty if he endeavours to extricate the attitude of the Yellow Caps regarding images from the mass of writing on the subject. Roughly speaking, the older sect suffered from no contempt for the flesh. Indeed, their art glorifies that dithyrambic joy in life which has been sung by some of our finest western poets and seers. There is no shame because there is no sense of guilt. Therefore, we must not be startled to find the creative act enthroned as the highest symbol of paradise in much Red Cap ritual and liturgy. There are no suffering gods in this Olympus—only figures of consummate rhapsody and joy.

Not so with the New Sect. Their priests made it their first duty to divest the gods of their participation in the Force behind the element of earth, and relegate them to a more decorous realm where the orchestra of the senses diminishes from a Wagnerian fortissimo to a thin departing echo on the circumambient air. In other words, the doctrine of the New Sect is much more in harmony with the abstract philosophy of the ancient Hindu scriptures than with the full-blooded riot of native Tibetan religious fervour.

It would be idle to pretend that the vast edifice of Tibetan Yoga is not without certain flaws in its masonry. There will always be a tendency, even in the most acute and fortified human nature,

13

to use power, not for the good of the race, but for personal, selfish ends. Certain sects of the Red Caps, such as the Dugpas and the Zokchenpas are associated, rightly or wrongly, with practices which seem to bear the hallmark of Hell.

It is not necessary here to analyse modes of worship which can only end in futility. For, in a world full of uncertainties, there is one very provable truth : when occult force is gathered and used for unjust and negative purposes, then nothing but evil can redound to the person employing it. There is no need to curse our enemies ; if they have acted without justice they will most assuredly curse themselves. Any tainted and malevolent thought will inevitably boomerang back on the individual sending it forth. This is the ultimate secret of all morality ; nothing that comes from without ourselves can ever harm us. We are at least the *potential* captains of our fate.

All Tibetan initiates should know enough about the anatomy of the soul to realise this fact ; but, in a land enjoying a widespread heightening of the spirit and senses, it is very easy for manias to develop. If the vessel is not strong enough to bear the full potency of the wine poured into it, it will on occasion burst into a thousand disintegrated fragments, any one of which may be taken to represent the whole truth. Tibet, like other lands, has sometimes to face the danger of division within its borders.

It is for this reason that the hierarchy guard most jealously many very delicate and dangerous truths. If dynamite is put into the hands of children or the mentally diseased, an explosion will definitely ensue. To enter the consciousness of another is a hazardous operation, full of pitfalls for the untutored and the unwary. To cure another by assuming his rhythm and his pulsations is a technique only to be used by virtuosi in spiritual healing. There are very exacting surgical operations on the psyche which can only be performed by the pure of heart and the level of head.

There are cases on record of adepts who have voluntarily left their own body without having taken sufficient precautions to enable them to return. The kind of death involved is not a pretty thing to contemplate. If one is to carry into practice this very abstruse form of telepathy, one must have the helm very firmly in one's hand.

The experts of both " Red Cap " and " Yellow Cap " Yoga evince a firm belief in what we might term in Europe " the communion of the Saints." It is only through the great teachers who have gone before us that we can see our way through the jungle of our own ignorance and immaturity. These " gurus " who find their highest representatives in the Buddha and subsequent perfected messengers are always at hand to comfort and sustain. If we invite them with sufficient grace they will take up their habitat within our own hearts ; and with their hand in ours nothing in earth or Hell can harm us further.

In the great prayer-systems which will be described later, these teachers assume their places in an order of priority based on spiritual distinction. The religious history of Tibet is rich in these guides to the mansions of the soul. Jetsün Milarepa, Marpa, Tilopa—these names conjure up a world of concrete, bejewelled vision to which we in the West have no parallel, except perhaps in hints given out at times by some of the most sumptuous examples of Spanish Gothic Art.

" May each find what he seeks! " It is impossible to wish anyone a fairer fate. And the casting of nets into the ocean which is Tibetan Yoga will only yield up what we bring to it. It will at least illustrate the inevitable logic involved in the evolutionary, reincarnatory process ; for even if we reject the theory of the Buddha, we must face the fact that none of us is ourself alone, but a series of deposits left behind by our ancestors since the beginning of time. Each of us has at one and the same time a personal soul, a race soul and a group soul. There will be no rest for us until we have resolved these warring components into some sort of harmony.

We shall meet the principles of Tibetan Yoga in many different forms. In " prayer," posture, dance, and even dramatic spectacle, the same laws will be at work ; the same forces at their invincible play. To reinforce the gaps in our Western civilisation with the Chintamani gems of these undisputed Eastern sagas would not be a bad ideal for a continent in the throes of its own unbalanced emotional life. World-health can only come from spiritual, bodily and mental discipline ; and while we curse instead of bless the god within our breast, the Dark Age will extend to our furthest bleak horizons.

Great strength may shock at first, and we may turn away our starved emaciated gaze from a splendour of imagery and conception for which we have been in no wise prepared. But, taken step by step the sections of this astonishing countryside will appear not quite so unfamiliar to some inner core of remembrance within the shrine of our religious subconscious; and the air of high places will waft us to a more sturdy virility, a more honest and consistent endeavour.

"Vouchsafe your 'gift-waves,' O Gurus, that the Four Powers may be conferred upon my mind.

Vouchsafe your 'gift-waves' that all things visible and existing may dawn upon me in the form of deities.

Vouchsafe your 'gift-waves' that the vital-force may enter into the median-nerve.

Vouchsafe your 'gift-waves' that the ecstatic warmth of the psychic-heat may blaze up."*

* *Seven Books of Wisdom of the Great Path,* edited by Evans-Wentz: p. 182.

CHAPTER II

Yoga Breathing and Meditation.

IF A YOGI were asked why he devoted so much of his time to sitting, standing and lying in curious positions, he would most certainly answer that he had his health to consider ; that the mind and spirit cannot function effectively unless the physical system is in a condition of equilibrium.

The sceptic may have his doubts as to the value of producing a condition of physical well-being in a world in which most of the delights of the flesh, legitimate and illegitimate, seem to be renounced. But the yogi has none ; for he knows that the attractions of this accepted, obvious world are as nothing compared with the realm " over the threshold."

It is not always realised in the West that the magician is still the medical man in many parts of the East. We are acclimatised enough to the idea that the tribal doctor is a primitive among primitives, eking out his prestige as black necromancer by some occasional commonsense in first-aid or the use of simples ; but most of us are little aware of the enormous number of quite miraculous cures which can be laid to the credit of these unfashionable physicians.

In Tibet, in particular, Yoga is practised very largely as a means of cure. Hence the great value of a knowledge of these processes to the Western world, which has for so long been marooned on its own island of voluntary divorce between mind and body. Until we are brought back to the elementary truth that the management of each nerve in our body is as important for our well-being as the topmost aspiration of our "souls," we shall not enter the Kingdom of Heaven of this earth. To cause ourselves or others the least physical injury either through vice or neglect, with our eyes open, is as reprehensible as to sully the mansion of the higher spirit. Our bodies are indeed " Temples of Reception " if only because of the fact that when their mechanism is hampered or impaired all our potentialities are brought to a temporary standstill.

According to the Lamas, there are three chief sources of disease. The chief of these is the faulty functioning of the nervous system. Here old philosophy joins up with modern observation ;

for it is a truism nowadays in medical circles that a vast number of morbid conditions, particularly those of a cancerous character, are directly traceable to this handicap. If gnawing fears and unresolved complexes vex our minds we shall first find our nervous organisation " running down," and then, perhaps years afterwards, we may develop symptoms of an apparently inexplicable character, but which a psycho-neural expert would diagnose as the result of some impediment in nervous direction.

The second cause of the malorganised system is the overbalance of the secretions of bile. It is a verifiable fact that evil, ungenerous desires and thoughts produce a state of physical lassitude," "malaise," and even prostration. That is why it is so essential to keep our minds in a constant attitude of acceptance, charity and positiveness. Otherwise we shall be paid back in our own coin : evil begets evil and good, good. Probably every one of us can testify in his or her own personal experience to certain periods of life when, our worse nature having got the better of us, we have allowed ourselves to become run-down and dejected, through our unwillingness to extirpate negative emotions, impulses and fears.

Thirdly, if we are to understand the curative aspect of Tibetan Yoga, we must grasp the doctrine of the "Vital Airs." The human system receives its sustenance not only from food and drink ; but also from the much more important sources of absorption of the various kinds and degrees of vitality to be found in the vast ocean of the airs which surround our world. These airs, which are, of course, also forces, are of an immeasurable character, except in so far as we can detect the interlocking relations between the atmosphere, of known chemical components and the various ever more subtilised ethers which feed body, soul and spirit with special grades of power.

According to the Tibetans, each separate element, earth, air, fire and water contains its own world of potencies. By concentrating on one alone of these. one can rise to great power and glory. But the balanced soul takes its fill from all. And air represents the most " spiritualised " and sustaining of these elements.

It is therefore of prime importance that the body should be trained for the intake of the essences of vitality, which can only be extracted from the airs. Otherwise we shall not walk through life as kings of this earth.

YOGA BREATHING AND MEDITATION

Besides these indispensables for functional health, there are many emanations from other planets, and from the Sun and the Moon. We are only members of one unit among many of the cosmic empires, and we must gauge our perspective accordingly. It is held that Mars, Venus and Saturn in particular have what may be called direct lines of communication with our world.

This personal health is reduplicated in the general health of races, countries and sectional divisions of mankind. One must figure the worlds as resting over the vast interlocked mechanism of forces which can be evoked by the correct ritual and the right orientation of effort. Sometimes these dynamic aids are seen in action when a country undergoes some tremendous uprush of vitality, or when some apparently inevitable Nemesis brings to a people the dire result of consistent evil-doing.

One may use the metaphor of the stoke-hold of a ship or the rumblings of a volcano to make this point clear. The surging elemental entities who lie in wait to sustain or destroy, make for racial and even world health, when mankind " follows their tide " and recognises their presence. But when our puny arrogance or pert irreverence seeks to deny the foundations of our safety, then the forces rush in through the breaches made by our folly, and we suffer decay and death.

It is important to state here that, according to Tibetan doctrine, we are living, in the æon of our development, in the *Kali Yuga*, or degenerate period in human affairs. The wars and rumours of wars, the mental decay, the restlessness of our minds and hearts is due to the fact that, not only races but all individuals are in some measure enduring a time of great trial. *Kali Yuga* is, of course, the inevitable result of our own imperfection in previous births. As we have sown so do we reap. There is no escaping this law ; and, if we really envisage its justice we should not seek to escape it.

But the conception involves an important corollary. If, through its misdeeds, contemporary mankind flounders in the bog of illusion and distress, it becomes all the more imperative to find a way out of its woe. In a purer æon a direct "rapport" with the cosmos, or with his higher self would come naturally and spontaneously to the individual. But, in the degraded state, the help of our own senses is needed. Hence the stress, laid by the Tibetan mystics on visualisation, "words of power" and a rapt study of our own limited bodily framework. It is impossible, in these latter days, to climb to the heights until we have disentangled our feet from the marshes of the lower self. Perfection, for most of us, is not gained without winning our laurels in the heat and dust of the strife.

The numerous diseases to which the modern body is subject; its frayed nervous reactions, its constant recourse to harmful and exacerbating stimulants, are all symptons of the furnace through which we are passing. Tibetan medical experts teach that certain of the heavenly bodies exert, in the form of gods, their influence on this world to the extent of causing or counteracting various diseases. For instance, *Ravi*, the Sun, causes eye-trouble and certain kind of fevers : *Chandra*, the Moon, is associated with ringworm ; *Shukra* (Venus) is the province of diseases accompanied by high temperature.

It follows from this theory that the Tibetans attach very great importance to the science of astrology. If our bodies are composed of the same chemical and subtle elements as the whole circumambient earth, it is natural that the two entities should interact to a complete extent. It is indeed most probable that the conception of benign or maleficent gods arose very largely out of acute observation of astrological fact. It is only when the planets are in a position inimical to man that care has to be taken not to draw associated forces on our own hapless heads.

Before describing processes of breath control, practised in Tibet, it is necessary to clear away a prevalent misconception. The Yogi who takes up his postures preparatory to entering into *samadhi* or ecstasy is adopting a very different technique from that of the usual western *dévot*. He is not praying, in our sense of the word; for he holds that the whole idea of beseeching any deity to bestow boons upon him is a monstrous fallacy. What we have prepared for ourselves by thoughts and deeds in past lives can hardly be avoided by a species of selfish subservience in this. The attitude of the Tibetan yogi, when he does his devotions, approaches much more nearly to stimulation. He is, in fact, paying homage to the highest possibilities in his own nature, and consolidating what he has already achieved in the way of self-knowledge and self-discipline. He is aiming by whatever process of breathing or meditation he may adopt, at that single-pointedness of mind which shuts off irrelevances and permits free activity to essentials.

The whole of nature is dominated by rhythm. The great elemental functionings of the world, the changing of the seasons, the alternation of variously-stressed epochs and dynasties, all move at a different rate and with a different " phrasing." The aim of the Tibetan masters is to inculcate in each disciple the imperative necessity for " getting on his own rails," or discovering that timing of metabolism which is most ineradicably his.

If we could calculate to a mathematical nicety the range of any individual's vibrational compass, it is probable that, granted a mastery of the technique involved, we could kill him instantly. *Per contra*, a *guru* appropriately equipped, by adopting the same principles of knowledge, could " tune in " the system of his pupil to an extraordinary degree of exaltation and receptivity.

The first essential, then, of correct breathing, is to endeavour to ascertain, to the best of our capacity, the natural ratio beween our own pulse-beat and that of the earth. To accomplish this with any measure of exactitude is difficult, and postulates a well-nigh perfect control of the nervous apparatus on the part of the student. But, for all practical purposes, commonsense observation will provide the best guide. If we feel comfortable and relaxed in all our limbs we are in the best position to carry out a yogic system of breathing. There is no need, at least at first, to learn the elaborate postures which have been evolved through many centuries as symbols of the inner resonances of the psyche. It must be remembered that, until we are freed from the tryanny of the body we cannot hope to encompass the higher flights of the spirit. It is, in fact, only when the body is dominated that it can be used.

That stance is necessary which allows the deepest breathing to be practised. In this world it sometimes happens that people fall upon truth and right technique by chance. If we are " lucky " we may have been breathing, and therefore thinking correctly for long periods without realising the fact. It is, for instance, a matter of common observation that the greatest singers, orators and men of dynamic and revolutionary action are one and all deep-breathers. In other words they have managed to formulate without apparent effort some at least of the recipes which lead to the control and diffusion of power.

For effective breathing there must be no taint of division. Although step by step the system must be charged with *prana* or vital air, at the same time the " greater breath " which includes the sectional revivification of the " centres " previously described should be envisaged as a whole; and it is better if there is no delay between these great energising sweeps.

The Tibetans have a very elaborate scheme of computation, by which numbers are associated in varying proportion with the respective centres. For example, a breath of six minor cycles should be concentrated on the *Muladhara* or Earth *Chakra,* whereas as high a figure as two hundred is given sometimes to the *Sahasrara* or topmost centre. The point need not detain us here ; as the Tibetans are not only mystics but mathematicians, and an explanation of the endless ingenuity displayed in juggling with a new interpretation of the accepted theorems would tax too severely the patience of the average reader.

What, however, is of paramount importance is to note the stress laid on the time-relation, which is an essential consideration of the process of breathing. This involves in every case a threefold operation : the in-take, retention and exhalation. The beginner commences his training with a low-time rhythm: the more advanced practitioner sets himself a longer period in which to vibrate each of the centres into life and consciousness.

The usual ratio for the beginner is $1 : 4 : 2$; or, in other words, if inbreathing takes one time-unit, then the retention and exhalation should take four and two respectively. This is enough to commence with, as a state resembling chronic intoxication will ensue if too much is attempted at once. The Tibetan mind is for the most part, cynical and calm as regards worldly conceptions of time, space and cause ; and so can afford to recommend patience and perseverance to its devotees. On the other hand, an increased breathing under intense technical control is frequently advocated by the Tibetans as a cure for many serious disorders, such as gangrenous swellings, surface cancers and multiple fibromatosis.

More spacious rhythms are undertaken as confidence increases, and a higher state of energy and consciousness ensues. When the ratio of $7 : 28 : 14$ is attained (and this is a good average for a practised yogi) the student is advised to imagine that his body becomes the entire universe. By this means a great sense of exultation is obtained.

Visualisation of many kinds plays a very large part in Tibetan Yoga, particularly visualisation of the parts of one's own body. The apperception of simple concrete things, leads, it is held, to a comprehension of ultimate and infinitely complex phenomena. And one must start at the centre, which is the inescapable gift of the physical shell or framework.

But concentration centres on that map of the nervous system

which has been described earlier.   The spinal cord (*sushumna*), the essence of this scheme, is all in all to the adept. From it branch, on the left side *Ida* (the moon) and on the right *Pingala* (the sun). It is the constant practice of the Tibetan mystic so to correlate these functional lines of energy with the general world around him, that the two manifestations become, as it were, interchangeable.

The process is not accomplished immediately. First, complete control must be obtained of each sector.   Quite early in Tibetan training, the novice is taught to visualise the body of man as a skeleton, with the essential nervous system clearly delineated. Piece by piece, each part of the main plan is weighed, appreciated and delineated until the eye of the mind has made it its own. Then the median nerve is enlarged until it assumes the length and size of an arm ; then of a man ; then of the entire world. Similarly with other canals and feelers of the system. These mental pictures synchronise, of course, with a well-calculated management of the breath.

The point of this particular exercise lies in its value as a protective adjunct. If we imagine that we are the world, and that the currents and cross-currents ebb and flow in our veins, then we are free from the ills which cause and accompany fear. Not to be equal in stature to the Gods but greater, and immune from change, frustration and decay. A sense of invincibility is only to be won by bathing at the fountain-head of all Force.

It is a truism in mystical philosophy that the rapt contemplation and understanding of one thing, even the smallest and apparently least important, elicits the understanding of all things. '' To see the earth in a grain of sand '' is no prerogative of the Western pietist : long before the devotional temperament showed its first glimmerings among us, the Tibetan sage was fully aware that every nerve and tendon, every segment of flesh and length of bone, was as necessary to our spiritual as well as to our bodily balance as the main architecture of our being.

Another common visualisation exercise among the Tibetans is to imagine the central spinal column to be Mount Meru — the mountain at the centre of the " Four Continents," as the massed worlds are called in Tibetan occultism. By this means an extraordinary sense of integration is set up in the devotee, due to a subtle and recondite deepening of what is called " *earth consciousness*." His strength is quadrupled and his senses, particularly those of smell and taste, develop an amazing acuteness.

Most of these breathing processes are accompanied by a species of pictorial intercessions which takes the form of elevating the guide, or *guru,* under whom the pupil has studied, to a position among the hierarchy of saints who preside over his destiny. The usual method is to picture this personage at first in a row of emancipated figures enthroned above the contemplative's head. Among these, popular Boddhisatvas, such as Avalokitesvara, and famous teachers of old Tibet, will assume a prominent position.

Here, too, must be mentioned the *Dakinis,* or Mothers, whose business is to dominate and direct the occult regions of the universe. In old symbolic paintings one sees these matrons, dire of visage, but strong to succour, fixed like marionettes at the end of streams of reflection emanating from the head of the seeker.

It is difficult to overestimate the importance of sound in discussing the concomitants of Tibetan mysticism. It will be recalled that, according to the secret doctrine of these regions, sound is the primal manifestation of Force. Under the name of *Shabda* primeval matter manifests itself in the phenomenal world. It follows, then, that we are ourselves partial manifestations of sound, and must react in various degrees of sympathy to the parent that begot us.

This reaction can be measured and calculated with regard to its influence on our bodily and psychic systems. It can be adjusted to calm us into a condition of acceptance or comatose stupor : on the other hand it may excite us to frenzy either deadly or divine. Its value as a stimulant to religious elation is incalculable. We may compare it, if we wish, to the modern engineering device of electric welding which has so effectively replaced the old rivetting method. Sound and its foster-child, music, is the great consolidator and unifier. The wounds and indentations of our inner self are magically healed when the subtle alchemy which arises from sound transports us from frustration to something like completion.

The Tibetan recluse makes use of the transfiguring power of sound. It is a not uncommon sight to see a yogi beating on a skull-drum, in order to induce in himself the requisite mood for successful concentration. The reverberations of this instrument undoubtedly set up in the subtle nervous system of the invocator a series of resonating chambers which can be drawn upon to increase the vitality already inherent in the " preparations " for meditation.

Again, the ringing of bells and beating of gongs are concomitants of many " corporate " yogic ceremonies. It is interesting to note how these accessories have been transplanted with varying degrees of success into our more sober and respectable climes. But it must be remembered that these things should be aids, not dampers to the spirit ; there is a danger that an insistence on inessentials may very easily obscure the real issues.

In the higher reaches of Tibetan Yoga, the postures are accompanied, too, by the use of *mantras* or Words of Power. Certain monosyllables, it is held, if reverberated through the cleansed psychic body are highly effective in banishing undesirable distractions and attracting the right elements from the external world. It is essential that these words should be inwardly intoned or chanted at the correct pitch. Otherwise, disintegration may follow.

The *yantra,* or diagram, is of equal importance. Tibet, much more than India, places great store on the concept of formal design. For meditation to be completely effective, the laws of geometry must be brought in to reinforce the control of the senses. The rules of correct and lucid thinking (and it must be realised that Tibetan Yoga is a highly intellectualised business) are inextricably interwoven with a due regard for creative design.

Tibetan art is rich in gorgeously elaborate conceptions which depict Gods or devotees sitting amid a veritable maze of intersecting triangles and squares. These impressive tableaux are sometimes known as *mandalas.* One sees them, frequently enough, on the walls of the cells of solitary ascetics, who prefer to have their paradise in advance !

The Tibetans in nowise despise this world. To indulge in any contempt for any aspect of manifestation, would be in their eyes the unforgivable sin. Far from contemning the base degrees of the ladder by which they ascend, these religious specialists regard as holy even the most " taboo " of our human activities. It is, perhaps, difficult for a European to divest himself of his prejudices to the extent of sharing in the bland indifference of these monks towards the frailties of the flesh. But, until he does so, the whole territory of Tibetan Yoga will be hid from his gaze.

To each centre are attached the forces and potencies belonging to one of the senses: for there is a world of sight, a world of taste, and worlds of smell and hearing ; above all a world of touch. The lowest, or " earth " *chakra* is associated with the domain of smell. To put it as simply as possible, each separate sense can be utilised as a transforming rotator which gathers up, in its own symbols, the general energy which is usually disseminated throughout the entire universe. Thus, delicately picking one's way through the débris of inessentials, one sees, hears, tastes—above all *touches* images of smell.

Crossing the threshold into another world of power, we find that the second *Svadisthana chakra,* leads us into the potency factors of taste. Now we are dealing in what seems to be another coinage ; and, as there is no force without compression, no strength without resistance, we shall find that the combination of breathing and thinking in these terms will increase our appetite for adventure among the remainder of these wheels of ecstasy.

The next two *padmas* or lotus-seats (for they are frequently visualised as thrones of the Buddha) are the centres of sight. One of the most common exercises associated with these is to use the lower (the solar plexus) as a visualising focal station for extending one's consciousness into an apperception of all sights of the past ; in this method the mental angle will be reversed with the higher or heart centre, and insight will be attained into the whole world of the future, Thus a very genuine clairvoyance can be developed in the practicant ; and he will be able to sharpen his faculties on the whetstone of two dimensional ambits.

With the most subtle psychological acumen, certain Tibetan adepts have shown that clairaudience and clairvoyance are extensions of the same faculty. To possess one is, more often than not, to be on the high-road to the mastery of the other. The apparatus of the tendons and feelers contingent to clairvoyance are part and parcel of the arterial system of clairaudience. It is therefore, not surprising that, in Tibetan eyes, the ganglia of sight and hearing are one.

The *Ajna* and *Visuddhi* centres, at the base of the neck and root of the nose respectively, cater for *touch.* Now this sense is far the most important of the lot. The word itself is just our way of expressing the fact that when we see, hear, taste and smell we impinge the feelers natural to these modes of perception on the surface of some realised object. All things resolve themselves, in the world of phenomena, into sensations of touch.

Concentration on the last two centres can do much to bring to fruition the abilities of those persons who have healing power in their hands. The present writer has had ample opportunity to study the growth of his own capacities in this respect. A delicate and highly-skilled series of breathing-exercises on these points will do more than almost any other move on the terrain of the subtle body to eliminate waste and bring a whole host of supporting occult battalions into action.

As we ascend the flower-strewn path from *Ajni* to the seat of the thousand-petalled lotus, discrimination yields to rapture, and the goal of all endeavour is in sight. The devotee is now inheriting the fulness and the power which he has fought for on his pilgrimage. He is encompassing in little, that which the best moments of all his lives have sought to accomplish on the major scale. It is not given to words to utter the ecstasy of this experience. One can only speak in parables concerning the full heritage of the Kingdom !

The usual technique for a " full-dress " meditative sitting is to travel the entire circuit by what we may call a tour of elimination. One makes use of the virtues inherent in each of the centres to reach ever higher into a realm in which they are no longer needed. But when our nature comes more and more surely into its own we can divest ourselves of the robes of audience, and can see the majesty of its own " Body of Glory " face to face.

To do this a kind of ratchet system is employed. Concentration is effected first on the lowest *chakra*. When this territory has been thoroughly traversed the assences culled therein are transferred *en bloc* to the next centre. By this means each vat is, as it were, emptied, dried and rested ; and later, the return journey will be correspondingly smooth and easy.

One important essential of this exercise must be made clear. There is not the slightest benefit to be gained from the practice unless the whole meditation is conducted in the *Subtle body*. Indeed, to stir up the *Kundalini* activity for the benefit of mere physical exaltation is to open the door to elemental entities whose one concern seems to be to enmesh the unsuspecting in bonds of his own making. The " seven devils " can only enter when selfishness and egotism have prepared the way. In this life we are helped by the mere idea of harmony ; and this conception cannot be said to be attained until we have made ourselves complete masters of our moral life. There are no " off days " in Tibetan Yoga— no concessions to our weaker nature in the shape of what the deeper conscience tells us is reprehensible. In actual fact, before the exercises are attempted, it is necessary to have so trained the perceptions and the will that none of the elusive and illusory baits of the world can tempt us to a betrayal of our glad mission, which is to rise from the realisation of phenomena to the enjoyment of undifferentiated bliss. Completely to find the Self is but the ante-chamber to the still greater joy of losing it.

The " Yoga of the Voidness " or complete freedom, even from the bondage of the perfecting of the senses, is the ultimate goal of the adept. Listen to the voice of *Prajna-Paramita*, to which all things flow in their appointed time. " The Sage has gone down into the depths of his heart. He has seen there—and here he fore-stalls our critiques of pure reason—the external world, in the phenomenon of representation, taking shape and vanishing there. He has seen the dissolution of all that we call ego, of the substantial soul, because Buddhism denied it, and of the phenomenal age, because its fall is involved in that of the external world. In place of this world of moral suffering and material obstacles, of internal egoism and external adversity, an apparently bottomless gulf opens in the heart—a luminous and as it were submarine gulf, unfathomable, full of ineffable beauties, of fleeting depths, and infinite transparencies. On the surface of this vacuity into which the eye plunges dazzled, the mirage of things plays in changing colours, but these things, as we know, 'exist only as such '— *tathata*—and therefore, are as if they were not."

"And once this mirage is dispelled, behold—in the intimate contemplation of that bottomless and limitless depth, in that unrivalled purity of absolute vacuity—behold all virtualities arising, all power emerging. What can now check the heart? It has broken its bonds and dissipated the world. What can check the mind? It is freed not only from the world, but from itself. In destroying its own lie it has overcome itself. From the unfathom-able gulf it now arises up victorious."

In consonance with this aspiration of the soul towards perfect freedom from what may very easily become the tyranny of the senses, the Tibetans, like the Jesuits, have their meditations on the futility and transitoriness of the flesh. There is at Lhasa the same odour of skulls and bones as at Manresa but with a marked difference. The Tibetan visualises his body in the skeletal form, sees it as a reticulation of fibres and cross-fibres, follows the course of blood and sap, not merely to criticise its imperfections and its imminent corruption ; but to trace out the connection between matter and spirit ; to seek, as far as it is humanly possible, those " sensual " clues which inspire the soul to a contemplation of the First Cause. In other words, the Tibetans accept rather than reject the gift of life, regarding it as the very necessary beginning of the evolution of the perfect human being.

The practice of regarding the physical frame as empty is, in fact, a constant in Tibetan meditation. This visualisation of vacuity slowly resolves itself into the landscape of the completed organism with every constituent part assembled. This type of realisation brings with it a remarkable degree of clairvoyant insight to the devotee. He feels his faculties extended in all directions; and experiences an inrush of "cosmic consciousness," or union with all manifested and unmanifested things.

One important element in the "Yoga of Non-Ego" remains to be considered. Not only humans, but elemental beings who have not attained even to humanity are included in the dispensation of benevolence which the adept radiates from this detachment. "May all those elementals who have not yet reached Liberation be impregnated with the Essence of Compassion and Mutual Affection, and may they soon attain Nirvana ! " Nothing is condemned; nothing is finally lost in this system, because there is no duality. To regard any sentient being as for ever outcast and accurst would be to isolate one's own righteousness from the general stream of suffering and ignorant humanity, and so incur the penalty of the misery that comes from separation. Unless we love all things we cannot inherit the strength inherent in all things; and there is no worse fate on this earth than to be cut adrift from the corporate spirituality of the world which is at once our very self and our home.

The reader may be tempted to ask what truth there may be in the numerous sensational rumours which ascribe to certain Tibetan occultists the desire to curse rather than to bless mankind. The answer is the old one: there are in existence adepts of an unbalanced type who stoke themselves up with hate instead of love. To explain how this inversion of the natural order of things can be brought about would entail a long and complicated analysis of the intricacies of psychism which would serve little useful purpose. Suffice to say that the weapons forged by malevolence, although sometimes efficacious enough in this world, earn their due retribution in future stages on the Path. "As we sow, so shall we also reap." The gods of destruction, the Judges of Hell of very ancient mythology, create their own kind out of the tainted emotions which have been offered them as placation and appeasement. Nevertheless all evil returns to its source, and the life of the ill-wisher will foreshadow his penance in the next Red Hell of reincarnation to which he, of set purpose, directs his steps.

The demonology of Tibetan mysticism is as thickly-populated as is its heavenly choir. It would be unwise for the average Westerner to venture too far into a province where symbolism can bear so close a relation to "reality" and where very thin partitions divide invigoration from a possible madness. It needs someone wiser than either Dante or Virgil to ransack the stores of this ambiguous and very unvirgin continent. It were better that the enthusiastic novice should confine his projections to the middle spaces of this strange three-storied palace of reflection, where height calls unto depth, and the sound of ram-horns and the insidious tinkling of millions of tiny bells proclaims the ultimate union of good and evil.

The *Kargyupta* School of Meditation, standing as it does between the Bacchanalianism of the "Red Caps" and the difficult, rarefied ascetism of the "Yellow Caps" is the best inspiration for the beginner. It avoids fanaticism and generates in the practicant a confidence in his own ability to help others. In particular, it recommends the cultivation of "psychic heat" so that the whole human race may be energised and uplifted towards a more spiritual destiny. "There is no religion higher than truth." This truth can be best demonstrated by the good impress we can make on the souls of our fellow-men. Equipped with the balanced occultism of the Kargyuptas, all men of goodwill can play their part in a most valuable and practical scheme of redemption.

CHAPTER III.

SOME EMINENT TIBETAN YOGIS.

IT IS PROPOSED in this Chapter to give some account of the temperaments and characteristics of certain masters of the spiritual life who have flourished in Tibet more than in any other quarter of the globe, for a number of reasons, some of which have already been stated.

The study of the lives of saints is not so pointless as some readers may suppose. There is a strong tendency among people of average virtue either to discountenance or to ignore fellow-creatures who have stormed the heights of moral attainment. Such examples, it is argued, are of little or no use to men " who have their living to earn," and for whom the visible world, in a very narrow and material sense, exists. It is true that some of the " saints " are to blame. Frequently enough, they belong to a type which forsakes the world after an extremely half-hearted attempt to realise it. They consecrate to God what is no longer particularly acceptable to man. In other words they are no real saints but rather disillusioned and discontented members of the world who have not been able to adapt themselves to the normal charities and sacrifices of humanity. It would be idle to specify instances ; but the whole history of certain religions is overladen with shadow-like beings who belong neither to this world, nor any other (at least with any weight or body to it). Their " idealism " starts at the wrong end of the stick : instead of planting their feet firmly on this earth, in order to ascertain the value thereof, they fly with averted gaze from anything resembling matter. And without apprenticing oneself, first of all, to the sphere in which one has the bad fortune or good fortune to be born, it is impossible to attain a true perspective of salvation.

With real experts in the mystical life there is another tale to tell. These people, one and all, have had the same record as you and I. They have erred, suffered and repented in common with the humblest of their fellow-creatures. Naturally, their potentialities were overwhelmingly strong ; the force of their emotional and intellectual capacity give them an unmistakable pre-eminence as personalities. Their progressions and regressions, even in the days of their noviciate, have revealed a voltage, a dæmonic and dynamic quality, which have set them apart from the mass. They have

31

suffered more because their destiny has decreed that their eventual ecstasy will be of a corresponding intensity.

There is no real sainthood without humility. One of the commonest faults of the pseudo-saint is his or her tendency to expect, with a savour of smugness, reward for services rendered. The good life, to these seekers, resembles more a profitable investment than an inevitable acceptance of ultimate truth. It is possible to reflect that, given a less definite hope of an over-tangible paradise, they might easily have taken a diametrically opposite direction.

It is not possible to apply such strictures to the adepts of Tibet. In their case, they have attained to mastery of the forces of nature for the simple reason that they have *gone with* nature, in a very deep and subtle sense. Also, it is to their eternal credit that they are understanded of the multitudes among whom they live and work. They are the elder brothers of humanity, who sympathise with all and forgive all, because they know all the weary stages by which the halting beginner ascends to a realisation of his real self. They are not different in kind, but in degree, from the weakest and most unresolved of all sentient strivers after Truth.

It is important to recall, in studying Tibetan Yoga, that it is essential for the novice that he should be guided on the path and initiated into the mysteries by a " guru " or master to whom he owes a tacit and life-long allegiance. Without help from one who has already trod the road little progress can be made. From the first tests of courage and endurance to the last whispered initiatory secrets in the ear of the pupil, the personality of the teacher dominates the course of the devotee. It behoves us then to observe as meticulously as we can, the training and discipline of those who are regarded as adept enough to control the spiritual fate of others ; and to learn what lesson we may from the contemplation of their aims and achievements.

Fame plays a big part in these reputations. It is more than possible that legend has crept in when truth has called a halt ; and due allowance must be made for the flattery of idolatry. Nevertheless, we possess very reliable records for the elucidation of knotty problems of individual psychology ; and our knowledge of rites and methods of development will reinforce some of the *lacunæ* of biography.

It is not necessary to say much here about Gautama the Buddha. Details of the life-story of this pre-eminent saint are to be found in a thousand manuals. But his influence permeated many layers of Tibetan religion ; and it is impossible to escape the Buddhist atmosphere in any region of modern Tibet. Indeed, it is the ambition of every Tibetan to make the pilgrimage to Bodh Gaya, in Bihar (Northern India) and there to meet with an international crowd of Japanese, Burmese and Ceylonese who have come to pay their respects to one of the greatest of all religious founders.

It can be said that the teachings of Gautama Buddha gave a philosophic balance and harmony to Tibetan religion, infused as it was with elements from Shamanism which savour too often of the disreputable. The old Bön faith had tended at its worst towards an indulgence in experiment for its own sake ; and there is evidence of human sacrifice and other unsavory details. It was humaneness rather than magic which was reinforced by the example of the Buddha; and certain sects in Tibet had concentrated on the latter while giving only a passing glance to the former. This had bred an occasional intolerance.

Tolerance is the essence of the Buddhist creed. When Gautama converted a general who had been a Jain, he gave him full permission to continue his gifts to the Jain monks. When among Brahmins, he expressed the deepest interest in their doctrines, and pointed out the similarity of these to his own. "There is a Middle Way, O recluses, avoiding the two extremes. . . . And which is the Middle Way? Verily it is the Noble Eightfold Path." It is this advocacy of moderation which has given to so many of the religious personalities of Tibet a quite singular and inalienable charm.

From the great religious universities at Nalanda and Vikramashila, on the North bank of the Ganges, there went out teachers and propagators to Tibet. There is a tradition extent to the effect that during the fourth century A.D. a chest containing sacred Buddhist scriptures fell on the roof of the palace of the King of Tibet. The monarch, who took up the right attitude of reverence to these gifts lived, in consequence, to the ripe age of 160. Whatever may be the truth of this, and similar stories, it is certain that the Buddhist spiritual concepts flourished, propagated their kind, and intermingled with the native beliefs of Tibet to form the richest mosaic of mystical speculation and practice that the world had ever seen.

The human personalities which arose from this pattern are distinguished one and all by an almost incredible knowledge of psychic technique and by extreme insight into the psychology of their fellow human-beings. Foremost among these fore-runners of the " superman " was the famous Padma Sambhava who is one of the great pillars of the seventh century.

This adept, whose name signifies " The Lotus-Born " is first heard of in connection with a crisis which had arisen in the country owing to the temerity of an abbot, who had offended the local deities by delivering a tactless sermon. These enfuriated Beings retaliated by sending hailstorms and plagues which devastated the locality. The superstitious argued that the whole trouble arose out of the introduction of Buddhism into the country. A conference was hastily summoned, and the redoubtable Padma Sambhava, who was in Bengal, where he had acquired an enormous reputation for miracle-working, was invited to try his hand at exorcism.

His methods were entirely effective. " By his occult magical powers he subdued all the spirits and demons, and bound them under to abstain in future from doing harm to men or to Buddhism." Following on this cleaning-up process he founded the first Tibetan Buddhist monastery at Sam-yet, which long remained a celebrated centre for studies of the Tantric kind.

Pictures of Padma Sambhava show him accompanied by his two wives and wearing a somewhat severe expression. "The precious Teacher," as he is known among the Tibetans, was no ordinary ascetic. According to his particular mode of belief, the union between man and wife was an essential part of devotion and meditation. It is difficult to convey to Western minds the workings of a creed which regards matrimonial union as holy in a very literal and dedicated sense. In northern India and Tibet, where the gods themselves participate in the more voluptuous human activities, love takes on a complexion and a colouring which places it in a more refined and transcendental realm than that allotted to it in our more self-conscious and prudish West.

Also, the position of women, both in society and in Paradise, is profoundly affected by this point of view. There is no reason at all why women, in the system advocated by Padma Sambhava, should not attain as much mastery over the forces of nature and of themselves as their menfolk. Indeed, owing to the profound psychological truth that woman has a great deal more dynamism than man—that she is in fact, the embodiment or that *shakti* or force which drives the world—she can claim a higher degree of initiation on the adept path. It is the Mothers who control the planets and usher the forces along their respective channels.

It is not at all uncommon to find a woman profoundly expert in the yogic arts. But, for seasons which will be stated later, history tells mainly of the learning and wisdom of men. It is not always the most advertised achievements which secure the most permanent results. We owe more than we are at times prepared to admit to the power that drives our internal dynamos.

The teaching of Padma Sambhava accorded well with the natural temperament of the Tibetans. They liked his peculiar brand of devotion ; and the uncompromising virility of his character appealed greatly to a people whose inborn propensity for fighting had received little encouragement from the more orthodox Buddhism, which had as its first injunction, the doctrine of non-resistance. Subsequent attacks on Buddhist monasteries and criticisms of Buddhist tenets, were the outward and visible sign of a strong sense of national idiosyncrasy clamouring for a wider self-expression.

One of the most remarkable men who helped to rebalance the religious life of the country and to infuse it with a new ardour for research into the life of the spirit, was Atisha, who lived in the eleventh century and who resided thirteen years in the land of his adoption. A Bengalese of good family he early abandoned the life of ease and comfort for the mystic search. He wandered far and wide in pursuit of the truth, living in the West and East, Afghanistan and Burma, before assuming the robe of a monk in his thirtieth year. For three whole years he was engaged in developing a process of expert mental and bodily concentration, which is still quoted with intense approval by present-day Lamas of the more intellectual sort. His reputation for learning spread far and wide, and in his maturity he became Chief Priest at the Vikramashila Monastery. Having amassed all the scholarship that the world of books could offer, he forsook the "last infirmity of noble minds" and entered western Tibet when he was sixty.

Atisha gave the Tibetans very much what they wanted. His outlook was essentially realistic ; and he seems to have silenced the vanity of bookworms by revealing to them the limitations of mere learning. With a temperament richly endowed with the dynamism without which life ceases to exist, he re-inspired Tibet with a passion for establishing the Kingdom of Heaven upon earth. He had seen by practical experience that books, unless they are made the gateways to a deep-seated instinctive and intuitional life are a useless encumbrance to the developing spirit of man. He was

35

witty, courageous and infinitely perceptive. It is little wonder that he was widely-loved throughout the land. A young man named Dröm-ton, who was later to play an important part in the religious life of the country, gave up all be possessed to follow him to the end. He had the supreme gift of attracting friendship wherever he went. The only persons he offended were those whose academic vanity obscured any commonsense they might otherwise have possessed.

The most interesting feature of Atisha's career from the yogic point of view was the graded series of initiations which he instituted for his followers. Equipped as he was with a quite extraordinary insight into character, he could tell in a moment how far a pupil was qualified to go on the path of salvation. He was never known to have made any error of judgment concerning the spiritual capacity of those who came to him. Especially equipped to detect presumption and immaturity in the spiritually ambitious, he suited his teaching to the comprehension of each individual aspirant. All through the most elementary steps in mind-training promulgated by Atisha, we can detect a valiant attempt to set before the student a clear view of the ultimate goal of all psychic endeavour—the realisation of the unreality of external phenomena and the necessity for taking one's pleasure in sublimated form.

Late in life, Atisha turned once again to translation, as he regarded the doctrines contained in certain Sanscrit texts as essential for the development of Tibetan religion. In these texts are to be found some most illuminating illustrations of the necessity for propitiating the deities who represent the essential balancing forces of the human psyche, if harmony is to be attained. It is said that the gods were so impressed by Atisha's respectful regard for their intervention that they caused Chen-re-zi, the patron deity of Tibet, to appear to him in person on more than one occasion. At any rate, They had cause to be grateful to him for his deference ; for Atisha, who loved colour and symbolism, did more than any previous religious genius to reinstate a whole pantheon of gods and goddesses with all their attributes clearly defined. A lover of decorum had made his home in a land where the idea of hierarchy and formalism had always found many supporters.

The Tomb of Atisha, twenty miles below Lhasa, is, like his life, rich, luxuriant, intriguing. Tradition has it that, in its base, repose thousands of little clay images over which the ashes of the saint are strewn. A fitting final touch for a personality singularly endowed with high emotional power and a grand and integrated rationalism.

After his death the philosophy of *Shaktism* took a firm root in Tibet. Expressed in very simple terms, this is a mode of worship which gives pre-eminence to the creative force inherent in Woman. *Shakti* is the great dynamo of the universe which brooks no let nor hindrance. This female vitality wins by the force of its own momentum. It triumphs over good and evil because it originates in a realm where these apparent opposites are both superseded. Even men, who have accomplished anything really significant in the world must, by the very nature of the case, be endowed with some of this incandescent quality. The division between the sexes is largely a division between the static and the kinetic elements in life. Without the instinctive passional drive of women, men would be for ever incurious, devitalised, dead. The more sensible tracks of modern psychology have followed the course laid down with unerring precision by Tibetan soul-doctors before psychology was heard of. The Yogi who would make the most of his devotions must transplant his psyche into the all-embracing aura of the Goddess-Woman.

One of the earliest stories concerning the development of *Shaktism* in Tibet concerns a brilliant young scholar who, when studying in India, was advised to return to Tibet, by a' sage. Once in that country, he was informed that he would "meet an incarnation of the Goddess, known as 'She who Saves.'" He was to take this lady as his wife; she would bestow on him the power to meditate on the Divine Wisdom, and would lead him to success and fame.

There seems to be little doubt that the suggestion was carried out; for Tibet soon became very full of sanctuaries catering for colonies who got to Heaven via the intercessions and the *savoir-faire* of their spouses. Dubious as this "approach to sanctity" may seem to our Western conventions, it is impossible to understand some of the more intricate mazes of Tibetan Yoga without probing pretty deeply into matters outside the range of the English religious sense.

A very remarkable figure of this time was Marpa, great translator, and one of the most influential revivalists and controversialists of his day. Marpa was most decidedly a "character." Far from being a stucco saint, this peppery and quarrelsome son

37

of Heaven stands out as one of the most difficile and irrepressible personalities that Tibet ever produced. It is possible to have two, or even more opinions about Marpa ; but there is no escaping the fact that he will always engross the attention of anyone interested in the structure of the soul.

He was born in A.D. 101 in the region between Lhasa and Bhutan, and was, from a boy, notorious for violent explosions of temperament. But somehow, these ebullitions alternated with moods of the deepest piety and curiosity, when something infinitely noble seemed to be released in his nature. Marpa, who, in his early life, got over his temptations by yielding to them, is one of the best examples in psychological record of the temperament which relaxes to receive. He seems to have understood from the first that life must be either hot or cold ; and by experimenting in extremes he yearned to find a mean.

His energy was indefatigable. Repeated journeys into the jungles of India provided him with intercourse with some of the most sincere and accomplished *gurus* of the day ; and Marpa had an extraordinary "way with him" when he met anyone of a genuine spiritual calibre. He was one of those people who hate any kind of cant, but respond immediately to the presence of worth. Like all men of his stature, he had a profound understanding of personal problems. His well-known gift of leg-pulling and practical joking was only the obverse side of his sympathetic charity.

His speciality seems to have been warding off evil influences from persons susceptible to this kind of invasion—or, in other words, he was a master of the art of suggestional therapy. None of his patients are alive to tell the tale ; but we may guess, from the atmosphere that surrounded his "visits" that here was no ordinary practitioner. He left behind him a constant trail of amusement mixed with deep satisfaction. If one may be permitted a colloquialism, he was one of Nature's "cards."

The recipes he has left for the attainment of mental and emotional health are distinguished, as we should expect, by extreme understanding of individual cases and by a system of central nervous "tonics" which make his teaching eminently valuable for our own overstrained day. Especially intriguing are his tips for protection against enemies by adjusting ourselves to their increased emotional rhythm. One touch of Marpa makes the whole world kin !

Contrary to the practice of most ascets, he had eight wives,

38

who acted as his headquarter staff, and who were popularly supposed to be incarnations of goddesses. Be this as it may, the whole travelling circus became widely famed through Tibet as harbingers of good luck and a panacea for all human ills, including melancholia.

Marpa's character will always remain something of an enigma to the formalist. It fits into no compartment and is not to be judged by the usual standards of normality. To follow its involutions is to find oneself in an atmosphere thoroughly Eastern in texture and tone—vivid, romantic, warm. The best thing that can be said about him is that he meant well by humanity ; for he shared its failings as well as its virtues, and saw both from afar. May his spirit be freed from the Wheel !

Marpa's life provided great inspiration to a number of faithful followers, balanced and otherwise. The radiant geniality and understanding which he could turn on at the shortest notice especially captivated the very young who longed to emulate the feats of the beloved physician. Some of these neophytes assumed names of a highly esoteric cast in the very natural hope of attracting virtue to themselves.

One of the most entertaining of them was " Magical Void-contemplating Lion "—otherwise Trul Zhik Seng-ge. This aspirant was marked out from the first for the religious life. At the tender age of eight we are told that he evinced extraordinary capacities for faith, meekness and love. It is not surprising to find that, at the age of nine, this prodigy had discovered all worldly things to be sheer illusion. But this revelation did not deter him from practising for many years the arts of compassion and philanthrophy. He was a saint of the desert type, having a particular love for the heart's development in solitude. One of the most delicate and complicated of breathing processes, called the " Meditation on the Heart's Drop," was the especial province of this initiate. Over his last years there broods a quiet and exquisite fragrance—the reward of a nature profoundly convinced that the only thing that ultimately matters in this world or any other is the Law of Love. Charity which, alas, in the case of so many pseudo-occultists begins and ends at home, was diffused by this slightly " rococo " spiritual genius as naturally and spontaneously as leaves fall from a tree. A non-temperamental, acceptant and utterly contented worker in Heaven's vineyards, the mere mention of his name introduces harmony and dispels all cynicism and fear.

With Jetsün Milarepa, we arrive on very firm and very illuminating ground. Milarepa, is one of the spiritual " illuminati " of the human race. Not only because he passed safe and sound through every experience, increasing in virtue as he grew; but because he had the intellectual grip to measure his own progress by the laws of a detached and recondite observation which is, in the best sense, " modern."

To study his life is to see a high-tensioned soul losing itself in experiment after experiment, clutching at all the shadows of worldly hope before renouncing them in favour of the peace that passes understanding. The blackest depths as well as the most serene heights were touched by Milarepa in the course of his pilgrimage. There is a candour about his autobiography which gives it nevertheless a singular freshness and purity. Here is a heart unfolding itself before our understanding with all its faults confessed. " It was written ; and it had to be. Behold to where it has led." If we care we can take some inspiration from the spectacle of a profound oriental mind coming to confession to the entire world. Milarepa had great capabilities of an occult kind ; but he had, as well, the far greater gift of constructive humility.

The life-story of " cotton-clad Mila " is accessible in many editions. The narrative was dictated to the monk Re-chung, one of his two chief disciples, and was penned when the bad days were over and the main lessons learned. Re-chung only joined the saint in the evening of his days, and had to rely on what he was told for the recapitulation of the earlier part of the life. But the whole record flows with the ardour born of immediate sympathy, and the account takes us as far as Nirvana, or the apotheosis of Milarepa. The preface gives the key to the tone of the book. " This is the history of the Revered Milarepa, the Holy One of the ascetics, Rich in Power, the deliverance and the guide to all knowledge. And with it is the Book of Songs. I, the ascetic, who roam about the corpse-grounds, clad in ornaments of human bones, have composed this writing and finished it on the eighth day of the waxing moon in the middle month of autumn in the year of the Earth-Monkey, in the wilderness of the great pilgrimage, where mother-goddesses and sky-goers collect, at the fence of the Snow Mountain. May this writing bring great vast benefits and happiness to all beings, until the Round of Existence be emptied. Blessing."

Milarepa lived during the latter half of the eleventh century, when India was undergoing her first Mohammedan invasion, and

William of Normandy was lording it over England. He was, in every sense of the word, a born Tibetan. When the people at large were fortifying their culture and their habits under the growing influence of China, Milarepa stands out as a thoroughly indigenous son of the Tibetan soil, patriotic, hardy and possessed of a magnificent will of his own.

A literary man himself, an inspired poet and a master of the national ballad, he is as valuable as a commentator on Tibetan life and culture as in his other and greater capacities. The Scriptures and the Commentaries are perhaps, more informative ; but their studied meticulousness and factual references are tame compared with the high vitality of Milarepa's hymns in honour of his country's greatness. To this day his songs are sung by high and low in courts and fields. There has never been a national hero who has called forth more general response than this sturdy marcher towards the light.

Milarepa was born in A.D. 1038 not far from the frontier of Nepal. His father, a merchant, who was away at the time, when he heard of the happy event, was so delighted that he ordered the boy to be christened To-pa-ga, "Delightful to Hear." There is a curious premonition here ; for Jetsün Milarepa was to possess a speaking and singing voice of great beauty. It is more than possible to argue that the uncanny effect which his company exerted on his associates in later life was due in some part to this gift. Everyone who wishes to acquire the Yogi power must learn to mould and use his voice to its best advantage. Sound, especially that emanating from the human machine, is the most potent of stimuli.

Misfortune came very early in the day. When Milarepa was seven, his father died, leaving the family to the care of cousins. These relatives proved unscrupulous and faithless. After a little time had passed, they succeeded in robbing the widow and children of all that had been bequeathed to them, and turned them out to fend for themselves as best they could.

Here commences the period of humiliation and resentment for mother and son. Fortified in their rage by the conviction that the persecutor of the helpless inevitably draws down the most terrible retribution upon his own head, they began to brood on the possibilities of revenge. Opportunity was not long in presenting itself.

One day, Milarepa, by now an attractive well-built youth of seventeen, came home slightly the worse for drink. Overcome with remorse for the grief occasioned to his mother by his licentiousness, he promised to do anything she commanded. Pouncing as if by instinct on the chance that offered, the widow made him swear to seek out a magician who could teach him the Black Art so that the miseries of the family could be avenged.

Nothing loath, the youth, together with two companions of better means, set off in search of some sorcerer of distinction who could instruct them in the art of killing at a distance and could tell them how to send ruinous hailstorms on the crops of their enemies. The magician, when found, was difficult and testy. He was awkward on the subject of fees, and it took all the strength of Milarepa's charm before he could be prevailed upon to consent to a course of instruction.

But the instruction, when it started, was effective enough. Before many months had passed Jetsün was able to try out his newly-won knowledge. His success was spectacular. His first feat consisted in bringing down a house in which one of his unjust cousins was celebrating his wedding-feast; thirty-five people suffered a painful death on this occasion. Milarepa followed up this " coup " by producing from nowhere a mass of noxious vermin which played their part in the destruction of others of his enemies. A blighting hail-storm completed the catalogue of his necromantic achievements.

It was not to be expected that happiness would follow this recourse to the Left-Hand Path. Like other men of immense curiosity and vitality who have been treated ill by mediocrity, Milarepa had poured all his energies into destruction rather than construction. He was successful ; firstly, because he had suffered genuine injustice ; secondly, because he was born with great intelligence and could apply himself with complete industry to anything he wished to learn. His prowess in magic was the obverse side of his capacity for virtue.

The heart cannot suffer its own desolation. Milarepa wearied of power without love : he yearned once more for the virtues of his boyhood, for the joys of the pure expectant imagination. So, he determined to wash himself clean of the past and devote himself henceforth to virtue. But first he must find a teacher.

In Tibet, it is taught that it is impossible to scale the heights of the spirit without the aid of a mentor or guide who is equipped with a full understanding of the Language of the Soul. Milarepa had heard of the fame of Marpa, and some voice from within told him that here was his destined teacher. Once he had made his decision there was no turning back. Another milestone had been passed in Milarepa's life.

He was thirty-eight when he came to Marpa. Better equipped in every respect than most, he had run through all the passions and all the illusions. He was tired and sought only for peace. But he did not find it all at once. First he had to show his mettle and endure the long and cruel process of the "breaking of the will."

Students of the system of the Jesuits will understand what is meant by this phrase. It implies much more than any mere temporary expedient. It involves the giving oneself body and soul, to a firmly-realised ideal. It gets to the roots of all egotism and all unbalance, and leaves the subject a kind of robot, ideally suited for the dissemination of certain fixed principles. To effect this process satisfactorily the novice is led through something like the valley of the shadow of death. No shred of his old idiosyncrasies and whimsies is allowed to remain.

Milarepa was tried in this particular furnace of adversity. But he came out of it not less, but more himself than before. Under the shadow of pain he learnt humanity ; and with nothing but his own will for sustenance he passed triumphantly into the full stature of his being.

Marpa was an expert at detecting any weakness in his disciples. If the aspirant showed a too strongly-marked taste for any specific activity, every care was taken to ensure that he should get no chance to practise it. If, on the other hand, he evinced distaste for any task he encountered, it was to this that he was forced to devote all his energies. Thus was self-will eradicated. Milarepa was commanded on one occasion to build a house. As soon as this was done, Marpa ordered him to pull it down forthwith and remove the bricks to the quarry from which they came. Sometimes he feigned drunkenness so as to test the faith of the young man. Beatings were common, and there were occasions when Milarepa would lie prostrate with dejection and fatigue.

On one occasion Marpa's wife intervened to protect the disciple, only to receive a scolding for her pains. Milarepa had many sins to atone for, and he had to do his penance. The lure of Black Magic, with its concomitant of temporary power and domination, is not to be banished in a single revulsion of feeling. Success in the practice of evil is only too often the seed of an insidious temptation which may lead to its continuance ; and some of the most ardent natures are the most prone to sudden changes of direction.

But bad times do not last for ever. There comes an end to the days of testing. One is reminded here of an instance from a different kind of virtuosity. The great diva, Adelina Patti, was trained for ten weary years by her *maestro* in Milan. Not once during this period did this most conscientious of artists receive a word of encouragement from her teacher. On the other hand, her daily meed was petulant criticism rising at times to quite hefty abuse. The ingenuous girl bore it all with resignation, convinced that she would never make a singer. At the end of the ten years the *maestro* called her aside. "You must go," he said; "I can do nothing more with you." She wept: she thought her career had now definitely come to an end. "What shall I do?" she entreated, "I have become so attached to my singing." "You must go," he repeated. "You are the greatest singer in the world." And she was!

So Jetsün Milarepa had learnt all his master had to teach him. When the day for the Initiation and the Teaching came, the two, *guru* and *chela*, drank out of the skull-cup and confessed all to each other. Marpa revealed all his strategems and ruses for converting the turbulent will of his disciple into the sharpest of weapons for the propagation of the truth. Milarepa, in his turn, laid bare the resentment and the doubts which had beset him since he had come to give himself body and soul to one who was more expert than himself in a knowledge of the Way.

Milarepa was now forty-four. Some ineradicable instinct drew his footsteps towards the home of his mother. She had long since died, and he found his boyhood's home a heap of neglected ruins. Under the rubble he searched for his mother's bones. With great reverence he gathered them into a sack. For the rest of his life he used them as his nightly pillow. He knew, that by the power of his sanctity he could redeem both of his parents from their imperfections and lead them into infinite bliss. To accomplish this act of natural charity and to help to protect the mass of humanity from their evil *karma* was the work of the rest of his days.

There are many who would condemn the life of ferocious asceticism to which Milarepa consecrated the remainder of his life on this earth. In doing so they would exhibit a lamentable ignorance of a certain kind of ecstatic religious temperament. Milarepa killed the body because had had no further use for its services. Resolved as he was to attain Buddhahood in one lifetime, he was going to subject himself to every mortification and pain of the flesh. Teaching was not to be his main province. He had chosen the harder way of solitude and meditation.

Harder, that is to say, in its beginnings. For when *samadhi* is attained, there is no question any more of comfort and discomfort: all is merged in bliss.

The last associations with home had to be cleared away. His aunt and uncle set their dogs on him, and he went away grieving that they should voluntarily pile up evil *karma* for themselves. He sought out a cave high up in the hills, where he could meditate undisturbed. It was so inaccessible that few visitors found their way up to his fastness. It was better so. Otherwise he might have been tempted to waste precious moments in useless preoccupation with inessentials. The soul could not breathe when it was hampered in its flight to its objective. Only his faithful disciple, Re-chung, and Dzze-se, the girl to whom his parents had betrothed him as a boy, came at times into his mountain retreat.

"Why don't you marry and live out your life?" he once asked the latter. "I could never have married anyone but you," she replied. "And there are few would take me, knowing your great power to curse." Milarepa smiled: the time for cursing was passed. Now he was preparing to let loose on mankind innumerable constructive blessings.

The stories of his hardships are manifold. He was so loath to lose precious minutes in eating that he never went down into the village for food, but subsisted on the nettles that grew in profusion outside his cave. His body came to resemble a skeleton. For clothing he had nothing but a thin cotton cloth, although the climate in which he lived was always bitterly cold. He must endure to the top of his bent. Then complete peace would come.

He was always criticising himself, constantly lamenting his own imperfections. He was so desperately anxious for Perfection that nothing short of absolute abnegation and control would content him. His tremendous humility had led him through a narrow gate into a very spacious place where the Kingdom of Heaven was seen in its terraced proportions.

" Grant that I may not yearn for the pond of the lesser peace.
Let the flower of super-consciousness be created in me."

Thus he sings on one occasion, when he feared that he might lapse into an acceptance of the secondary virtues. He knew that it was his destiny to scale the topmost heights.

In the early days of his great adventure it sometimes happened that his physical vehicle gave way temporarily under the strain. He laments at one period his inability to generate at will the psychic heat which supports and propels the elaborate mechanism of the subtle nervous system. There is a story which rings true in connection with this need.

One night, during one of those meticulously-chosen dreams in which he had made himself so expert, there appeared to him three Goddesses who showed him how to gain complete control of the heat-potentialities of his body so that he need not hunger, nor thirst, nor shiver any more. Henceforth, the Way, as regards the manipulation of the more cumbrous self, was much more easy. He never refused offerings of food and drink:—he could up to the end derive a very subtle tonic from the very occasional eating of meat. But a constant recourse to the deeper recesses of his self had made him practically independent of aid from outside. He had entered the portals of the pure intellectual light, and from now on his food was *amritsa,* the ambrosia of the gods.

It may interest those persons who are wont to look upon all intensity of life as "morbid," to hear that Milarepa was by temperament and conviction a man of the utmost cheerfulness, thoroughly fit and sturdy until his voluntary death in his eighty-third year. In no sense did he manifest any neuroticism or unbalance. He was in the habit of breaking into frequent flights of song, and there was no impatience in his composition. An amiable and perfectly charitable insight characterised his dealings with his fellow-men. There has never been a saint who was less of a prig than Milarepa.

In these years his magical powers were enormous. Like other yogis of high development, he could perform the most astonishing feats not only of the moral will, but also of the mind. He could transform himself into a flame of fire, a bird or running stream. At will he could leave his body and visit any one of a number of worlds in which he would listen to discourses by masters of the spiritual life, and return to illuminate this world with their precepts. He knew that all is Mind ; and when this fact is completely realised it is easy to project and control all phenomena. He had no need to impress this particular truth on his countrymen ; for the Tibetans are by instinct and nature believers in what we in the West are pleased to call "the miraculous." But he saw that his achievements as a magician would attract an undesirable attention and popularity. People would forget the end of all wisdom, and would seek to elicit his powers for mere worldly ends. Accordingly he decided to transfer his abode to a place of greater isolation and peace. Leaving his cell, "White Cave of the Horse's Tooth," he set out for the vicinity of Mount Everest, where he settled for the time left him in a spot called "Between the Rivers at Lap-chi." Here he was certain of rest.

> "My growing aged unknown to friends—
> My sister unaware of my last illness—
> If I can pass in this solitude
> This hermit will be well content."*

But even *he* never hoped to avoid altogether the carping envy of men. He could only teach them by example that the baser emotions are the surest Hindrances. Here is one of his parables which illustrates his method of exposition. He tells of a certain man who was obsessed with the most potent and disruptive of demons—that of Egotism. The sufferer finds it difficult to believe that all the disharmony and unhappiness of his nature is caused by his yielding to self-centredness of the wrong sort. Milarepa offers to give him a practical demonstration of his folly. This is accomplished by transferring the vice from which he suffers to a door. Immediately the wood bursts asunder under the evil force to which it is subjected. Bringing it back in its undiluted form into the body of the egotist, he causes him an agonising and very salutary pain.

When Milarepa died, more than comets were seen. The sky took on the semblance of a *mandala* and showers of flowers fell from all quarters of the firmament. Some time afterwards fabulous and wonderful things occurred in the neighbourhood of the cremation-ground. Still to this day the places on which Milarepa walked are sanctified and productive of astonishing and revivifying phenomena.

But his main achievement lies in his power to live in the minds and hearts of men of good-will. There is nobody in Tibet who does not believe that his chance of salvation is augmented by the fact that Milarepa fasted and meditated and desired the good of all sentient beings. He was one of the great radiant messengers of universal love.

* *Tibet's Great Yogi Milarepa* [edited Evans-Wentz: p.206.]

" Hold your peace, and no lawsuits will arise,
    Maintain the Condition of Undistractedness and
        distraction will flee away.
    Live alone and ye shall find many friends ;
    Take the last place and ye shall find the first ;
    Hurry slowly and ye shall soon arrive."†

The contemplation of the life of such a one as Milarepa should convince the most sceptical that yoga is no mere cult, but the concentration and essence of all religious faith. By its light we are vouchsafed a glimpse into realms one iota of whose bliss is enough to orientate our moral life in its right and proper direction and teach us the imperative necessary for right thought and right control. A properly-constituted religious fortitude is, in the last resort, the only healer and the only solace for the manifold apparent contradictions and miseries of the temporal life.

† *ibidem* : p.273.

CHAPTER IV

TIBETAN YOGA AND THE ART OF DYING.

THE TITLE OF THIS CHAPTER may seem morbid enough to those readers who are not yet attuned to the fundamental concept behind all the more developed theses of Yoga—namely, that the practices are advocated mainly with the intention of generating various degrees of happiness, reaching at the highest to complete ecstasy, in the student. If happiness is natural and possible to man in what we call "life," it should follow that the process of "dying" is no violent jolt to the engine which we have trained to serve us with the maximum of efficiency and the minimum of waste ; but a changing of gears, at is were, to facilitate the crossing of the bridge over the river which divides us from the bourne of our hopes. There is no break in perfected Yoga.

Indeed, as we shall see, the coming of "death" threatens us with no necessarily painful ordeal, enmeshed with all the trappings of woe, but with the opportunity for an exploitation of some of the most delicate and exquisite apparatus of our highly complex framework, ranging from a skilful use of the brakes and levers of our defensive system to the full throttle given to our capacity for calculated, directive flight.

The fear of death is largely dependent on the associations with which it has been accompanied in most parts of Europe. It would seem that a decadent imagination had, since the beginnings of things, done its utmost to make us terrified of everything that savours of this transition. For very few of us have ever had the temerity or the ingrained pessimism to be really convinced that the coffin or the incinerator spells anything but the beginning of a new adventure. It is not the possibility of extinction that we fear ; but the prospect of entering upon a new pilgrimage, with a new scheme of values, to which our conventional timidities and reluctant obscurantism have in no wise prepared us. It is significant that races and peoples with the least fear of death are those which are lucky enough to possess a religious framework which allows for logic as well as for reverence. If our beliefs do not permit of a willing acceptance of the tests to which they inevitably lead, then we are of all men the most unhappy.

One of the most satisfying aspects of the spiritual life of our day lies in the fact that writers and thinkers are at last being

49

conceded the opportunity to speculate before a rapidly-growing public on the forms that the after-death state may take. No longer are people content to forego the proper functioning of the imagination in this field: more and more, theories are being adduced to explain a fact which has always been self-evident to mystics—namely, that there can be no extinction of the soul, only transformation and re-adaptation.

The growth of the various spiritualist societies in Europe has been at least a move in the right direction. When people sit up and take notice of the findings of a sincere and balanced psychic research, then there is hope for the spiritual life of the race. The bad old custom of leaving all the ecstasy and excitement to the priests is giving way, little by little, to a condition in which all may participate, according to their capacities, in the fun of the psychic fair. What concerns all should be the province of all.

Mr. J. B. Priestley, in his admirable play *Johnson over Jordan,* is an inheritor of the spirit of the age. He has been able to pick up, as it were, from the glamour and fret of the day, the distillation of a secret desire. Unashamedly and with a due regard for logical possibilities, he sets before the spectator, a plan of life and death which has all the appeal of novelty while retaining the tested harness of traditional morality and reverence.

A quite average citizen is shown in his progress through the *Bardo,* or after-death state. As soon as he has breathed his last, a flux of grating fears and anxieties stirs him into a bewildered self-examination. The ghosts of an unresolved conscience plague him with incessant importunities. Then he escapes from his turmoil into an even more exhausting and deceptive realm of "pleasure." The lure of gross fleshly delight vanishes at last in a realisation of its emptiness and decay. At last he can go forward; his system has been cleansed, and he sees before him something resembling a Way.

Now, he approaches nearer and nearer to a conception of the laws of his real self. Now, his fate carries him through the most fragrant memories of his past. It is the essential beauties of literature and life that engross his attention at this stage of the road. His wife appears to him with all her temporal imperfections removed: the beloved figures of the creative imagination take on a local habitation and name. But he cannot linger in this semi-paradise. He must climb ever higher and higher until he attains his full stature. The last act shows him bracing himself in stoical solitude for the ascent of the furthest mountains of the spirit. The readiness is all!

The perceptive student will see here an immemorial tradition taking on a Western dress. The parable is writ in English ; but the spirit that breathes over this landscape is redolent of heights far removed from Cotswolds or Chilterns. Here, in fact, is an aspect of Tibetan Yoga, watered down, perhaps, for our consumption, but with all the main features present. To see such a play in such transitional times as these is to realise that the world is gradually approaching to a new philosophy and a new unity. It is good that East and West should join. The two sides of the globe are mutually complementary and mutually imaginative : what one lacks the other supplies.

But owing to the fear and misinterpretation of death described above, there have been few attempts in European literature to delimit and define the areas of those transcendental modes of consciousness to which the adventure called Death is the key. It is not to be expected that a terrified and subjugated world would take a very alert interest in a condition which most may think to be little more than a continuance of their present pain. The method of the coward and the cynic is to deny. Even if saints and martyrs have sung of the rapture of approaching bliss, the plain man has usually made secret reservations in his heart about the desirability of entering on an hypothetical experience for which he is very little prepared.

Most of the early records we possess in painting, music and sculpture of orthodox conceptions of the afterworld are distinguished either by a gruesome insistence on the apparatus of revenge, or, at the other extremity, by a cloying and backboneless picture of jubilance which terrifies rather than attracts anyone eager for an extension of his vitality. It is as if faith, too insistent on escape, and afraid of its own fulfilment, has posited in front of itself a mirror of its own weakness. European man has fallen into the bad habit of making not only his god, but also his heaven and hell out of his own image. Blake was called a lunatic for seeing that the essence of salvation is rapture ; and his clear and confident vision has done little to remove the cobwebs and the blinkers from the eyes of those less mystically gifted than himself.

There have been, of course, exceptions. It would be strange indeed if out of the passionate interest in death and predestination which was one of the dignities of our ancestors there had not sprung some methodic approach to the problems of the continuance of the route. The slow, sad booming of the "Dies Irae" must, sooner or later, have set up resonances which would help sincerity rather than mere wish-fulfilment along the road. Sometimes, life was so bitter for those fathers and mothers of old that there bloomed out of the devastation of their earthly hopes a poignant admission of a logic and a method which should rob the dreary business of half its terror by showing it to be capable of being turned to immense profit.

Apart from the Tibetan ideas we are going to study in this chapter, there is at least one European work of importance. It is the *De Arte Moriendi* (The Art of Dying), and it was known throughout the Middle Ages as a sage and humble handbook for those who would search out the mystery in all its channels and ramifications. One may also mention, in passing, the contributions of other civilisations to the subject. No diligent student of the literature of the Death Process could afford to neglect the great *Book of the Dead* of the Egyptians, which provides us with a whole universe of speculation ; or, for that matter, the Orphic treatise, *The Descent into Hades*, whose every word is alive with a fervour and a hope which is, alas, not always natural to the Greek genius. Then again, the Hindus, in the *Garuda Purana*, possess a manual of inestimable benefit to those meticulously reverent minds who like to combine their mysticism with a due and decorous ceremony.

Reference should also be made to Swedenborg's *Heaven and Hell* and Rusca's *De Inferno*, although these works may more legitimately be classed as studies in the psychology of ecstasy rather than as balanced progressive guides to the art of dying. There are also a large number of tracts and chapbooks which would be included in a purely literary review of the subject but which have little spiritual merit. It is enough for our present purpose to state that the Tibetan *Book of the Dead* excels all other competitors in its keen apperception of the whole medical-spiritual significance of dying, and the calm, detached reverence of its style.

It is good that man should learn the transitional stages of his being. Much harm is done by the general lack of differentiation regarding the true constituents of vitality. In our part of the world we suffer much from false ideas concerning bodily vigour. If we waste a sufficient amount of time in kicking various kinds and sizes of balls about muddy fields we are regarded by our friends as creatures of "high vitality" instead of lost souls strangled in our own stupidity. It is not by physical restlessness that peace and balance come, but by a realization of the necessity for organising our resources in the most efficient and economical manner for their full play.

Many of us die long before we are nailed down in any coffin. We accept so many false conventions, befool ourselves with so many clouded ideals and cramping terrors made to look like hopes, that the sap of life dries up prematurely in our veins. Our physical energy as well as our mental and spiritual resilience sag and wither instead of growing more powerful every day ; and our last state is decidedly far worse than our first. This condition can be cured. It is by a perusal of such systems as Tibetan Yoga that a new capacity for observation and a new grip on our possibilities can be attained. Also a great danger can be avoided. If we refuse to pay any heed to the accentuations of our consciousness, there is a possibility that we shall not appreciate the "death" state when it comes. There is a well-known case in spiritualistic circles of a soldier, killed in the first World War, who passed over into the astral world without realising that his grosser self had left him. The result was that he still imagined he suffered from an excruciating bayonet-wound received in action. Although the pain was self-engendered, it was imperative enough for him to complain bitterly of its "reality" to the medium who contacted him at several sittings.

That popular play *Outward Bound* illustrates the same situation. Here two lovers arrive on the "other side" without waking up to their deliverance from the flesh. Their bewildered agony is extreme. One could quote instance after instance from the annals of psychic research of similar avoidable states of feeling. The lesson they convey is a wise one : if we would avoid the risks of entering the lost property office of the astral world we must take every care to inform ourselves regarding the nature of the mists and the boundaries which separate our world from the next. It *can* be done ; and the energy expended will be rewarded by a sense of focus which will put all things in their proper perspective. To know the laws of deliverance is to feel deliverance already in the air.

The control of death is, for all practical purposes, the control of the imagination, using the word in no loose sense, but in its true meaning of constructive thought-building. Tightly held and realised, there is no "miracle" which this profound occult activity cannot evoke. The man who has, even tentatively, speculated on his hidden capacities to build out of his dreams a fairer and more tangible world than that which he is forced to inhabit, will inherit more virtue than the materialist whose hopes are set on nothing beyond the outcome of his gross appetites. Most of us face fears with a gloomy and whole-hearted diligence: we give full credence to any philosopher who assures us that we are damned. The positive attitude is, perhaps, more difficult to cultivate; but a great deal more efficacious in its results. It has, moreover, a host of evidence to support it. A serious scrutiny of man's destiny leads inevitably to the acceptance of some beneficent law and order rather than to the postulate of a revengeful, malevolent despot behind the scenes of the universe.

The Tibetan mind has no doubts in the matter of the ultimate goodness of the scheme of life. But it posits a wise cunning and caution in accepting values which cannot be tested by experience. The extreme importance of Tibetan Yoga to a world grown weary with a false and vapid view of eternity lies in its patient questioning of all those "dwellers on the threshold" who hold the keys of admission to the various complications of our psyche which confront us as we abandon the plains for the hills.

The *Bardo Thodol*, or "Book of the Dead," the main source of our knowledge of the Tibetan attitude to death, is of very remote antiquity. It is impossible to name any single author who may have been responsible for its compilation. It would seem that there were many fingers in the pie. It is one of those productions which have grown up, as it were, out of the self-examination of an entire people. Many intelligences may have contributed to its formation, as many separate influences go to make an atoll; but the result is thoroughly cohesive, beautifully interlocked. Only an academic precisian would waste his time on the nicely-calculated less and more of authorship, when there is so much subtle occult matter to digest and enjoy.

The central objective of Tibetan rites for the dead hinges on the "extracting of the consciousness-principle" from its more or less deeply-rooted seat in the gross body, into a position from which it can view the spiritual world in a true perspective. Forty-nine days are taken for the culmination of the process. The number is not accidental. It is the square of seven: it will not be necessary to explain to the occultist that, in the psychic world, as in the territory of unrefined matter, there are seven planes of evolution, each with its special conditions and laws. In a sense, the newly-dead pilgrim has to "start again" (although he has, of course, ascended to a new mode of evolution). Just as the amœba has to work its way slowly up the scale until it arrives at man, so the questing spirit feels its feet on the lowest rungs of the ladder which looms when the flesh has been cast off. It has to breast the battle and temper the wind by energy, concentration and the gift of Grace.

The appurtenances of the process are important. They are reminiscent, in their studied minuteness, of those elaborate ceremonies which gird about the death of a pope, in Europe. The two chief celebrants are the officiating priest and a professional astrologer, whose business it is to cast an horoscope so as to determine which persons may be permitted to have an interest in the disposing of the body; where the corpse is to be laid, and what measures are to be taken to ensure that the correct rites are performed.

As soon as death has been proved, all doors and windows are sealed up, and the priest commences his vigil by the head of the corpse. All lamentation is forbidden: complete quiet ensures that the dead person will not be harassed in the beginnings of his flight. A white cloth is thrown over the face. The priest commences a long and intricate chant which has a deeply hypnotic effect on everything inhabiting the atmosphere. Prayers are said for the flight of the soul to the Western Paradise.

When the lama has made certain that the spirit has departed the body, he plucks three hairs from the top of the skull of the deceased, at the spot known as the "Aperture of Brahma." So the freed spiritual body is allowed to depart on its pilgrimage. The time allotted to the period of waiting is usually about three days.

After this interval has expired, the corpse is sat bolt upright and is placed in a corner of the death-chamber. The position in which mummies are found in several sarcophagi of ancient Egypt and Sumeria suggests that a similar ceremony accompanied the funeral rites of these civilisations. The relatives are called in, and there follows a feast, in which the corpse participates. It is offered the essences of all the food and drink consumed.

Next, an effigy of the deceased is made out of wood, and this object is dressed in the clothes of the former. For forty-nine days it stays in its appointed place, and various lamas take it in turn to chant the appropriate liturgies before the image. Then, hung with symbolic ornaments representing the invisible powers of the five senses, the effigy is dismantled. The departing ghost is solemnly warned that it must not come back to haunt the body.

The funeral ceremony itself is full of interest for the lover of the occult. Cremation is the favourite form of dissolution among the Tibetans, as they believe that earth-burial may result in the dead person surviving as a vampire. The procession to the burning ground is led by a number of lamas who blow on trumpets made of human thigh-bones and tinkle many types of small bell. This to make manifest the cleansing and concentrating efficacy of sound.

There is much in this procedure to recall the treatment of the *ka* or disembodied spirit in ancient Egypt. Readers will also recall in this connection the Parsee custom of burial. Like the latter, the Tibetans frequently favour that kind of burial which leaves the dismembered parts of the corpse to the mercy of the birds of the air. In a cold dry climate, such as Tibet, this manner of burial is practicable and healthy.

But the letter killeth, the spirit giveth life. It is the inner esotericism of the obsequies of Tibet that can teach us much concerning the nature of the soul. The perception of the "clear Light," or the unformulated astral substance out of which progressive manifestation appears, is the beginning of a system of perceptual training which will eventually end in complete balance and deliverance for the emancipated spirit.

Most dead men attain only a momentary glimpse of this Light in the early stages of their exploration. If they could endure its ecstasy for long, they would already have attained to the spiritual development of a Buddha. In the majority of cases, the Light bears some resemblance in its effect to the rapturous halo which surrounds all things when "cosmic consciousness" is experienced in the life on earth. The same feelings of surety and confidence, the same belief in the ultimate salvation of all things, enflames every nerve of the mystic. It would seem that the scent of fields of asphodel will linger for ever around the feet of the happy pilgrim.

But "such beauty does not last," unless we are ready for it. The "being ready" would imply that the dying person was able, as it were, to die consciously. With one leap he could cross over into a perception of truth, and, out of the experience that "shackles accident and bolts up change," he would pluck the flower safety. Most of us are so cluttered up with the vain illusions of the world that we have not attained our spiritual sight to the requisite degree of keenness necessary for this quick deliverance. The majority of men must hurry slowly if they would arrive.

The proper choice of an officiating priest is an important consideration in the early stages of the death-process. If possible, the *guru* who has watched one's spiritual progress in this world is the best sponsor. If such a one is unobtainable, then any convinced member of the Faith will be able to take his legitimate place. What is needed above all is a person deeply convinced of the tremendous importance of the duty entrusted to him—one who "thinks nobly of the soul."

Much stress is laid on the awareness of the dying person just before the coming of death. He is laid on his right side in the so-called "Lion Posture" (incidentally the best position for normal sleep). The arteries of the neck are pressed so that consciousness does not flicker out before the celebrant has whispered his instructions in the ear of the pilgrim. It is imperative that these admonitions should be accompanied by the utmost regard for the precarious balance of the dying man on the hinges of his own destiny.

Not once, but many times, the *guru* admonishes the wayfarer to prepare for the confrontation of Reality. He must shake off his tendency to sleep and try to rise with rapture to the possibility of dwelling for ever with the Good, the Beautiful, the True. In words, chosen not for their intellectual meaning alone, the dying man is told that before him is the Light which shines in darkness and which takes away the errors of men.

In the ritual of "Setting Face to Face with the Light," the whispered directions are protracted until a dim yellowish luminosity is seen to extrude from the body. The strength and the duration of this emanation are largely dependent on the nature of the worldly existence of the deceased. If he has led an idle, wasteful and dissipated life, then the phenomena will be of the shortest duration: they will vanish in the twinkling of an eye. If, on the other hand, he has anticipated Heaven by the sanctity and intelligence of his pilgrimage, then the aureole will be perceived for a longer period, and no foul odours will tell their tale of corruption.

The Tibetans have studied the gradations of dying so minutely that they profess to follow the passage of the released spirit back through the elements from which it sprang. The immediate business of dying is largely the giving back to the earth what is its due. So it comes about that the scheme of the elements is traversed before the first landing-stage is reached. The last breath of the body of decay preludes the process known as "earth merging into water," and the system is weighed down under a heavy pressure.

Then the body feels itself in a cold, soaked condition, and shortly afterwards an intense heat quivers every part of the frame. This is known as " water sinking into fire." The second stream has been forded. Lastly, the whole system feels as if it were suddenly blown to bits. The element of air is entered, and the process of dissolution is finished. Fire has been consumed in air.

It is to be noted that each of these steps in deliquescence is accompanied by a corresponding weakening in the purely physical capacities. Sight and hearing fail ; the breath comes in gasps ; the muscles lose their tenseness in complete relaxation. The organism is resolved into the basic energy from which it was originally composed.

It is the case of M. Valdemar, with inevitability instead of horror as its accompaniment.

The sceptical may ask how these postulates can be proved. The answer is provided partly by trained empirical observation. For the remainder, recourse must be had to the evidence compiled from the mouths of dying experts, who have had sufficient detachment to observe every change of mood and configuration in their departing "vesture of decay." There is no reason at all why people of sufficient will and stoicism should not be able to forget any possible pang there may be in death by observing its concomitants with the careful eye of the soul-physician. The witness from the horse's mouth is worth a cartload of metaphysical conjecture.

If one is to remain in the " Clear Light," a glimpse of which is the lot of everyone, a great moral endeavour must be made. The Law of Love prevails here as well as in every other walk of the spirit. The only way to attain liberation is to make up one's mind and will to consecrate all one's energies to the betterment of the human race. This is the real test of moral worth : can one leave the world a fairer place than one found it ? The priest adjures his charge to do his utmost to climb up to this peak of the creative will. If this effort is successful, the cleansed soul can at once get in touch with persons who need help on the physical plane and appear to them in the guise of some profound religious personality with whom their prayers and thoughts have made them best acquainted.

Actually, the condition here adumbrated is equivalent to living in the realm of pure creative force in which there is no shade or shadow of turning. It is the realising of the immanence of the Great Mother, from whom all things flow, and to whom all things return. But a high moral aptitude is the only key which will turn the locks of this place of transcendence. It stands to reason that practise in visualizing this condition by Yogic exercises during the earthly life is the best preparation for continuing in it after "death."

The usual course for erring men of the world is to relapse quickly enough into a less heightened sense of ecstasy, known as the Secondary Clear Light. When this experience occurs a significant change takes place in the subtle body. The concentrated psychic fluid which has collected in the great median-nerve commences to infiltrate other duct-paths of the system: force is weakened by a loosening of compression. Sensation builds on a lower level. Persons who find themselves in this particular "pocket" are advised to concentrate their visual energies on the formation of an image of their tutelary deity, so that they may have some support to enable them to remain at this corner-stone of their being.

This comparative realisation, too, passes for most men and women. Their lack of any concentrated spiritual development during their life binds them to the Wheel for longer trials, further essays and adventures. After the first or *Chikhai Bardo* is ended, a new phase of development takes its place. Now we find ourselves in a territory, confusing enough at first, but with its own peculiar necessity and utility. In this second crystallization (the *Chonyid Bardo*) we see something like an awakening. Or, to express it more lucidly, a new world of dreams, based on our habits and associations in the life of the flesh, supersedes the more refined climate of the preliminary experiences. We are rapt away this time not to a unified and transfiguring paradise, but to a situation in which we shall have little difficulty in recognising the lineaments of our own illusory corporeal being.

This is the preliminary to a new birth in the world of phenomena. But first, the requisite law must be fulfilled. Time and tide must be equated and foregone before the fresh course is ready for the next endeavour. This stage is not invariably a pleasant one.

The sting in the tail of this condition lies in the fact that there is usually no reciprocity between the dead man and the things and people he has left behind. Although he has sloughed off his earthly skin, it by no means follows that he is content with his position, as it were, between earth and heaven. He would desperately like to make himself visible and audible to the relatives he had left behind ; but this is not often possible. He alternates between moods of despondency and exaltation : his nerves are set on edge with the indecision which wraps him round.

It is the urgent duty of the *guru* to solace and support him with admonitions which will guide him in the way of peace. The sounds, lights and rays which vex and weary his senses are not to distract him ; but are to be viewed as a test which the calm indomitable mind will resolve into security. One must trust the pre-ordained scheme of things.

The admonition consists largely of a recapitulation of the spiritual experiences through which the dead and dying man has already passed. He is exhorted to keep his balance ; for what has happened to him is the lot of all men. " Thou wilt achieve nothing by casting longing glances in the direction of the earthly life. To yearn for that field once more is to confess weakness. The beginnings of final deliverances will only come when worldly things are realised as illusion."

The essential necessity for the dead man is to recognise that the things for which he longs are nothing but the product of his image-forming mind. There is no reality in the *sangsara* existence. " Pay no heed to thine own thought-forms. Thou hast tasted the joy of the Pure Truth, and this should teach thee that there is nothing to be gained by retracing thy steps. Be confirmed in the Setting Face to Face and look ever upward."

As the deceased now finds himself in a world of duality, his future death experiences take on a more gorgeous and elaborate hue. From this stage onwards, we are in the company of deities and figures of a strange and terrible significance. Heavens and hells alternate on this scene with a dazzling array of furnishings of the most compelling and evocative character.

A knowledge of the Tibetan pantheon is not necessary at this juncture. It is sufficient to keep in mind the fact that there are deities of the upper worlds and the nether worlds who represent adequately enough the various " pulls " on the imagination and the fears of men. It may be argued, too, that crystallization of forces into forms robs them of some of their terror. At any rate, there is something in the mind of the average man which compels him to give a local habitation and a name to much that lurks in the dark marshes of the unconscious. There is nothing to be gained by debating what there may be of tangibility in these figures of beneficence and rage.

The Coming of the Peaceful and Wrathful Deities is, therefore, the next apparition which greets the gaze of the one enduring his trial. The Gods of Peace are the first to appear on the horizon of consciousness. The first is the "Buddha of the Central Realm." He is accompanied by his spouse, who represents the Female Principle of the Universe. Seated on a throne girt round with figures of lions, he holds in his hand an eight-spoked wheel, representing absolute power. Around this vision shines a clear blue light.

It is imperative, on this first day of contact with a Divinity, that the heart should be fully equipped with faith. Otherwise, fear and irresolution will drag the mind down to the World of the Devas, from which shines a dull white light. Once this fall from grace occurs, one is back again at the strident delusions and harsh ironies of earthly existence.

"O travelling one, keep before thine eyes the joys of the Central Realm from which all the seeds of things flow. Who would drown the perception of reality in the vapours which rise up from the territory of the Six Imperfect Worlds? Hold tight to the centre and abjure the lower impulses within you."

Thus ends the first day of the appearance of the deities. The second, as we should expect, is even more intense in tone. This time it is the heroic "Buddha of the Eastern Quarter," Vajra-Sattva, who will rise out of a great expanse of water. He, too, is accompanied by his female counterpart. Around them is a court of attendant Boddhisatvas in attitudes of adoration.

It will be difficult for the average soul to face these apparitions without flinching. Anger at finding itself over-impressed and bewildered will lead to aversion for the searching white light which emanates from these new presences, and a furtive longing will arise for the thick smoky flame which seems to appeal invitingly from the direction of the hells.

Here again there is a chance to attain immediate deliverance. It is only necessary to put one's complete trust in the intensity which can save rather than in the beckoning flames which offer only the appearance of refuge.

Slowly there opens up a diagram of an inevitable justice-pattern. As each day passes a Buddha is added to each cardinal point of the compass, the whole presided over by the omnipresent Deity of the Central Realm. The third major apparition to meet the wayfarer's gaze is the Buddha of the Southern point, the repository of all that constitutes the essence of Beauty. The colour is a rich effulgent yellow. There is nothing here to fear: only the pilgrim may be repelled by the sight of so intense a perfection and may seek again for false echoes of home.

At last the fatal warning comes. If the mind is sufficiently duped by the call of the lower influences, then the whole dreary process of rebirth will inevitably recommence. Birth, old age and death will once more be the lot of the soul which is not stout enough to realise its greatest good. "It is thine own egotism, thine own accumulated 'karma,' which lures thee into this stupid adventure. Do not confuse habit and custom with the things which are most fair to know. The real Mother awaits thee not on Earth, but in the realms above."

There is still more of the Setting Face to Face in order that the spirit may have full opportunity to envisage its possibilities. The fourth day brings on to the scene the powerful God of Fire, the Buddha Amittabha, wrapped around with a red light, and seated upon a peacock-throne. The light signifies Wisdom, and it comes from the heart of potential existence.

There is a danger that if the journeying soul does not abide in contemplation of this vision of glory, it may fall downwards into the damp and discontented world of hapless ghosts who do not enjoy even the ambiguous harmony of humanity. The symbol of redemption used here is the cluster of hands armed with hooks which seek to pluck the soul from disaster like a brand from the burning.

By the fifth day, the state of the pilgrim is beginning to get a little precarious. He has had several opportunities to rid himself of his baser inclinations; but still he hesitates. There are more chances yet. These increase in intensity as the landscape unfolds itself. The figure who appears now, the Buddha of the all-performing Wisdom, rising out of the colour of the element Air, is an apparition which the eye can scarcely endure. The counter-pull is exerted by a dull green light which smokes up from the poisonous swamps of jealousy, calling him back to imperfection.

The sixth day brings matters to a climax. Instead of single or dual deities, there appears a whole *Mandala* of Divinities representing, with their appropriate consorts, the four elements, earth, air fire and water. Opposed to these shine forth the *Wrathful Keepers of the Door*, the field-marshals of Hell. Against this terrific psychic orchestra the devotee must direct his particular instrument of faith and piety. He must choose and hold fast to the good.

From this stage onwards the Wrathful Deities dominate the

scene. These gorgons spring out of the brain-centre of the pilgrim. Speaking theologically, they are the destructive aspects of the Peaceful Divinities above described, although the emanations from their personalities bear no obvious relations to each other. It would appear that these judges are even more difficult to face than the ambassadors of beneficent splendour. But such is not the case. Actually, because of the concentration or "one-pointedness" demanded in focussing these deities, the subject is helped, in that he pays far less attention to the "call of earth" than he would in the case of the first batch of apparitions.

If the voyager can only recognise that these frowning emissaries are nothing but the coagulation and concentration of his own evil deeds in life, his path will open out straight before him. It is not often easy for this conviction to become self-evident. So many prejudices and inhibitions stand in the way. It is better if these blood-drinking furies have been meditated on while breath is yet in the body. Otherwise, fear will emperil safety.

On the eighth day the sinister Buddha, Heruka, hung round with skulls and serpents and drinking from a skull filled with blood, dawns on the aspirant's gaze. The sight must be borne unflinchingly. Otherwise, on the ninth day the even more grim gods of the Vajra Order will arise to admonish him. They will be accompanied by Shaktis even more forbidding than themselves. On the tenth day the tenor will be increased by gods of more subtly complicated accoutrements—tridents, bells, scalps and gems.

The representatives of the formidable Lotus Order which appear on the eleventh day are not less awe-inspiring. Still, these are merely the deposit of one's own dark-shadowed thoughts. Every nerve must be tensed to regard them as such. Thus courage will be gained to face the bevy of goddesses who dawn balefully on the twelfth day. They are green in colour and their weapons are as terrifying as their expression. But even these apparent harpies will turn into messengers of peace if they are rightly interpreted. Similarly, on the thirteenth day, animal-headed presences, engaged in death and destruction, are to be treated as esoteric harbingers of salvation.

The climax comes as a fourteenth instalment, when the four female Keepers of the Door, headed like Sows, Tigers, Lions and Serpents, advance into the centre of the tableau. If they are seen in their true light, they will all merge into the form of the Queen of the Pantheon, the all-embracing Maha-Kali. On the other side of the medal of destruction is the image of maternity and succour.

A spirit properly equipped with *Mantras*, or Words of Power, will have a considerable advantage above those not so prepared. These whispered words soothe, placate and heal. There is on record the case of a man who ransomed his mother out of one of the hells by an application of this rule. The gods are pleased by the reverberations of sound.

The remainder of the injunctions given by the *guru* are concerned with reassurances as to the preferable nature cf the subtle body. Unlike the earthly vehicle, it can accomplish the most miraculous feats of insight and projection: it can dispense with the limitations of time and space, and can control many phenomena. Yet psychic power, even in this release, must be used with the greatest hesitancy and precaution. A minute account of the possibilities of existence in the "intermediate state" follow.

Here life is lived in a murky opalescent atmosphere, from which the light of the sun and moon is absent. There is no bond of friendship among the dwellers in these spaces; for the banked-up mutual distrust conserved from the earthly life keeps all hearts asunder. Sounds of catastrophe rend the air : beasts of prey and hosts of demons seem to pursue the abandoned soul. Snow and hail fall continuously; precipices loom before the fleeing spirit.

The way out of this condition is granted by prayer. "Lean with all thy might on the bosom of the Compassionate One." Repent if fault has been mortal. Rejoice if reward has been earned by good deeds. Beware lest ye be "neither hot nor cold"; else purgation will take command, and the unhappy ghost will exist as one knowing neither esctasy nor regret—all will be merged in a stupid and lustreless indifference.

It is not possible for the ghost to stay long in one place, as the subtle body, dominated as it is by desire, is carried with the speed of lightning from one alighting-place to another. This is a freedom which has at times an unpleasant irony in its tail. When the soul would tarry a while it is often carried by a kind of absentmindedness to confines the furthest removed from its hopes.

The experience before the Bar of Judgment is of a shattering awe and magnificence. The Lord of Death looks in the Mirror of Karma, and all one's past is revealed. Evil deeds are counted out in a series of black pebbles. Presently, a host of Furies will rush on the defendant, and he will be subjected to dismemberment, torture and destruction. And he will not die!

All these trials are, in the last resort, mental. They are the logical outcome of the deathless Good within us, which arises to judge and condemn those deeds and tendencies which reveal our spiritual failure. Our conscience is the arbitrator ; and, by the force of its union with divinity, it cannot err. It possesses the infallibility of perfect vision, and it knows that not by one jot nor tittle can man escape the results of his own wrong-doing.

It is well here that the pilgrim remember the sacred "name of initiation" which was given him by his *guru*. By the reverberation of this word a secret occult bond is established between him and the principal Lord of Hell. Thus the human and the divine elements in man are united.

The final opportunities to renounce any longing for the phenomenal world are at hand. The spirit looks down on the life of his relatives and friends on earth. He sees sacrifices made for his benefit: the smell of burnt oxen reaches his nostrils. The weaker sort will sigh as they gaze on the old excitement of the flesh. But the disciplined mind will realise that "all *that* existence is over and done." Even if he wished he cannot go back whence he came. A further birth will set him in a new context, with none of the old comforts to sustain him.

The will is helped by the developed faculties of even the most average deceased. He can look before and after, and see as in an extended landscape the whole course of human joy and woe. He should have no illusions as to the desirability of following that path again. The Buddha and his knowledge can alone bring peace.

Alas, perfection does not come to most men at once. The generality of humans will, by sheer force of bad habit, rest unconsoled until they inhabit once more a human womb. Once the inner decision is made, the light of the region in which they will again be born begins to dawn upon them. The chemistry of the body will begin to answer to the elements of earth. The child wanders by the law of its nature back to the doors of a womb. Even here, at the eleventh hour, escape may come.

With a tremendous effort of will, the individual may fight off his doom by a sudden gathering up of all his devotion and a heartfelt prayer to the highest Buddha within him. "Link up the chain of good deeds. Remember that virtue is the only road to deliverance."

If this fails, at the very gateway of rebirth, a further device is recommended. Imagine in the place of the vision of the male and female in union, which urges one towards the brink, the transsendental transports of the divine Father and Mother. On no account should one stray between the earth-bound couple.

If one is going to be born as a male, there will be experienced a great distaste for the father and a corresponding love for the mother. The converse will occur if the female line is taken. One must endeavour to shrink from this tainted condition. "There is no comfort within the circle of this flesh."

When rebirth is accepted as inevitable, at least choose with care the associations of the mortal lot. Seek out the fairer places of the earth: avoid grinding toil and helpless poverty. Temper the wind to the reckless soul. Breathe a benison upon the mother who is to bear thee. There will be observed through all this web of direction a graded progressiveness which the superficial may find meticulous after a rather sacrilegious manner. They may cavil at a curiosity which refuses to "let go" at the moment of apparent extinction. But *they* are the irreligious and the doubters.

The preoccupation of the Tibetan with the meaning of death is the best evidence of his intense natural reverence and his complete regard for the laws of cause and effect. "To bring a taper into a darkened room" is in no wise to dispel any holiness which may exist in the atmosphere of the place. It is the best tribute we can pay to the possible extensions of our own being.

CHAPTER V.

THE GODS OF TIBETAN YOGA.

IT MAY BAFFLE certain types of reader to hear that the most complicated Yogic system in the world has an equally complicated hierarchy of divinities. It is embarrassing to certain minds to admit complication into a system of meditation and development which puts in the forefront of its programme a superb and unflagging simplicity. These people will have to start by ridding themselves of some clogging prejudices.

One way of envisaging Tibetan Yoga is to regard it as a mother which clutches to its bosom every richness and achievement of the phenomenal world. The structure soars, not by elimination, but by a clustering and crowding from base to summit of all the lovely things the mind and senses have created for their own delectation. The traveller who has seen the Cathedral of Burgos will know what this means ! Elaboration becomes justified by the decorum of its final result. A luxuriant message demands a luxuriant medium : style is the expression of content.

There is no need here to detail the differences between the " pure metaphysics of uncorrupted Buddhism " and the superstructure erected on these premises to satisfy the comfortable limitations of mere man. It is probable that Gautama Buddha himself foresaw that his original " message " was too difficult a proposition to be swallowed by the average human being without some gorgeous hint of liturgy and ritual to take down the pill. He was speaking immediately to the East, and he must have known the yearning of the countless thousands around him for an enhancement of life by dwelling on its lovely concomitants. At any rate, certain legends have grown up, not without evidence to support them, which give an air of probability to this conjecture.

Chief among these is the story set going by Nagarjuna, in the first century to the effect that the system knows as "The Middle Path " or " Greater Vehicle " (Mahayana Buddhism) had been hid among the Naga Demigods until the time was ripe. This had been named the *Prajna Paramita* (Means of arriving at the other Side of Wisdom), and contained recipes for the cultivation of exquisite pleasure by means of the practice of certain esoteric rites.

From this time dates the deification of the Buddha in the " Western Paradise of the Sun," as the Boundless Life which brings all solace and joy. In one sense he is the highest of the gods, the recourse of all who find life burdensome and weary. At this date too he was given two " archangels " as counsellors and guides, Avalokitesvara (the Down-Looking Lord, the Saviour) and the Goddess of Infinite Mercy, Tara, who dispenses comfort and hope, and who delivers from the snares and traps of the world. Thus was erected a Trinity of deathless beauty.

It is significant that the first Buddhist pantheon concentrated on the beneficent rather than on the dreadful. It is held in these chapters that the essence of the higher Yogic faith is based, not on abnegation, but on a *realisation* of all that is really succulent and desirable in the earthly lot. To worship correctly is to inherit an inexpressibly rich and vibrant sense of the glory of actual things. The Tibetans have taken at least this leaf out of the Buddhist book—they meditate not only on the transience but also on the potential rapture of the Path.

Gradually this aspect of godhead became enriched and complicated by an encirclement and delimitation which comprehends many facets of existence in many types of world, heavens, hells and intermediate spaces inhabited by experimenters who have not yet found their destiny. The position of hell in this map of man's pilgrimage need not disconcert the student. It is merely another illustration of the fundamental precept that everything is born and dies within the consciousness and imagination of the individual, who may himself attain to godhead if he can muster his forces in the right array and discipline. There is no pain which cannot be borne, if we utilise the force it gives us for constructive and humanitarian ends. Better by far that we " suffer " now, than heap up for ourselves an agony of discontent in a future existence because we have not anticipated the rules of the game.

In the Tibetan religious system each universe is placed in unfathomable space resting " upon the face of the waters." Around Mount Meru, which from time immemorial has stood as the centre of all things, are ranged the " Four Continents," with their respective satellites, all reposing on bases of solid gold, shaped like tortoises. These are separated by seven concentric circles of precious metals, alternating with seven oceans of celestial milk, butter, ghee and sacred juices. The whole is girt round with a huge iron wall.

Between Earth and Heaven dwell the Titans, who are the " fallen angels " of this cosmogony, strong in character and achievement, but poisoned by their own envy. They spend their time in warring with the Gods, who dwell one hundred and sixty-eight thousand miles above them ; but all their efforts are fruitless ; for they lack the spiritual freedom which might win them their desires.

The deities, who enjoy illimitable peace, are protected by the "Guardian Kings of the Quarters." These sentries dominate the various points of the compass. Their colours signify their capacities. White for the East, green for the South, red for the West and yellow for the North. As well as these stalwarts, the gods *Agni* (Fire), *Indra Yama* (Death), *Varuna* (water), *Vayu* (Wind) and *Soma* (Moon) have certain functions to fulfil. The Heavens themselves are divided into the Region of Desire, the Region of Form, and the highest and most ineffable of all, the Region of Formlessness, in which all opposites are united and the soul "goes no more a'roving."

This realm is near to Nirvana, the unspeakable bliss.

Into these paradises the gods are born without spot of defilement. They sit in supreme contentment, an aureole of glory round their heads, enthroned on lotuses to symbolise their perfection. A sacred cow, a magnificently caparisoned horse, peacocks, lions and elephants wait on their every whim.

"The Gods themselves die !" It is said in Tibet that the Buddha was born twenty times as the god Indra and four times as Brahma. There is an ultimate end to every paradise except Nirvana. The deities, like man, must needs know the highest when they see it, and it is argued that they always aspire, even within their heavens of approximate perfection, to that tremendous end of sensation which spells the True Beginning.

Inscribed over the portals of the entrance to the hells is a statement more dire, and certainly more just, than Dante's "abandon hope." It expresses to a nicety the conditions of temporary damnation, and, by implication, the recipe for deliverance. "Not in the heavens, not in the midst of the sea, not in the clefts of the mountains, wilt thou find a place where thou canst escape the force resulting from thy evil actions." There is no unsuspected horror here—only the logical outcome of wasted energy and illicit lust.

It is true that the picture of this diversified Tophet is not for weak nerves. There is too much insistence on an embarrassed helplessness and on the spicy detail of variegated torture to please those sentimentalists who have been given to understand that the Buddhist system promises to every initiate a bouncing rapture on a perpetual bed of Liberty lotus-bloom. Rewards have to be earned here as well as in the more fear-ridden evangelism of the West. If we have asked for hell we shall most undoubtedly get it. And again, and yet again, if we do not train our curiosity to observe where bogs and ditches lie !

The hells are partitioned, according to taste, into the hot and cold varieties. They reach to a depth of forty thousand miles below the earth, and each has four gates, outside of which four minor hells cater for the neither hot nor cold. Due consideration is made for right degree of punishment to fit various defects and crimes. Scandal-mongers, traitors and fornicators—each take their medicine in doses, homeopathic or otherwise, as their special case may dictate. A special section is reserved for those who grumble against the weather !

Nothing could better symbolise the contrast between our worse and our better selves than the classical Tibetan pictorialisation of forms inherent in human development. To gaze on a huge visualised parable which depicts, with equal voluptuousness, the nicest techniques of pleasure and pain, is to learn a spacious and most salutary lesson. Better to sport with a goddess (or god, as the case may be) in the shade than to drift forwardly into that Chamber of Horrors in which our every error and vice is mirrored until such time as it will leave us free again.

Out of this antinomy of symbolised sensation arises the intensities of Yoga, which knows no defeat. It is difficult to say exactly when this synthesis of the religious instincts detached itself from much that was merely ornamental. " Miracles " began to be performed by expert students, and pomp gave way, in many places, to concentration. Above all, the doctrine of creative energy gradually began to find many adherents. The soul could best save itself by solitary meditation and insight. With concentration of the bodily forces would come command not only of self, but of friends and enemies. *Mantras,* or Words of Power, began to creep into individual devotion. The senses were sharpened to a pitch superb and vibrant. The world within merged into the world without ; and man sought to become, even in this life, the absolute controller of his destiny. Erotic vitality was seen to be, not a necessary hindrance to psychic expansion, but a tremendous medium for pure force which could be skilfully engineered to make the spirit soar. " There is no loss."

The monk Asanga was as instrumental as anyone in propagating the rich and splendid Yoga which many Tibetans still use. Of exalted and luxuriant temperament, he outlined the significance of a whole pantheon of gods and goddesses who were to be visualised and hearkened to in the intercourse of the Self with the Self. The position of woman was perceptibly accentuated in this new dispensation. Henceforth modern " depth psychology " was anticipated (and far surpassed) by isolated pilgrims in Tibetan deserts, who yet enjoyed the earth and the fullness thereof. The Buddha, it was said, had foretold a day when the religious should rejoice exceedingly in the full-blooded play of the creative imagination.

Woman, as representing the procreative energy of the world was raised to a position of pre-eminence. In her aspects as mother, avenger and destroyer, she came to stay as the chief mediating power in the world of contending forces. Without her aid the individual spirit would perish ; for she alone can pour into the parched and fainting vessel that ichor which is brewed from the electrical possibilities of matter. The " Eternal Feminine " beckons us on in more senses than one. She is all that makes for dynamism rather than decadence: resurrection rather than decay.

We must not therefore be surprised to find goddesses figuring rather more prominently than gods in some departments of Tibetan mythology. In India, rites connected with Shiva are illuminating on this score. Parvati, the consort of the god, is the dominating partner in this alliance. The reasons for the apparent irregularity will be explained later. Sufficient for the moment to say that the Tibetans, like the Tantrists of North India have adhered in all the main particulars to the " ladies first " principle in their more intensive religious communings. The phenomenon has nothing to do with politeness, but a great deal with esoteric fact.

There are three treatises extant which provides us with much information on the subject of the Tibetan hierarchy. " The Means of Obtaining the Hundred Gods " ; the " Hundred Precious Appearances " and a voluminous work on " The Nature of Demons " are a good working guide to the elucidation of problems concerning precedence and sanctity. But unforunately these tomes are inaccessible to the West.

In Tibet, images and pictorial representations of the deities are " as thick as autumn leaves in Vallombrosa." Not only in innumerable temples, but also on boxes of all shapes and sizes, on amulets, signposts and on the title-pages of books, look out the various visages of saviours, saints and devils. The artists and worshippers who construct images of deities are particularly careful to execute their work on auspicious astrological occasions, and to invoke the due blessings on their achievement. The greatest care is taken with the representation of the eyes ; for, to be incorrect in any detail, is to cause these orbs to glow with a malicious patience. The name of the god is only to be uttered with the most careful circumspection.

The Buddha Image itself admits of several varieties. In its " mild " or beneficient aspect, it depicts a calm, serene figure, clad in the threefold ascetic's robe and with hands in the " earth-witnessing " posture. (This position of the hands typifies the victory of the soul of the Buddha over the demon Mara, who was driven away when the saint summoned up the forces of earth to his aid.)

In his " angry " aspect the Buddha is transformed into a figure of menace and vengeance, with severe countenance and with weapons in his hands. When we come to the "Fiercest Fiend" embodiment we are in a wild world of rage and destruction. The popular Western conception of a figure of illimitable mildness has given way to a being with disproportioned head, a third eye in the middle of the forehead, scowling fearsomely, half-seated upon an untamed animal, tongue lolling out of the mouth. The hair is of a yellow or red colour, and is frequently fringed with a coil of snakes. Several appurtenances, such as necklets, armlets and skins made from human corpses give final effectiveness to the apparition.

The corresponding Goddesses are equally " macabre." If anything, their appearance is even more sinister, as it is supported by the inherent psychic force referred to above. Like Medusa, in Greek mythology, their hair is encircled with snakes, and it would be a stout cynic who should say their glance can be disregarded. The Dakinis, the more ferocious of these matrons, emerge out of tongues of flame, standing triumphant over a writhing victim, chaplets of human skulls falling as low as their breasts.

In many parts of the country Buddhas are worshipped in groups. These divisions are of two main kinds. The first includes those deities whose chief concern is the right guidance of the human race. The second consists of more genuinely high and mighty divinities who, not deigning to concern themselves with mundane matters repose in solitary state wrapped in their own perfection. It is taught that these latter, out of a sense of divine compunction propagate, as it were, their lesser representatives to further the interests of mankind. They are known as the Celestial Buddhas, and their chief is Amitabha, the " Boundless Light," who is a kind of sun-god.

One of the most interesting groups of the Earthly Buddhas is that which displays the seven forerunners of Sakya Muni, the " historical " saint who sat under the Bo-Tree. Prominent among these is the first teacher of Gautama. Mention should also be made here of the three series of Buddhas arranged according to the mystical theory of the " three Bodies of Buddha," the body of Law, the adorned Body and the " changeable " Body.

It would confuse the reader at this juncture to analyse all the phantasmagoria of the visualisations of the Buddha. What is meat for the ritualistic palate is only too often a surfeit for the simple kind of taste. These are matters for the delectation of a peculiarly pliable type of imagination whose appetite is satisfied only with the richest of fare.

But something must be said about the various " hand-postures " which accompany the stances of the god, particularly as these are of such essential importance for the right correlation of Yoga with the technique of evocation and exorcism.

There is a whole occult system inherent in the correct application of the laws of gesture ; and the hands are in this sense, even more than the eyes, "the mirror of the soul." The pre-occupation of so many great artists, such as El Greco, Albrecht Dürer, Sargent, and of course the incomparable da Vinci, with these expressive terminal points of the anatomy, should make the ordinary man at least aware of the power that can flow from the fingers. Good pianists, too, know much that they do not reveal concerning the hands as electrical transmitters.

In the higher occultism of Yoga much can be learned of the exact parallelism between the motions of the mind and will, and the changes in the various currents of the body. In veiled hints the pose of the hands in the images of the gods gives us an inkling into the subtle doctrine aforesaid. Magicians have worked more marvels with their " beckoning " or " banishing " gestures than with any other weapon in their arsenal.

When we look at representations of Buddha we see that there are nine main variants in the manipulation of the hands. The word is used advisedly ; for in the ideal world of thought-forms the eman-cipated body passes through all the dancing moods of its own ecstasy. Some purpose will be served by enumerating these symbolic counters of control.

The " Earth Witness " posture is the best-known, and betokens command of forces which work their way up through crystals, minerals and plants. The " Impartial " attitude is marked

73

by the resting of the hands over each other on the lap in the middle line of the body, with palms upwards : it signifies the acceptance of all the trials that life may bring. In the third or " Gesture of the Best Perfection " the first finger and thumb of each hand are joined and held almost touching at the level of the heart. The " deepest thoughts " come from all-embracing charity. The fourth or " Turning Wheel of the Law " is a more imperative admonition, and calls attention to the irrefutable reaping of effect from cause. It is a dogmatic attitude and the index-finger of the right hand turns down the fingers of the left.

The " Best-Bestowing Charity " extends the right arm to its full length. In token of universal compassion, the hand is directed downwards, with outstretched palm to the fore. In the "Refuge-Giving" gesture, on the contrary, the arm is bent, and the palm is pendent with the fingers held downwards. In the seventh or " Blessing of Fearlessness " the arm is again bent, this time with the palm and the fingers directed upwards. The " Preaching" posture differs from the previous one in that the thumb is bent to touch the ring-finger. There is an irresistible truth inherent in the message of the Law.

The last " Gesture of the Pointing Finger " is much used in necromantic conjuration, and is not in favour with the holier type of yogi. Readers who have seen *The Dybbuk* as interpreted by the remarkable Habima Players will recall how, in the last act of this highly " macabre" piece, this menacing " pointed finger " is used by the chorus of exorcists with a singularly diabolical and chilling effect. Force drives out Force when there are more atoms on its side.

While on this point mention should be made of the significance of the weapons carried by many of the Tibetan Gods. These are not arbitrary ; but stand for influences and forces directed along certain channels. These same weapons, grouped in certain designs, have also a great power to generate the very high-wind of magic. To meditate on these symbols and formations is to walk for ever unconquered.

For instance, Manjusri, holds in his right hand the Sword of Truth with which he cuts the tangled knot of error. Among the weapons carried by other gods are the thunderbolt, the hand-drum, the alarm-staff, the wish-granting *Cintamani* Gem, the banner, the water-pot, the bell, the iron-goad, the skull-cup and the thigh-bone trumpet. Much occult meaning is concealed within the material sound and purpose of these accessories. Some of the

Tibetan gods, notably Manjusri, are allowed no *Shakti*. They are sufficient unto themselves ; for these deities, for the most part, carry in their glance the power and pomp of the superficial actual world. They are not concerned in driving the machine, but merely proclaim the splendour of its parts.

But when all is said and done, the spiritual richness of Tibet can very largely be correlated with the pursuit of the great ritualistic system, sometimes known as Anuttara Yoga, sometimes as the Religion of the *Agamas* (Sacred Texts). This approach to the universe, which seeks more than any other religion or philosophy to inculcate unmitigated joy, has been elucidated by the present writer for the first time under the name of *Psychoshaktism** with the hope of applying to the spiritual, mental and bodily diseases of the day an explanation and an alleviation, culled from remote Eastern quarters where wisdom is not tainted by craft and expediency. Already some most happy results have been seen, notably in cases of nervous breakdown and profound neural disharmony.

The therapeutic and philosophic system above adumbrated is ruled over by the God Shiva, who is, of course, one of the three supreme figures of the Hindu trinity. In the minds of the ignorant this God is often associated with the idea of a destroyer. And, indeed, in so far as it is often necessary to destroy the evil in order to build the good, the designation will stand. But Shiva is also the great restorer — the mender of broken hearts and disillusioned lives. He is the gift to compensate the soul for its false starts and misguided adventures, and to lead it into a new promised land. (It is significant that the word *Sciva*, in Sanskrit, means " kind, gracious.") He is the God of the Arts, particularly dancing ; for his profound occult movements represent the ecstatic joy of the Absolute in Its own creation ; and He promises the seeker an abounding and uninhibited vital happiness.

Again, in his ascetic aspect, the complete figure of controlled resignation and austere penance and meditation, Shiva is the worker of miracles, the teacher of magic. Unless the devotee is willing to subjugate his baser passions, to think the world well lost for the infinite reward of the Undying Vision, he can hardly expect to make his psychic presence felt among his associates. The glory of the Kingdom of Heaven is, in the last resort, reserved for those who abjure the lesser consolations and deliberately choose the greater and more enduring.

* *Psyche*—The Soul. *Shakti*—Creative Energy.

A difficult point has to be explained here. The student who undertakes the Shiva Yogas is obliged to face his task with a considerable degree of reverential caution. To put it in the simplest manner possible, he will be dealing with the counters of pure force. One has seen several nasty smashes in the case of persons who have ventured recklessly into fields for which they were not prepared or attuned. The gods are not tamed, and they seem to reserve their malediction for those who would defy the mystery with their arrogance and ineptitude. High-tension conductors are to be acknowledged for the forces which they carry, not wantonly grasped or underrated.

One might put it another way by saying that in this sphere of activity, there are no frills and furbelows. There are certain fundamental Laws to be observed, all of which subserve a definite and relevant purpose. Although the surface of devotion may be encrusted with the most enchanting of gems and frescoed delights, yet the inner discipline is arduous, coherent and completely logical. It is fatal to mistake the surface for the reality. The formidable appearance of the Dark Gods is nothing but the secret strength within the capacity of all who would sharpen their spiritual faculties on the whetstone of a disciplined insight.

The consort of Shiva, who is best known under the name Parvati, has very many aspects. These must be gauged according to the functions she fulfils—either as destroyer, restorer or healer and miracle-worker. She is known too as Durga, Kali and Yogini. In the symbolic statuary consecrated to the representation of these figures, they are usually depicted in a transport of unabashed joy. When the human being realises the correct balance of the active and passive possibilities in his own nature, then is his cup of happiness full. He knows neither self-reproach nor self-analysis : all is lost is perfect consummation.

It is no paradox to say that these two all-important gods are, in the last resort, one. Certainly they can be meditated on separately; and great assistance, it is taught, can be obtained in our various earthly troubles by becoming one with the various powers and virtues which inhabit the God-figure in its different forms.

Yogis in Tibet have an especial devotion to Tara, who is the Feminine Principle in its beneficient form. The Tibetan Goddess of Mercy is the " Cherisher of the Poor," the " Subduer of Passion," the " Giver of Prosperity." She is usually imaged as clothed in white with a green complexion. Her uncovered head gleams with jewels, and in her left hand she carries a long lotus-flower. There are twenty-one variants of this Dispenser of Peace in Tibetan worship. Sometimes she is loaded with adornments: then her efficacy is of a more subtle sort, and she is credited with unfolding and comprehending the most tortuous mazes of our being. She fills the dried-up channels of our disillusion with the living waters of constructive hope.

At the opposite end of the picture is Marici, the dreaded Goddess of the Dawn whose male counterpart is horse-necked, and who carries within her veins the irresistible energy of the sun. " The Adamantine Sow " as this being is rather unflatteringly designated, is said to be incarnated in the ruling Abbess of the Convent of the great Palti Lake. She has three faces, and eight hands. She carries an axe, saw and snare and sits in the " Enchanting " pose. She is drawn by seven swine.

An even more repellent conception than this harbinger of agitation is the lady known as " The Queen of Warring Weapons " (Lha-mo) whose unholy business it is to let loose the demons of disease. She is slightly more easy on the eye than Marici ; but her appurtenances are even more startling. Enveloped in flames she rides on a white mule caparisoned with a covering of human skin, flayed from the body of her son. She drinks blood from a human skull-cup, and wields the trident of Power in her right hand.

This ambiguous Female is reverenced by the Tibetan contemplatives for seven days at the end of every twelvemonth. Curious articles of diet, including the fat of a black goat, wine, dough and butter are offered up to placate her wrath. Some of the less reputable sects gather her strength for the practice of sorcery ; but, in general, she symbolises for the worshipper the dire judgment which awaits those who do not put the requisite energy into their deeds of atonement and piety.

While on this subject of the representatives of the darker shades of the Tibetan hierarchy something should be said of the various cohorts of demons who act as a kind of chorus to the enthroned Gods and *Shaktis* in their destructive aspects. The Demon-Kings, the Demon-Generals and the Lord-Demons fulfil their several offices as agents and emissaries of the full-dress manipulators of pure energy.

The last-named are popularly recognised as the " Lords of the Black Cloak." In most particulars they can be viewed as similar functionaries as the " Lords of the Dark Face " who group themselves around the magic-working Thoth in the secret records of ancient Egyptian occultism. They stand for the amoral undergrowth of man's being ; for the possibilities which can be recognised by all who have their psychic senses developed; but which plunge the soul into the deepest hell of corruption—a corruption so intense that it cannot realise its own ultimate impotence.

Nearly every Yoga sect of Tibet has its own tutelary demon. It would seem as if, in a mental and spiritual world which seeks the highest spiritual good, there exists a tendency to remind onself at frequent intervals of the abysses which loom before the faint heart and the weak will. Also, in a more subtle sense, enjoyment and health depend very largely on the invigoration which comes from the clash of opposites. It is only when we have experienced pain and dismay that we can realise the full liberation of mystical pleasure. The nature of humanity stands between the heights and the depths. Who shall forbid the seeker to leave one vestige of the adventure unexplored?

The Lady-Demons (if one may give such a conventional title to beings of such primeval intensity) have an equal lack of compromise in their composition. " Hell hath no fury like a woman scorned "; and, to judge by the expression on the imaged faces of these beldames they are more than competent to admonish and correct those foolhardy enough to dispute their sway. They are the projected embodiment of all that is implied in the idea of the " Evil Eye." Their strength is especially reinforced by the fact that they carry as by a special prerogative some deeply significant articles used in the more esoteric Yogic rites.

Prominent among these are the flower (*Pushpa*),—the symbol of the essence of purity ; the shell-vase of perfume, which is offered up to the idealised God-Union ; the mirror, which reflects the living shadows cast by all phenomena, and the lamp which transfers to a small circle the untold potency of light and fire. It cannot be too sufficiently impressed on the reader that the altitudes of Yoga are largely concerned with the meticulous investigation into the laws governing the extension of the senses. In a very definite connotation the art of Yoga is the art of bringing the dead to life. At the present day many of us wilt because our senses are being tempted into a decline and a decay. So much of our hearing is done for us by the amplifier, our sight by spectacles and our motor responses by the aids of artificial transport that we have forgotten that the purpose of life is that it should be enjoyed. We are inheritors of the lovely banquets of the world, and we are content with a mess of utilitarian pottage !

Much misconception prevails on the subject of the offerings made to the gods in yogic devotions of the more ritualistic sort. Human nature being what it is, it is of course inevitable that abuses have crept into a mode of worship which was formulated with the intention of freeing the soul from the more obvious encumbrances of matter. It is not to be expected that the priests of the temple will always flee from corruption. Sufficient to explain here the true inwardness of the five *markaras* (the "Five M's" as they are sometimes called) which are consecrated to the Great Mother of the World in Tibetan Yoga.

God-Union, wine, parched pulse, fish and meat are one and all symbolised or used as part of the central ceremony which celebrates the inexpressible joy of the worshipper at contacting the all-embracing strength and fortification at the heart of the world. There is, in general, no licence and no lapses of taste at these (to Western eyes) rather flamboyant proceedings. All is tensed up with reverence for the Spirit which will breathe its benison over all inhabiting the surrounding space, and which will carry into the lives of ancestors, parents and children some echo of a dream fulfilled.

The men sit with their womenfolk at their side ; for they know that women inherit by their nature the kingdom of creative energy, and are blessed in consequence. According to the terms of this conception marriage is doubly sacred : it has been sanctified by the wise tradition of ages, and, more important still, it re-enacts the creative transports of the Divine Pair, of the sun and the moon, from which life is created, and to which, in due course, it will return.

The meat stands for man in his bodily bondage. Until he has shaken himself free from the lusts of the flesh, he will never find his true, indomitable Self. He must master and analyse his physical integument. The fish represents the first evolutionary life to possess a spinal column. (In the most ancient mythology the first god took the form of a fish.) It must be recalled that the spinal column is the territory in which the spiritual lotuses are meditated upon. The gift of this food to the gods is the best thanks one can tender for the structural miracle of salvation within ourselves.

The parched grain-seed, in its turn, has a living significance for the aspirant. The practice of *puja,* of concentrated and decorous meditation, consumes all unseemly desire, as chaff in the furnace. Likewise, the stimulants of desire are overcome by the more convincing spiritual erethism of the soul. Never again will the energy empty itself into unworthy channels.

The wine comes last of all. He who drinks of this cup will not thirst again. Here the intoxicating drink is a dim foretaste of unity with the Beloved. By virtue of its properties, certain layers are uncovered in the subconscious of the worshipper, and all the chords of his being vibrate in unison with the eternal music. For the enjoyment of the real Self it is necessary that the heart and mind be free. The liberation of the mind from puny fears and the baser inhibitions is no mean preparation for the banquet which the heart shares with its own expanded capacities. In an obscure Sanskrit manuscript there occurs a passage which may be translated as follows : " A husbandless woman (for example, a widow) abandoned her own home and rushed up the high road. She became intoxicated, but reached her lover's house, and was enwrapped in enjoyment. This is the true wisdom." Let those who would search out the mystery ponder this passage !

The reader may ask to what extent this Group-Yoga, if one may coin a term, surpasses or falls short of the more solitary communings of trained mystics. The answer is that, in the former case, there is often a special purpose served, by convening a number of suitable persons together to lift up their minds in praise and contemplation. The Tibetans' point of view is singularly up-to-date and " scientific " on this score. It holds that forces can be concentrated into something like electrical batteries. And the Tibetans go further than most modern scientists by asserting that thought, particularly when purged and fortified by the clean wind of genuinely passionised emotion, is the strongest force on earth. A group working in concert and harmony will, in general, produce a more effective influx of this power than the solitary individual, unless he or she be a person of quite preternatural dynamism. Particularly when the male and female elements are, so to speak, aligned together and allowed to complement each other by a process of active and passive retraction and assertion, will this formidable vitality steam out of the *Kaula* (Circle) like the essential distillation of some fine perfume. It behoves the pious to use this refined and concentrated energy for the best possible purpose.

The energy may be said to be, in its intrinsic nature, amoral. Voltages of the psychic power-house have no percipience in their constitution. They can be employed indifferently for the furthering of the ends of the highest virtue, or for the propping-up of motives brought from the pit of Hell. It is only when the controls are sound that a safe journey can be promised to the adventurer brave enough to travel in the company of heavy-weight potentialities. Disasters and wreckage ensue, if there is any confusion in the issues involved. The theory of the *tulpa*, or thought-form, has found a fertile soil among Tibetan yogis. It is natural that a people so preoccupied with the mechanism and utility of thought should evolve doctrines of transference and domination which are calculated to make the timid shrink.

It is believed that these *tulpas* can take the shapes of men of any other projections which the ascetic may care to send out from his store-battery.

Thus there are many cases on record of entities of a purely psychic origin being disseminated through the world with comforting or disturbing results to the peace of mind of humanity. Evil *tulpas,* deadly *eidola* of wild beasts, or bristling myrmidons of the Gods of Vengeance, are sometimes despatched by outraged lamas against their enemies. But, for the most part, it is the practice of the Tibetan *dévots* to use their accumulated powers to propel emissaries of a more attractive and helpful kind. With this end in view, a remarkable system of telepathy has been organised by which groups all over the country communicate with each other for their mutual religious edification. It is called " sending messages on the wind." By its means yogis in Lhasa are made aware of the findings of Nepal and Sikkim ; and a whispered hint of beatitude in Tashi-lun-po can be increased to a swelling chorus of jubilation in the farthest corners of Bhutan.

To the developed yogi the dream-world and the " real " world are not dissociated, but the mingled parts of one pattern. Sleep, it is held, frequently reveals the hidden tracts along which the wheels of our volition guide us to our destined end. It follows that if one can project oneself into the sleep of another person, it is possible (granted the requisite expertise) to direct him or her, by a skilful adjusting of certain psychic knobs, much more surely along the path he or she should go. Also, a weak mind can be taken under the protection of a stronger by being drawn into the ambit of a carefully-woven imaginative pattern into which the senses can be poured.

The materialisation of demons plays a large part in those branches of Yoga which are connected with keeping the baser world at bay. There must be no confusion here. It is not that the yogi wishes to ally himself with any improper agency : on the contrary, he is desperately anxious to keep far away from his inner sanctuary all things that " go bump in the night." He knows that the spirit can only rise when the more acrid and strident emotions have been sloughed off. But, at the same time, he realises the necessity for keeping the adytum clear from the surreptitious " gate-crasher " who would defile the temple with his ignorance and incapacity. Therefore figures of dire menace and admonition are projected and erected, frequently outside lonely hill-hermitages and the tents of ascetics, to scare away the impertinent and the unwary. There are many devils at large in Tibet: they focus attention on themselves while the religious experts carry on their work undisturbed.

When this method fails, there are more drastic measures. Closely guarded in one of the more inaccessible Tibetan monasteries, there exists a manuscript written many centuries ago by the great Padma Sambhava (referred to previously), who reconciled the primitive Tibetan religion with his own version of Mahayana Buddhism. This purports to be a collection of magical spells and conjurations of enormous power and efficacy. It is referred to, sometimes as The Great Doctrine, sometimes as The Secret of the Thunderbolt. The present writer has seen one of the few available copies of the original script.

The *dorje,* or Thunderbolt, is perhaps the most weighty of Tibetan religious symbols. It stands for the massed strength of the Gods, the " fortissimo " aspect of domination and confidence. It is to be wielded only with the fullest knowledge and respect. But the reward which is promised to the initiate who becomes master of the spells which it governs, is commensurate with its potency. By the incantation of the mystic words one can escape the otherwise inevitable round of rebirths, and Nirvana be entered long before the normal time. All obstacles are removed from the path : The " eightfold powers of the *Siddhis* " (supernormal gifts) are speedily acquired ; and enemies will be swept away as chaff before the wind. No human guile can turn away the wrath of Chana Dorje, the Lord of the Thunderbolt.

The associations of this invocation may well remind us of some of the more colourful episodes in medieval witchcraft. The initiate is adjured to choose the right time and season. " Select a night when thunder rages. See before your eye the great Chana Dorje riding the skies. Hold in your hand His all-powerful weapon, the Thunderbolt. Prostrate yourself before His image on a mirror cleansed by the purifying waters of the ascetic will."

Next, pressure is brought to bear upon the god by the utterance of one of the most formidable of the Words of Power. The

reader will note here the subtle repetition employed. One of the
fundamental laws of esoteric hypnotism is implicit in this device.
" Meditating on the majesty of the God, meditating upon the might
of the God, utter three times the mantra ' Heegh,' the holy Word,
the ineffable Word, the Word which summons the all-conquering
Bodhisattva from his home in the storm-lashed Heavens." When the
word is repeated for the last time the thunder will cease. The
initiate is now secure in his knowledge that the God has passed into
the image. In token of the transubstantiation, the *dorje* is
held to the sacred lips of the image. Then it is advised to pronounce
the Great *Mantra,* the mysic syllable *Om,* which compels all gods
to hearken.

" Look intently into the eyes of the Image. Although the lips
will move, the teeth gnash, and the eyes gleam with all the terror
of the Heavens, fear not. Still gaze on. Remain in your position
until cosmic bliss passes into you. Then you inherit the power of
the God Himself." It is not surprising, when one studies invocations of this calibre to find that several yogis in Tibet are quite
convinced that, by the mental power they amass during these ceremonies, they can " kill at a distance." Either by auto-suggestion
or by occult fact these manipulators of the psyche are able,
not only to predict the future with amazing accuracy, but to cause
the punishment to fit the crime by casting in front of those who have
mocked the symbols and images held sacred, a tangled and nebulous
landscape which leads sooner or later to the brink of a pit. It is not
proposed here to discuss the rationale, the questions of abstract
justice, involved in these incidents. Suffice it to say that there is
ample evidence for those curious about such matters ; and it has
been held from time immemorial that to harm, or seek to harm a
Tantrik is to incur woe and calamity in this life and intolerable
suffering and disappointment in the next.

Beyond the Himalayas, in India, the fulfilment of Shiva
shows him dancing : at the end of the corridor of pain, a door opens
into the sunlight of Love. It is a virile and optimistic faith which
posits as its central core the idea of a rapture which is careless
because it is so complete. It must be repeated that the ultimate
harvest is good.

Shiva, and his various Tibetan analogues are best viewed as
the Saviour of Mankind, the Destroyer of the Unreal. It is not for
nothing that his throat is painted blue in the usual images one
comes across in countless temples and groves. When the Gods
churned the Ocean of Nectar and fomented a poison so strong that

the three worlds of gods, men and demons were wellnigh destroyed, he held the venom in his throat so that we all may live. It is the worst of errors to assume that he represents the abandonment of mortal passion. For he will have none of earthly passion : of that he is the Destroyer, and of all things that make for it. And the phallic emblem is the concentrated symbol of all that cannot touch Shiva—lust and the disruption that comes from lust.

In the note-books of a very old Yogi we found the God addressed thus : " Shiva, Light of Lights, austerity of austerities, fruit of all holy things, the calmness of the calm, the Knower of the Knowledge, the self-controller of the self-controlled, the wisdom of the wise, the seer of auspicious things, yogin of yogins from the worlds have issued once and for all." This is not the language of hysterical licentiousness, but the very voice of the highest spiritual chastity.

The *Tantrik* yogi, when meditating, frequently carries the image of this God in a kind of conducted tour around all the spiritual centres of his psychic body. Shiva is worshipped in the heart, the head and in the abdomen. His light shines along the avenues which pass through the junctions of the *chakras* to the very root of the Mystery. His strength, drawn upwards on the white horses of the waves of desire, sinks down at last on the weight of its own bliss. Likewise, over the rocks and boulders of the defeated senses his consort is brought to meet him, until, in the rapture which passes understanding, yogi and god and goddess are one. The refined and subjugated sense apparatus is brought into this psychic fugue after a manner which will strike the more timid Westerner as excessive. The god is absorbed through every sub-tilised extension of sight, hearing, smell, taste and touch. Often, the image is destroyed afterwards, because it has no further use as a medium. When the palace of the Self is ablaze with the glory in the heart of a god, then everything in this world becomes little more than an echo heard from afar. To keep the ladder on which one has ascended to the stars would be an unnecessary piece of sentimentality.

It will not be amiss to end these remarks on the splendour of the dancing Shiva with a reiteration. Vivid as may be the appeal of the religious habits outlined above, it must be remembered that they have no ultimate value except as a stepping-stone to higher things. To linger too long in the outer courts is to run the risk of forgetting the inexpressible perfection of the hidden figure within the shrine. It is not every cripple who needs a crutch. There are some lucky and immediate mentalities on whom the Light shines without speck or mote. It will not be necessary to tell these emancipated ones that their road lies straight before them : their desire will shoot to its goal like an arrow from a bow. It is to the weaker brethren that the injunction is addressed: to follow, at all costs, the Gleam.

The huge and sonorous orchestra will one day die down. The rites of propitiation and expiation will leave no trace on the desert air. The gods themselves will vanish in the rounded completion of the Scheme of Things. " On the burning-ground of Kali all worldly desires are burned away. She is naked and dark like a threatening rain-cloud, for She who, as Herself beyond all expression reduces all living things into that worldly ' nothingness ' which, as the Void of all which we know, is at the same time the All, which is Light and Peace."

If the reader wishes he can build his own Mount Kailasa on the purity and simplicity of his best and most unselfish aspirations. There is a passage in the *Bhagavad Gita,* that sublime Bible of yogic devotion, which gives the recipe to all who can read. " Abiding alone in a secret place, without craving and without possessions, the good-man shall take his place upon a firm seat, neither over-high nor over-low, and with the working of the mind and of the senses held in check, with body, head and neck maintained in perfect equilibrium, looking not round about him, so let him meditate and thereby reach the peace of the Abyss : and the likeness of one such, who knows the boundless joy that lies beyond the senses, which is grasped by intuition, and who swerves not from the truth, is that of a lamp in a windless place that does not flicker."

CHAPTER VI.

INITIATION INTO TIBETAN YOGA.

BEFORE DEALING with a subject of such a recondite nature as the above it is necessary to hold up certain warnings. Initiation is a word and a concept which can give birth to the wildest extravagance and fantasy. It is rarely used in the West without some association of ambiguity or even scandal.

Before one can initiate people into rites one must possess rites to initiate them into. So often these latter are invented, or to put it mildly, culled from highly doubtful quarters, in which numbers of markedly neurotic individuals live in a condition of artificially exalted and completely imaginary converse with a godhead. No names are mentioned ; but the reader cultured in these matters will unhesitatingly cast his mind not too far back to organisations, surreptitious and otherwise, which, after payment of a very definite and, for the most part, quite inappropriate fee, "initiated" the novice into exactly nothing, or at the best, into a sodden marsh, in which his wits, like his feet, slipped into a frequently irredeemable chaos.

It is dangerous and confusing to take it that East has the same technique as West in these matters. No one with the slightest acquaintance "East of Suez" will attribute to the oriental mind the sogginess and misconception on spiritual matters which seems so often to be the inalienable birthright of the Westerner. The difference resolves itself at the last resort, into an economy and a powerful sense of direction. The Tibetan, in particular, refuses to waste his time on things which do not appear to him essential. He rebels too against any suggestion that the game of mumbo-jumbo is worth playing for its own sake. Unless he can see something for his money in the shape of a definite increase in spiritual garnerings when he gives himself to the life of consecration, he is, like Queen Victoria, " not amused." He is nowise willing to be ushered into back-basements for the thrill of coming face to face with an Adeptus or for that matter with an even more equivocal Adepta. He does not hold that the Kingdom of Heaven resides in the hearts of persons who are chiefly concerned with the uncharitable business of cutting each other's throats, and who seek to surpass each other in the pompous assertion of occult

86

superiority. In other words he is not interested in competing in such company.

Initiation into any mystery can only come when the mind and heart are ready for it. Only too often, in the West, the entrance is sought because of some peevish and discontented attitude towards the actual world. It must be remembered that it is not always the individualist who leaves the world. *Au contraire* the world sometimes leaves the individualist; and the world is not entirely to be blamed. Many persons demand an attention quite out of proportion to their moral and spiritual weight. When they fail to secure what they regard as their due, they are apt to retaliate by shaking the dust of the ignoble compound off their feet. But the compound carries on as usual in its daily round; and the task, though common, is a task.

Not so with the self-humiliated aspirant. In revenge for his neglect by the lesser brethren (or worthless rabble) he seeks out some group or society of an esoteric cast. His wounded pride can only be solaced by the conviction that some home awaits him which has nice snug hearths for a select few (among whom he will one day be pre-eminent). Little or no thought is given to the breadless multitude outside the portals: except to contemn and devalue and, if occasion permits, to make use of them—a policy in which the whole Council of the Elect raise up a voice in full accord.

It is little wonder that the word "initiation" has come to be anathema to the genuinely enquiring individual whose trials and troubles have not been assuaged in the bosom of any of the orthodox Churches. Rather than submit himself to rites and rituals in which his frequently sound common sense does not concur, he wanders disconsolate among the bleak purlieus of arid pseudo-rationalism, or worse, tries to sink all his spiritual strivings in a despairing acceptance of the conventional lies of the day. So souls are left unfulfilled, "hang still, patchy and scrappy," and the drooling deities of materialism add another victim to their fold.

It is unfortunate that so much insistence is made by occultists on the difference between "the Western and the Eastern tradition." As far as the present writer has been able to ascertain, by long and patient research in these matters, the origin of all secret or semi-secret rites of any validity is to be found in the Eastern genius for religious technique. Both scholarship and sound intuition go to prove that, for all practical purposes, the organic conception and realisation of the forces of nature which is at the heart of the deepest religious experience had a definitely Eastern provenance. Maybe in the Nile Delta, maybe in some jungle of Northern India or in some upland of Tibet, there arose, thousands of years since, certain of the sons of men freed by nature and appointment from the illogicality of the animal, whose mission it was to prove that there is a constant of perfection in humanity, in no sense limited by the boundaries of time and space.

One must beware of sentimentality. The East, at least on a surface observation, is made up of many idiotic traditional observances, many abominable varieties of climate and a multitude of bad smells. There is no reason to assume that, taken man for man, the average Easterner is wiser than the average Westerner. But it can be categorically asserted that the atmosphere he breathes can, if properly assimilated, conduce to a more reverent and comprehending attitude towards the universe.

In Tibet, in particular, there is little to distract the mind from the pursuit of Truth. A country with a singularly bracing and hardening atmosphere, surrounded with mountain ranges of an indescribable majesty, is little calculated to appeal to those who like their religion *couleur de rose*. With numbers of enclosed monasteries as its only architectural relief, the whole landscape contains no suggestion of the morbid and flurried overcrowding which has made Europe the cockpit of so much that is doomed to destruction. Communications with the outside world are practically non-existent. The religious novice inured to this physical and spiritual clime is scarcely likely to waste his energies in thinking wistfully of the insensate striving and epileptic hatreds of the foreigners beyond the hills.

It follows, that we find in Tibet no strictly-drawn line of division between laity and clergy. Every calling merges at some point into the religious life of the community ; and every religious dedicatee realises to the full his obligation to the less initiated workers around him. If any merely earthly region can be said to have attained harmony, it is this territory consecrated from time immemorial to the pursuit of the things of the spirit.

The naturalness of religious reaction is its most attractive feature. The humblest and most pedestrian Tibetan would never dream of regarding those more spiritually developed than himself as isolated and aloof in some prim sacerdotal domain. On the other hand, he has recourse to the lamas on any occasion for which he feels his own powers insufficient. At the same time the reader must not commit the error of thinking that the religious expert is regarded by the Tibetans as the representative of any supreme anthropomorphic deity. Rather, communication with any Godhead must be viewed as getting in touch with some particular aspect of Power. Different grades and types of the priesthood cater for different desires and aspirations. In the blackest depths of activity, a priest-sorcerer is sought; in the serene heights, a guide is approached because a fair city has been espied in some rapt moment of natural exaltation, and added energy is desired in order that the vision may be made constant.

The process is that of a magnetic chain. At the summit of the ladder of attainment are the Buddhas, with their various graces and gifts. Next comes the supreme *guru,* Dorje-Chang, the Lord of the Thunderbolt. He, too, holds in his hands many keys to many doors. The line of celestial *gurus* who occupy the next place in the hierarchy are intermediaries between His all-encompassing might and the apostolic *gurus* on earth, whose lives are consecrated to the task of directing and organising the religious possibilities of this world. Under these are the lesser gurus, who know much, but whose destiny it is to get more in touch with individual, striving humanity. Lastly, the neophytes bring up the rear. They are the beginnings of the initiatory process—the clay in the hands of the potter which is shaped for a divine end. Once the first step has been taken, the first vow spoken, there is no going back. Even if the novice is fated to err against the illuminated inner conscience within him, it is impossible that he shall be the same " man of the world " of the past. No matter how halting the step, it is set irrevocably towards the heights.

Nevertheless, it is not every aspirant who can climb in this life to the topmost crags. Sometimes it happens that the will and the conviction, although sufficient to prompt the beginner to a new orientation of his mental and moral life, is not strong enough to warrant entry into the higher teachings. In these cases, after the usual period of trial, the initiate is reserved for the lower functions of election. Generally speaking, the probationary period, save in exceptional cases, lasts for one year.

It is important to point out here that women as well as men may be *gurus.* Tibet knows no bars of sex or caste, granted that the heart and mind are ready for the Great Work. Indeed, in some respects, women, owing to their greater sense of realism and their profounder sensuous intuitions, are by nature better equipped for the intricacies of inward religious research than is the more unimaginative and adamant male. Also, it cannot be too often emphasised, they are the copies of the Great Mother of the World, from whom all phenomena flow.

There is no chopping and changing once one has found a suitable guide. There is nothing in Tibet which corresponds to the neurotic game of General Post which is so disconcerting a feature of the "salvation racket" in Europe. Very proper precautions on both sides must be taken before a working harmony is established between the two partners to this momentous contract ; but once it is seen that virtue can be given out on one side and assimilated on the other, then there is no necessity for change. Consistency and perseverance are frequently the best preparations for eternity.

Of course, it sometimes happens that a pupil is so gifted by nature and so diligent in his application that the *guru* finds himself in the position of having no more to give. In this eventuality a new *guru* is recommended, of greater knowledge and experience. Very occasionally a pupil is so developed on account of his good karmic record that he arrives very quickly on what Buddhists call the "Short Path." This implies that he needs henceforth no especial guidance except that which comes from within his own serene inner conviction.

It must be noted that, in Tibet, there does not exist the same relationship between teacher and disciple which persists in Southern India. Frequently, a relationship is established without further ado on the basis of first impressions. One of the most remarkable features of the Tibetan mentality is its capacity for judging what is really important in human character. People "of the same wavelength" often come together without any unnecessary preliminaries of conventional investigation. The best judgment is of the heart, not of the head. By Western standards, the Tibetan *guru* is by no means always a person of impeccable morality. Polyandry is tolerated, even in the most spiritualised circles; and very few Tibetans would raise the prudish eyebrow at the more obvious and primitive urges of the flesh. Curiously enough, serious exception is taken to marriage between cousins, even at the fourth remove. What the disciple usually seeks is some deep layer of psychic power which is strong enought to annul any surface vices.

With apparent cynicism he will sometimes turn from his master, when he has learnt all there is to know in that quarter. But his renegacy is not due to any sensation-seeking folly, but to the conviction that, like himself, the *guru* is human ; and that, when one species of vitality shows obvious limitations, then it is time to transfer one's attentions to another. The whole relationship is dictated by the commonsense realisation that it is useless to take up with any teacher who does not understand one's own particular case. Only those who have walked the same hard way as ourselves, in this or a previous incarnation, are competent to guide us. Otherwise a subtle battle of cross-purposes will negative progress.

Among Tibetan initiates faith is a power in itself. To put it in a slightly exaggerated form, it does not matter so much what one believes, as the result of the process of believing. When we give all our heart and soul to a vision, we erect for and around ourselves a vast protective barricade enclosing untold possibilities of releasable energy. To "enter the stream" is to project our whole will into its fulfilment, from any jumping-off board which may be to us the most natural and handy : and predilections are essentially personal.

It follows, that among certain yogis much stress is laid on those aspects of ceremonial initiation which have for long been associated with this accumulation of psychic energy. A balance must be obtained between knowledge (*chesrab*) and its application (*thabs*). Recourse is naturally had to those symbols of power which, although devoid at first sight of any ultimate significance, yet propel the mind to the world of balanced opposites on which deliverance rests. The *dorje* and the hand-bell (*tilpu*) which have always stood with the Tibetans for the polarisation of the male and female elements in life are given to the novice. He clasps them in his right and left hands respectively, and proceeds to associate all his life and energy with the forces inherent in these two concepts. For the remainder of his life on this earth he wears on the little fingers of both hands rings bearing the emblems of the immemorial instruments of occult attraction. Thus is his mind poised between void and desire: remembering that the secret of life resides in the injunction "Be What You Are" he dedicates himself with all his heart and will to the finding of his own strong level within the planes of concentration.

For the purposes of our exposition we may divide the initatory ceremonies of Tibet into two main categories—those of an orthodox character, connected with the established monasteries, and those of a more individual and, for the most part, more intricate character in which the ceremony takes place in some remote fastness, some desert retreat, where the soul has, perhaps, more chance to expand. It is necessary to realise that in Tibetan practice the usual order of things is reversed. In this land of religious specialists, where so many young men feel the call to a life of abnegation and aspiration, it is customary for monasteries to be entered almost as a matter of course. There is no natural irreverence among the young intellectuals of Tibet, no "rationalism" of the more deadening and stultifying sort. An organised centre where many eager spirits are gathered together is regarded as the natural goal for those seeking to expand their faculties. But even the monasteries do not profess to cater for the more hardy mountaineers of the spirit.

These latter sorts frequently leave the roof of their "alma mater" and seek development at a further remove. They need a more solitary climate, a more invigorating air for the spiritual lungs to expand. The monk's cell sometimes leads to the ascetic's retreat. Tibet is full of anchorites who look back on their novitiate in Ghum or Gan-den as only the first tentative beginning of their pilgrimage.

Leaving aside, for a moment, the regular accepted forms of initiation, we may dwell with some profit on the less accessible rites of the solitary gurus who have cut themselves off from the orthodox tradition of the great centres. These may be roughly classed under the headings of Esoteric and Exoteric.

Chief and most subtle among the first group is the manner of initiation by telepathy. There are several cases on record of a delicately-tuned relationship between teacher and disciple which is able to forego the usual procedure of physical concourse. Mediating in solitary silence, often separated by great distances, each "picks up" what the other has to give. Herein lies a valuable lesson for the Westerner who has no opportunity to visit what may be his own spiritual home. He can "tune in" his mental and psychic apparatus to a chosen friend yearning to help all mankind, although divided physically from most of them by the towering Himalayas. Much peace and harmony of mind will follow, once the requisite power of concentration has been established. "Ask and ye shall receive."

Another order of yogis teach by gesture. Most of us have no idea of the enormous power of "pantomime." It is a device which the East has brought to the finest of arts. Once the correct *rapport* had been found with the pupil, there is no end to the constructive configuration on the psyche which can be performed by a master skilled in the suggestive manipulation of those bodily limbs which are the limbs of the cosmos. The *yantras* or geometrical diagrams which have been explained elsewhere, perform something of the same service to the rigging of the intelligence and will.

A further method of training popular in esoteric circles is the "Meditation on the Wheel." It should be recalled that the *Chakras* of the psychic body may also be regarded as re-duplications of the Wheel in miniature: the course of man's life follows, in its broad outlines, the astrological rotations of the worlds. To study the broad impulses in the nature of things is to lay the foundation of reformation in our own being. The visualisation is carried to each of the Centres, and, floated on the waves of absolute cause and effect, the student attains to a wide serenity in which his vision is remarkably expanded.

The usual expression of the symbol in Tibet differs from the orthodox Buddhist emblem in marked particulars. It is much more minatory, much more powerful in texture and tone. As one would expect from artists educated to paint with the palette of intensity, there is more insistence on the admonitory than on the benign. It depicts creation in the grip of Mara, who, as the embodiment of Desire, lords it over his three daughters, Lust, Stupidity and Anger, which are painted at the hub in the centre as a cock, a hog and a snake. There are six compartments. That on the right is devoted to the heavenly realms, peopled with celestial beings and with all the concomitants of bliss: also with hints of that divine species of suffering which springs from the satiety consequent on every enjoyment except that of the Inexpressible. On the left are shown the human worlds, each with its special characteristics and limitations. Next to these are the territories of the Titans who strive ineffectively against the dominant gods. In the space below the centre come the hells, blazing mementoes of destruction. Left of these we see the astral worlds of disconsolate ghosts, undelivered from their febrile cravings. Right, live the animals, waiting patiently for their unfolding.

The outer circle or tyre of the design conveys a lesson in philosophy. Written here in twelve segments are the "causal bonds" which keep us tied to the illusions of the Wheel: Unconscious Will, the insensate striving of our inner resolution after the false delights of the flesh ; Conformation, or an equally fatuous acceptance of the ambiguous standards of the world ; Consciousness, Self-Consciousness, Perception, Contact, Feeling, Desire, Indulgence, Individual Existence, Birth, Atrophy and Death. Here are deployed both the lures and the psychological framework of actual life.

Attached to the rite of the "Wheel" Meditation are certain apothegms of Padma Sambhava, venerated as one of the greatest Apostles of Deliverance. These should be enunciated slowly, with due regard for their deep occult import, during the concentration. The following are among the most popular. "My body is like a hill, my eyes are like the ocean: my mind resembles the sky." "When I pass the bridge, lo! the water floweth not ; but the bridge floweth." By casting back one's mind to the thoughts of one who passed triumphantly through all the trials of life one is inspired to new renunciation and new endeavour.

A very interesting initiation is carried out in silence with master and pupil facing each other in appropriate postures. The distractions of the world eliminated by a concentrated one-pointedness of mind, both exert all their inward energies to establish a subtle pontoon of union between the reservoirs of dynamism which constitute their respective personalities. The *guru* sends out his Gift-waves of grace towards his disciple and the disciple in his turn answers mentally with what he has to give of the essence of his youth. The technique consists in the former releasing from the *chakra* between the eyes a radiation of beneficient vitality which is "caught up" by the latter and absorbed by the *Manipura chakra* in the region of the solar plexus. It is incumbent upon the pupil that he tell no man of what has passed: there are capacities which become all the stronger when a veil is drawn over what cannot be expressed in the province of analytical language.

Sometimes the above initiation ends with what is called "the ceremony of the rosary." This aid to meditation consists in Tibet of a hundred and eight beads, to each of which is attached some special significance in the higher development of concentration. The reader will not have to be reminded that the intense absorption in any physical object leads, if successful, to a very definite psychic "release." In a subtle way the contact of the fingers with a smooth surface helps to raise the mind to a more liberal plane. It is not by accident that the more "hypnotic" religions of the West have made full use of this device: the suggestion of the circle conveys both an inevitability and an escape. In the "silent" initiation the guru places the fingers of the disciple on each of the beads in turn: then he consecrates the act by going over them with his own. Thus is a psychic and spiritual communion established in one rhythm. And the master is able to reinforce both batteries by "drawing from" the voltages of his own *guru* in the past, even if the latter is dead, that is one step further on the Road. The "triumphant dead" can help in more ways than one.

Perhaps the most picturesque of the secret or semi-secret rites is that which may be translated as "The Devotion to the Altar." Particularly when it is realised that the appurtenances described have, one and all, their own inalienable and ordered significance. Indeed, this ceremony is as important as any in unrolling before the student the extraordinary meticulous methodology of the Tibetan technique for inducing the esoteric forces of the over-worlds to manifest themselves in the world of men.

So exacting is this celebration that it is necessary for the officiating priest, no matter how confident in his own virtue, to give himself up to a long and arduous period of preparation. He will be handling fire, and there is no man who has no need to tremble in the courts of the Lords of Life and Death. Solitude and self-examination are the preliminaries for the confrontation of the stoked-up energies of the Altar. Sometimes the lama is in retreat for as long as two or three months.

The first step to be taken is the construction of a *mandala* or sacred block. This is a square structure with length and breadth calculated from the distance between the elbow and middle fingers of the lama. It must be as smooth and equable as a mirror. With five separate powders, of the colours white, yellow, green, red and blue, the block is divided into five sections. At each corner of the contrivance is a small door, and in the centre a blue disc, on which gleams an eight-petalled lotus. In addition, four bars are traced—white towards the East, yellow to the South, green to the North and red to the West. Within this enclosure are placed different offerings: and there is much figuration, meant to represent various climes and inhabitants of this world.

A number of *dorjes* (symbols of the aggregate of force in all matter) surround the design, while at each corner and in the middle repose five ritual vessels. These contain mixtures of water and milk, grain, medicinal plants, perfumes, the "three whites" —cream, cheese and butter—the "three sweets"—honey, sugar and treacle. Further adornments include the "five mirrors," the five pieces of rock-crystal, five images of the mystical Buddhas, arrows, variegated silks and the feathers of peacocks.

Once this paraphernalia has been gathered together and put in its correct position, the ceremony gets under way. Black tea or grain brandy is set out as an offering to the gods: ritual cakes are placed on the square: the bowl made from a human skull is placed in the disciple's hand. As a final preliminary, magic daggers are set at each of the four "doors" and four knives are driven between the "bars."

Now ensues a liturgical dialogue between the celebrant and the novice. It usually takes this form:

Lama: "You are content to remain in the dwelling of the Presence?"

Disciple: "I am most content."

Lama: "Then know that the Buddhas, the world's wisdom and the wisdom of the starry spaces exists entirely within thyself. Prepare to feel within thee the volcano of thine own force."

Next, a ring of parti-coloured threads is tied to the candidate's left arm. The water-pot, as symbol of purity, is placed in turn on the four vital centres of the body—on the head, throat, navel and heart. This is signified the participation in sacred vows. For an initiate to go back on what he has promised to his own essential nature would be to incur unspeakable misery and torment. Although his monastery, like his "Kingdom of Heaven," is within himself; yet there is a superficial discipline as well as one of a more fundamental cast hidden within the organisation of his indissoluble body-mind. The dedicated life is none the less stringent because it owes no allegiance to anything outside the circle of its own profound experience.

As an accompaniment to this diverse procedure is heard the roll of muffled drums. The instruments, played by the lama's assistants, made as they are of human skin, serve a double purpose. They at once put the candidate into the semi-hypnotic condition indispensable for the impressionability required; they are potent to summon the most intractable forces from the depths of the mineral and crystal kingdoms; and, finally, by their volume of sound they call the mind to one of the most dominating principles of the higher Yoga metaphysics—namely, that the elemental Force which deposited the worlds in its wake manifested Itself first as *Shabda* or sound.

The ceremony becomes even more dramatic. The candidate is now blindfolded, and a flower is put into his hand. He must cast it on to the *mandala*. Much will depend on the direction of the throw. Among other things the new "confirmation" names which the disciple will assume (in Tibet of a fortifying character, testifying to certain realised powers on the candidate's part) will be selected on the basis of this singular version of "the red and the black." There must be a full trust in one's guardian angel to guide the hand aright.

If the flower falls to the South there are certain virtues and graces which follow inevitably in its train. For men this will be vital and abounding joy—a constant flow of an intense cosmic-consciousness: for women, a brilliant light on the architecture of the mind and will. If the North is favoured, there is promised to men complete liberation from the fetters of the unresolved senses ; to women, a directive stream of energy extending equally in all directions. Similar connotations accompany the other compass points.

The conclusion of the rite draws near, and the candidate is allowed to remove the bandage. The lama tells him, in sacerdotal language, that the blinkers of ignorance have been removed from his eyes. A great gush of rapture ensues, and the lama, in the dazzled awareness after the blindness, is seen as a beam of light. So is the ascent made from dedication and resolution, through the multifariousness of matter to the Body of Light which knows no diminution of its flame. The demons are conquered and the soul can continue gaily along its self-appointed road.

It may be said in passing that very great expertness is necessary for the correct construction of the *kyilkhors* or diagrams which serve as the concentration-ground for all kinds of mystic initiatory processes. Indeed, there exist in Tibet a number of small training-institutes which specialise in teaching the exact manufacture of these aids to power. As well as the square type described, there are circular, triangular and rhomboidal designs in general use in ceremonial practice.

The least error in correct delineation is viewed with considerable apprehension. It is held that psychic adeptness of the strongest kind works its way out into the open only along thoroughly determined and delimited channels. To make any avoidable mistake in delineating the elaborate setting which is laid down for supernatural entities, is to bring down on one's head a whole avalanche of undirected energies. The magic of symbol and formula answers to the magic which connects the ordered gradation of our own bodily " descent," from the causal and mental forms in very lofty spheres, to the gross deposit here below. An error in the projection of outward form is equivalent to a defect in the alignment of those mutually supporting parts which make up the efficiency of the ego. A bomb can explode from underneath us as well as from above us : it behoves the wary to take good care that they do not trip up or go astray on the psychic mine-fields.

It is of course, imperative that the *kyilkhor* should be traced by an initiate. Little reinforcement could come from one not attuned to the subtle emanations which arise from artfully-drawn line and angle. All that would result would be a dead formation, without reference or meaning. A full knowledge of the energies and relationships involved in colour is also essential to the practice of the craft. Colour can stimulate towards the most abounding health or can lower the vitality to disintegration point. We have enough proof of this phenomenon in several experimental therapeutic clinics. The East has known from time immemorial what we are just beginning to rediscover.

Very often the first concern of the novice after his initiation is to make himself adept in the art of *mandala* building. When he has acquired the necessary proficiency in this branch of his psychic preparation he can go on to the even more difficult business of constructing the figure of the god who is to inhabit the *yantra*. This exercise demands as well as considerable imaginative force, a very tight control of the most recondite of the breathing processes.

First, seated in the appropriate attitude of veneration, he must picture to himself a god or goddess arising out of the centre of the substructure. Just as the sculptor moulds his clay, so must he envisage, section by section, the feet, limbs, torso, and head of the deity. No part must be overlooked, no centre of energy allowed to refuse its quota of " gift-waves." And all must be absorbed into the etheric body of the adoring postulant. He must remain long in contemplation of this objectivised picture of a swelling reality in his own subconscious. He will not tire.

With loving tenderness he will take all this beauty into himself. Little by little a further miracle will happen. Out of the one benignant or minatory figure will spring lesser Gods in miniature. Apparently from the head and shoulders of the image these minor representatives of the Law will enter to play their part in the drama of the aspirant's quick rumination. Often there are four of these myrmidons to be pondered on : in the higher grades of meditative exercise there is, however, no limit to their number.

A double process takes place in this exercise. The " court " of the sovereign god is projected, but it is likewise reabsorbed into the heaven from which it came. One by one the little shimmering figurines disappear into the parent stem. The worshipper is left alone once more with the God he has summoned from the depths of his own mind. This figure too begins to take its leave. It departs as it came : first the feet, then the rest of the body, until there remains on the tremulous air nothing but a dot. This may be a luminous astral speck or a tiny floating circle of some definite coloration.

There is no space here to enumerate the copious occult interpretation given to these phenomena by Tibetan esoteric scholars. It is enough to point out that the place in which the dot seems to enter the body of the disciple is of the utmost significance. The future course of training of this particular type of devotee is largely determined in this way.

A word may be said on the use of the " Meditation in Darkness," so frequently advocated by the good psychologists among the *gurus*. The Tibetans are total strangers to the normal Western reactions in this respect. They fear neither darkness nor solitude. To minds accustomed from childhood to regard the riotous outside world as illusory, there is nothing more tranquilising in their eyes than the life of " elected silence." Indeed, they are able to communicate their tastes in this matter to foreigners. Any Western traveller with enough sensitiveness in his composition finds himself very soon falling into the " lonely " ways of the inhabitants of this strangely beautiful land. He no longer dreads the " monotony " of his own society, but finds in it the key to a vast, unexplored, infinitely absorbing psychic territory hitherto undreamt of.

A hint can be picked up here by all who would seek some freedom from the galling bonds of the lower self. There is no tyranny like that which comes from the nagging insistence by the outer world for conformity to its own attitude in matters affecting the alleged "cheerfulness," which is supposed to come from the false daylight of continuous social "amusements." Study to be quiet ! A great French mystic has told us that he who can sit at peace alone in a small room has learned the whole secret of existence. If he had added that the room should be in darkness the setting would have been improved. It is perhaps only when the heart is left to its own devices in the all-absorbing sense of release which comes when night has fallen that the full beauty of life is realised ; for then we are forced to find the hidden glory within ourselves, and the discovery can be fraught with the most ecstatic joy.

The human imagination is loaded with the very highest possibilities. Thoughts, of which the imagination is the propeller and " only begetter," are enormous forces if directed and motivated aright. The chief essential is elimination. We must help ourselves by cutting gradually out of our lives all that makes for waste and distraction. To cultivate the habit of darkness, if only for ten minutes during each day, is to experience tremendous influx of power, which may bewilder at first, but which will soon settle down to suffuse all the creeks and crannies of our inner being. And as we are fed and sustained by those emanations which gush from the more eternal parts of us outside the visible body, it follows that the more we cut ourselves off from the customary sight of stereotyped physical objects (including our houses, gardens and the frequently boring apperception of our physical frame and appearance) the more ready shall we be to enter the Kingdom.

Nature in light or darkness is the great healer. The most hardened soul knows at times the rejuvenating power of solitude in some woodland glen or some lonely hill around which the waves of the sea emulously surge. Here the worries of existence can be forgotten while, in a kind of divine hypnotic trance, we allow the vitality which belongs to crystals, quartzes and all the multitudinous life of plants and flowers to course through our veins.

A very trying initiation consists in lying on the back and staring fixedly at the sun. This is not to be recommended to the ordinary novice as the strain on the optic nerve is great. Also it involves a considerable degree of a rather curious kind of occult meditation. The Tibetans are a very hardy people, and what would appal our endurance strikes them as a trifing concession to the bounty of the gods. What, they argue, is a little discomfort, compared with the rewards of enduring peace ?

Following the directions of his guide, the disciple should gaze at the orb until the dancing points of light which blind him at first resolve themselves into a single dark spot. When this latter stays motionless, he is confident that his mind is " fixed "—that is, open to receive certain visions and visitations. These assume the form of innumerable combinations of deities and occult circumstances. From the results of his teaching he interprets these apparitions, whether favourable or the reverse. He takes the omens as encouragements or corrections to the particular line of application which he has been pursuing. If a single image of the Buddha is seen, then he knows that the gods approve of the innate wisdom within himself.

This " ecstasy of the infinitude of space " is regarded by the Tibetans as one of the most valuable of mystical states. More than most experiences, it puts us, they hold, *en rapport* with the great lake of peace at the base of our innermost being. To absorb the fullness of the heavens and then, in on alternative rhythm to " look in our heart " and see there reflected the glory to which we aspire, is to have a foretaste in this earthly lease of what is enjoyed by the dwellers in Elysian groves. For the correct fulfilment of this communion it is necessary that there be nothing in the landscape to divert the attention. Flat land is best ; and virgin soil will give us an added strength !

Very wonderful things are done in Tibet from a knowledge of the manifestations of the sun. It may not be amiss here to describe a remarkable feat practised by adepts throughout the whole districts of the Himalayas. It is the extraction of various kinds of perfume from the refraction of the rays of the sun. For the achievement of this wonder the adept needs only a burning lens which will deflect the rays on to a piece of material. Once the sunshine is focussed it will form a series of clearly-defined circles on the fabric. In a few seconds the material will be redolent with the perfume desired.

There is nothing obviously hypnotic in this " miracle." It is not performed, as so many bemused sceptics suggest, by bamboozling the wits of the observer. It involves, of course, a very acute knowledge of the laws of integration and disintegration of components ; but there is no element of hocus-pocus in its performance. As all life may be said to originate (in our planetary system at least) from the vital rays of the sun, so it should not surprise the balanced student to discover that the vitality can be divided up into its component elements, and that these elements can be knit into various patterns which will correspond to the " octaves " of colour, perfume and sound. The therapeutic importance of these combinations is enormous.

The famous " *Mani* " Initiation may carry a slight atmosphere of familiarity to the Western reader as it is bound up with the well-known mantram " *Aum Mani Padme Hum* " (the Jewel in the Heart of the Lotus). It is an excellent initiation to study, conveying as it does such an admirable idea of the metaphysical side of Tibetan occultism—its merging of the territories of sound and significance. It is performed alone in the silence by master and candidate, repeating after each other the sacred words of power.

Each syllable has its special interpretation. *Aum* (" The Stay of Meditation " as it was termed by the great commentator Sankaracharya) while implying the Three Persons of the Hindu Trinity—Brahma, Vishnu and Siva, in Buddhism signifies the means by which the puny individual mind attains to the inexpressible glory of the Absolute — the ladder from the " I " to the all-inclusive " *That.*" With a deeper meaning still, it awakens thoughts of the creative sound which first brought the worlds into existence. In this vibration are contained all other actual and possible manifestations of sound from all possible sources. Its colour is white, the emblem of the great light which comes from the sun and which illuminates the higher instincts of all who come into this world.

Mani Padme, the Jewel in the Lotus, comprehends the spheres of Titans, men and animals. Taken syllable by syllable, *Ma* signifies the colour blue, with all its occult potencies. *Ni* is yellow, and controls the mechanism of constructive activity. *Pad,* evoking green, summons the whole bewildering life of the animal populations of the cosmos, in its place in the plan of evolution. *Me —* engrossing all the activities of the agitating red colour, signifies the *Yidags* or "unhappy ghosts" who toil and spin in a realm of unsatisfied occult desire. *Hum,* with the colour black, gives vent to the dwellers in the purgatories. It is a bellicose syllable, full of a " banishing power " : by its aid the system is cleansed of the muddy ferments which obstruct the path to the Goal.

After the hundred and eight requisite repetitions of this exercise it is usual to ejaculate the vowel *Hri.* As far as one can put these subtle connotations into words this syllable conveys to the initiate the fundamental essences of reality when all elimination and exclusion has been practised. It is the final clearing of all decks —the embrace of the Self with the Secret behind the worlds.

During all the auto-hypnosis induced by the constant repetition of the formula the colours above-mentioned are circulated through the etheric body with an alternating motion. Merging through all their shades of transmutation they are carried on the breath in one nostril and out of the other. Rapid variations are played on this ground-bass: sometimes the theme is contracted or lengthened ; sometimes the imaginative aspect of the device is stressed, and the six worlds shine brilliantly before the mental eye in all their living profusion. One essential feature of this psychic cleansing is that the phantasmagoria of the creative visualisation must be seen to be illusory. The One abideth !

It will be realised that the doctrine is enhanced by the breathing method employed. As one inhales with the imagination working at full pressure there is collected into one compass every fragment of the usually scattered image-forming faculty. The exhalation of this plethora of pictures automatically figures forth the best projection of its ultimate Emptiness. We breathe in the universe like men eager for disillusion: we breath it out like Gods tired of Their handiwork. " The readiness is all."

The meditation on the lotus itself is more than a mere *point de repère*. Such an antique symbol must be packed with more than we readily imagine of significance and edification. It should go as follows. In the lotus-flower (the whole agglomeration of the worlds with their problems and sufferings) there exists the redeeming doctrine of the Buddha, the jewel of our hopes. Again the lotus is the "eternal mind": the longer we gaze into its depths the more quickly will come our deliverance from the transience and disquiet of phenomena. It is said by many Tibetan mystics that Nirvana itself resides in the heart of the world or worlds we know. To find after long search the core of fire at the centre of all matter is to pass through ecstasy to deliverance. Little wonder that there are a large number of prescribed formulæ in Tibetan initiation which hold fast to this conception.

To pass from the esoteric initiatory systems of Tibet to those of a more orthodox character is to make no great leap. Here may be seen something of the same insistence on preparation and meditation, the same meticulous observance of certain strictly delimited modes of approach to God-force and God-benediction. The only important difference resides in the more open and acknowledged ritual with which these Powers are approached.

The Chief Lamas themselves are, in some sort, supreme initiates. Although their lives are girt around with an apparently very worldly ceremony, yet their very election has a deeply occult connotation. A brief description of the functions and characteristics of these dignitaries will not be out of place here.

The Dalai Lama is the religious descendant of Tsong Kha-pa, the founder of the " Yellow-Caps " (Reformed Sect). He rules over the huge monastery of Potala, where the cream of Tibetan youth is trained for the religious life. He is both a temporal and spiritual ruler. It is this which distinguishes him from the Tashi Lama, who has no temporal sway, and who lives for the most part in retirement in the province of Tsang. There is also trained a traditional Grand Lama who manifests as a woman. The repository of this honour lives as the Lady Abbess of the convent near Lake Yamdok in South Tibet. In contradistinction to the "unreformed " Red-Caps, all these Heads of the Faith enjoin on their followers and on those whom they initiate into various forms of specialised yogic devotion a strict celibacy and general ascetic mode of living.

With the risk of incurring the charge of over-simplification, we may divide the major initiations presided over by these organising directors into three main Vehicles or modes of approach. The first and most popular may be defined as the Vehicle of those who work for the welfare and betterment of present-day humanity. No great knowledge is required here—only the pure and sympathetic heart.

At Gyantse there is an enormous Hall of Initiation with nine priceless symbolic frescoes on the walls. Here the candidate, accompanied by his friends and sponsors, comes to offer a *khadag* (ceremonial scarf) to the officiating lama, and to lay down the more momentous gift of his body and soul to the service of humanity. All around him the Buddhas of beneficence and compassion smile encouragement on his elected way. He listens to the Sacred Scriptures and drinks in their message. Ranged on both sides of the altar are assistants, who, in antiphonal chant, adjure the candidate to carry out the highest dictates of his conscience. Experts, skilled in soul-examination, thresh out by repeated questioning the wheat from the chaff. After this ordeal, the novice takes his place among the rank of circumspect young men who have subdued their passions in Service.

The entry into the Vehicle of " Pure Intellectual Truth," the second of the exoteric initiations, is accompanied by no such pomp and display. In this case there is no public celebration and no public and obvious jubilation in the candidate's heart. Those who enter the path by this turning are usually of a naturally austere and even frigid cast of mind. Not for them the warmth and homeliness of the Temple in the middle of the market-place. Their one desire is to " flee the press " and take up their abode in some isolated library where they can pursue in peace their study of the rigid laws of cause and effect. The " Jnana Yoga " as theirs is called, the Yoga of Knowledge, is the approach through the pure reason. It is the best way for the born metaphysical philosopher: the worst for the realist who is blessed or cursed with the average supply of emotion.

The last Vehicle, known as " The Supremely Excellent," is the most elaborate and the most exigent of the exoteric initiations. It demands both great knowledge and great application in the arts of charity and peace. The candidate must burn with love for all sentient beings: he must also give his days and nights to the probing of problems connected with the Buddhist philosophy. At all costs he must do all in his power to advance the cause and the theories he serves.

A very high degree of mental training is the lot of these candi-didates. They must learn to pare down the necessities and activities of their lives until these have reached the maximum of efficiency and the minimum of waste. The end of every day should show some progress in the tautness of the grip they have elected to exert on their own wasteful impulses and intellectual indiscretions. They must sharpen all their weapons so that they may be foremost in the fight against torpor and indifference. Their light must so shine before men that all will be in some measure inspired by their example. Every faith needs these initiates ; for every faith lives by reason of the energy put into it by its devotees.

The initiate of the " Supreme Vehicle " has to accomplish a very difficult task. He has to learn to meditate, not alone, but in the full company of his fellows. The group of novices is given every day a certain theme for analysis. With lowered eyes and concentrated minds they brood on the subject till its hidden meaning becomes clear. Each initiate is questioned in turn by the director who can see at once if the problem has been " sucked dry." Until this has happened the pupil is not permitted to go further.

There is no help, in the obvious sense, given by the master. If a meditation proves too difficult to comprehend it is, as it were, thrown back into the pupil's mind until its meaning has become apparent. This is what the Buddha meant by his remarks about "the noble silence." Gradually an immense intuitive understanding is established between master and pupils. There is less and less occasion for speech. In the glance of an eye the progress of the disciple along the Path can be detected. There is no finer discipline for the linking of a chain of expert minds into an indissoluble unity.

The " sermons " to which the initiate of the Supreme Vehicle listens are remarkable for their terseness and seeming ambiguity. Actually they are most skilfully formulated announcements which seek to pass beyond the world of the intellect into a dimension where truth is seized on, pure and undefiled by words.

The exoteric, like the esoteric, initiates do not always practise what they preach. Human nature is frail, and there are cases on record of Grand Lamas who have voluntarily weakened from a specious and plausible motive. They have excused their back-sliding on the pretext that it is necessary for them to produce off-spring so that the line of lamas shall continue. At times, too, an not proposed here to expatiate on the moral rights and wrongs of initiate and a woman will come together for the same purpose. It is customs so very alien to our conceptions of propriety. What is frequently repellent to Western prepossessions is treated by most Tibetans with a tolerant shrug. They do not invest the flesh with the same aura of frightened taboo with which we are wont to endue it. The attitude constitutes the main difference between occidental and oriental modes of mental orientation.

Which of the systems of initiation is the best ? This question we must leave the reader to decide for himself. They all purport to lead the same way eventually, and who shall lay down laws on the efficacy of the route? But that there *is* a route, "steep and thorny, beset with perils of every kind " though it be, is incontestable. On this point all fair-minded venturers will agree. Also, it is certain that once one's feet are set toward the goal there is no turning back.

There was once a young shepherd in a province of Tibet, smitten with the dread disease of leprosy. Bereft by one fell stroke, of wife, friends and livelihood, he sought out, in his desperation, a *guru* skilled in the art of understanding.

The *guru* heard his story, took from his hut a little image of the Lord of the Worlds in transport with his consort, She of the skulls and garlands. He told the young man to find some solitary cave and to immure himself for the remainder of his life meditating on the symbol.

The shepherd knew nothing of self-development ; but he had unfailing trust in his master who, he could see, meant him well. For twenty years he lived in his mountain cell, every particle of light excluded, and contemplated the image. Imperceptibly, the symbols began to live: from an æsthetic pattern they commenced to enact the great drama of the universe. The shepherd saw epochs and dynasties dissolve, and re-enter the womb from which they had come. He gazed with awe on the spectacle of lust and striving trampled underfoot by the co-ordinated resolutions of the ever-gentle gods. He gazed and his reverence grew.

Then one day there came a seismic disturbance, and his cave was blown sky-high. The shepherd wandered down the hill and chanced to look in a pool which mirrored his face and body. To his amazement he was clean. Gone was every sign of weakness and disease. He was handsome, healthy and strong.

For one moment a natural impulse seized him. It would be very pleasant to confront his old associates and show them that he was fit to live among them once again, not as their peer but as their superior. Then Reality returned !

The shepherd smiled and turned his steps in the direction of the hills. Now he could at least go forth and seek another *guru,* one even wiser than the first — one who would dispense with symbols and guide him stage by stage to that complete Nirvana for which his simple and uncorrupted soul had always longed.

CHAPTER VII

TIBETAN YOGA AND THE WORKING OF MAGIC.

TO DISCUSS the magical implications of Yoga is to walk, perhaps where even Archangels may fear to tread. There is no aspect of human activity which is so bound up on the one hand with abracadabra and a general sloppiness of intellect, and, on the other, with impulses and habits which the healthier taste of organised society has tacitly agreed to shun. For the whole question of necromancy has never yet been surveyed and studied with a proper regard for the evidence on which its extraordinary claims are based. Hence the misconceptions (and worse, the fears) which prevail when such a subject is mooted among persons of average stability and intelligence. Unable to envisage a scheme of human development which makes possible and tangible powers usually ascribed to the remote figures of folk-lore and fairyland, they prefer to regard as completely outside the normal province of sanity the feats and fables which reach their ears occasionally at certain lurid Christmas firesides, or through the columns of some of the more adventurous Sunday newspapers.

Yet sooner or later every circumspect man must give the matter thought. For alas, in the midst of life we are not only in death, but in the interstices between dimensions which may carry off the most unsuspecting to " kingdoms yet unborn " in the rigid tensity of their conventional minds. It is better that we wake up, before it is too late, to the evil in our midst. Only thus can the forces of disruption be adequately circumvented ; and only thus can the average citizen protect himself against what is, in effect, very germane to his particular case· For one of the most verifiable facts in connection with the practice of the darker magic is that its tactics are particularly successful against the bluff, the hearty, those who relentlessly proclaim that they have " no nonsense " in their constitution.

The reason for this deplorable state of affairs lies in the fact that the ordinary man is ignorant, not so much of magic, but of what should be common or garden psychology. Our knowledge of our own mental processes is still in a very rudimentary stage: we are far too content with the conventions we see, and not half curious enough about the psychic facts which have no visible surface, but which impregnate our every thought and emotion. We live over the simmering volcano of our own inner forces ; and who shall say when these elements are near to eruption or placidly biding their time in the underworld kingdom from which we draw so much of our vitality ?

It behoves the *homme moyen sensuel* to look out for squalls from the direction of his own suggestibility. To walk in the fool's paradise of " a fugitive and cloistered virtue " is to court a disaster which may be irremediable if proper precautions are not taken. And the only proper precautions which can be taken by all and sundry, students and non-students alike, are the schooling of the intelligence in a little of the knowledge which tells of the limitless power of the mechanism of the mind to work us either good or ill.

Many persons are protected from malevolence by the natural opacity and stultification of their minds. But this cannot be accounted to them as a virtue. The cultivation of insensitivity is a double-edged weapon which may kill, much more than save or cure. We are not put on this earth for our faculties to " rust in us unused," but to explore every particle of our being with the object of securing for ourselves the maximum of constructive and responsible fulfilment and the minimum of useless and pointless waste. And even this unsatisfactory protection can be broken down by an intelligence sufficiently crafty and subtle to disclose the Achilles heel of fear or prejudice, which is to be found in the most robust and impercipient of constitutions. Handed down, perhaps, by some ancestor, or left behind by some less balanced incarnatory experience, there exists in every one of us a weak or a blind spot in our psychological equipment which can be used with devastating effect by one skilled in the technique of the psyche.

This is the actual province of the " magician " of the *darker* sort. To drop a small pebble into the well of the subconscious and thereby set up a calculable type and series of eddies is the most effectual way to wreck and distort the whole structure of a mind. This is a knowledge as old as the hills; but we are fortunate nowadays in possessing enough empirical data and mechanical information to convince even the most hardened Western sceptic that whatever may be the provenance and associations of Black Magic it still has its old power to curse and thwart. It is not " explained away " by a knowledge of its laws: rather is its venom forestalled and effective counter-agents set up by the realisation that we too know the tricks of the trade and the turns of the screw. Evil is defeated by good much more when natural laws are sedulously observed in all their varied rhythms of cause and effect than when a mere recourse is had to a probably rather faulty set of moral adjustments.

The bad people frequently know their job a great deal better than do the good people. In the nature of the case it is imperative that they guard against the more clumsy kind of mistake. A false slip will very easily bring their house of cards tumbling about their ears. For evil-doers a reliable technique is more than a desideratum: it is a necessity. Not so with the *unco guid* who allow themselves a great many more off-moments than do their more satanic brethren, and who consequently expose themselves to certain kinds of flank attack. Indeed, if the virtuous forces of the world could unite with the same consistency and vigour as do their opposite numbers, and with the same determination to succeed, then the business of living would be for all of us an infinitely more happy experience.

Therefore, let him that thinketh he stand, take heed lest he fall ! The study of the very natural laws that constitute the achievements of magic, white or black, is the only prophylactic against attacks on his own mental safety.

The reader may well ask what the connection may be between the elaborately constructive Tibetan Yoga hitherto enunciated and the practice of disintegration. The answer is simple. The one is but the obverse of the other. It is often enough the same force, in itself outside any moral argument, which can be used for constructive good or diabolical evil. So much depends on the motive and the integrity of the operator.

If this force is sufficiently strong to cause any change in the circumstances which surround it, our instincts will tell us that it is there. There is no need to be " psychic," to detect the smell of Mars in the ether ! The " hunch " of the need for self-preservation or, better still, the recognition of some supernormal stability and confidence is quite unmistakable to one who has to live with his wits about him in the world. But whatever be the moral (or immoral) impetus behind this manifestation, we can be sure that it can never exist in any potency without a quite preternatural degree of *control*.

Now what, in the last resort, is Tibetan Yoga but an elaborate system of self-control? A control which is not self-subsistent in any narrow, isolated sense, but which draws unto itself a multitude of aids and accessories, many gathered from other planets than this. A highly-developed yogi controls not only himself but a whole cohort of powers and presences in his psychic vicinity. The fact that the most sure-footed and consistent control comes from the love of virtue, by no means abrogates the fact that there is a very potent control which usually has as its starting-point the love of power for its own sake.

This is a vice from which people of psychic constitution are peculiarly liable to suffer. There is probably a higher percentage of megalomaniacs among occultists than among any other section of the population. The reason is not far to seek. When a sense of " difference " and imaginary distinction get the upper hand in a personality of no more than average moral fibre, and when this false idea of dedication is reinforced by the inevitable attendant isolation, then common sense and common decency frequently fly out of the window.

Unfortunately, these people are not always fools (at least as far as our sphere is concerned). They have the ability to frighten persons with less impudence than themselves, and the type often possess a rather repellent but nevertheless very effective kind of *savoir-faire*, or low cunning, which not only protects them from the overshort arm of the law in these matters, but also convinces the disciples they collect round them that they have in very sooth discovered the newest and best of new Messiahs.

The hold they actually exert on these unfortunates increases after the manner of a rolling snowball. From mouth to mouth is passed the word that the source of all wisdom is at hand; and the legend of omniscience grows in the telling. In a short time what there is of discrimination vanishes in the artificial light of Psychalia, and the mind of the student, become by now " a big, booming, buzzing confusion," is left open and suggestible to every whim of the " Master's " capricious will.

It should be evident that this kind of thing constitutes a very grave public danger; for the legion of the frustrated and the blasé, continually seeking " a new thing," is peculiarly open to the infliction on itself of a partly self-induced, partly dominatory fantasy. In other words, the dissemination of dangerous lies is not the least of the evils which may be laid down at the door of the " magicians " who employ the art of the knuckle-duster for the propagation of esoteric truth.

In truth, fantasy, though an invaluable weapon for cutting our way through some of the more unpleasant jungle undergrowths of this world, is the least fool-proof of any of the interior aids. Used as a temporary stimulant or soporific it can be invaluable;

but interpreted as absolute truth it is the most effective way to hell. It is, of course, axiomatic that people cannot stand more than a certain amount of truth at once. The tonic must be taken in minute and homœopathic doses if it is to have any effect. In most lives there will have to be long rest-periods when the old lies are resumed as a palliative. A false idea of " romance," erroneous notions regarding individual destiny, take a long time to die. And there is usually no purpose served by trying to hurry the process.

But, sooner or later, each one of us has to face truth in its reality, and further, to realise that this perception constitutes the only happiness. Whether in one lifetime, or in several, we shall have to reach the one point towards which all ways converge. Before we get very far along the road we have to suffer greatly, to make a drastic revision of the nebulous concepts to which we had formerly clung. Life has to be regarded as a testing-place for souls, not as a frolic-fun-fair for the exploitation of imbecile emotions and the following of the meanderings of half-baked " intellectual " systems, existing at a very inadequate remove above a set of highly insanitary and unresolved emotional complexes.

Control can exist on different levels. There is the lofty variety which harnesses and disciplines itself so that the greatest good may be disseminated along its lines of direction. There is also a low kind which takes good stock of the gullible material it sets out to dominate and sets its traps accordingly. It is this latter manifestation which is the bane of occultism, and which it is the duty of the wise sociologist to reveal for the foul thing it is.

Actually, not much control is needed to hoodwink and bamboozle seekers who are desperately beseeching someone to lead them by the nose. And, seeing that there is such a market for auto-intoxication it is little wonder that the voice of the quack is loud in the land. However, even for this ignoble "leadership," a certain amount of energy and drive is needed, and this equipment is often derived from sources which are Yogic enough in character. That is, they owe their existence to a perception of the laws of association and relationship which are the mainspring of psychic powers ; and, guided by the requisite intelligence, can cause untold havoc among the unsuspecting.

Strictly speaking, no one has much to fear from an evil occultist if he keeps his eyes open. All that the go-getter magician can do is to bring to the surface the weakest and most timorous aspects of a man's nature and allow him to hoist himself with his own petard. There is a safety-catch, a law of automatic protection here. To exert sufficient external pressure on another human being so that he becomes a mere projection of the other's will would be a task of such magnitude that it would demand not only occult super-prowess of an almost incredible order, but it would involve too, such a lofty tensing of the moral will that the desire to do harm would itself cease. It is not without significance that the oldest of Tibetan apothegms says that there is nothing which cannot be accomplished by the human will, once the *desire* to accomplish has left us. In the last resort it is only the corruptible who can be corrupted. The weak are more often than not protected by their innocence, than which there is no more effective rampart against evil.

The remarks we have made on the dangers of Western cupidity and malevolence, equipped with a little occult knowledge, apply in a rather different way to the more philosophical climate of Tibet. In this more spiritually favoured part of the world the darker magic is perhaps less perilous because its workings are more clearly understood, and also because there have been evolved a whole host of exorcistic rites and counter-measures which have been proved to be of singular efficacy and durability.

Also, it should be pointed out that many Tibetan necromancers and black sorcerers are given a professional status which curbs, maybe, what may otherwise have developed into a widespread malignity. When a natural magician is sponsored by the ranks of respectability it may be argued that his temperament takes on a more humane colouring. The Tibetans are so pantheistic in their outlook that they feel a pressing need to employ expert psychic conjurers to alleviate and control climatic moods and deficiencies. Acting on a well-established psychological principle, that like is amenable to like, they reason that the demons who bring famine and pestilence in their train can be best mollified or put out of action by personages who "speak the same language." Some of the best detectives have been recruited from the ranks of crooks !

Thus it has come about that for the banishing of drought, the modification of the sun's rays and the staying of storms, yogis of an especial calibre are employed even by the most orthodox Tibetan centres. Usually a sorcerer it attached to a monastic establishment rather as a Poet Laureate is attached to a Court. His duties are not onerous, but he must always hold himself prepared to turn on his necromancy when occasion requires. In the case of smaller establishments this personage is not regarded as a member of the fraternity, lives outside the monastery, and is permitted, if he so wills, to marry.

It is extraordinary what a hold these rather dubious professionals exert over a large section of the Tibetan populace. Needless to say they frequently take advantage of their position to the extent of performing individual "turns," calculated to infuse the brains of the ignorant with a false notion of their prowess. These often take the form of knife-swallowing and fire-vomiting, exhibitions of legerdemain which startle the popular mind into acquiescence in more hypothetical revelations of virtuosity. One of the commonest feats of psychic " contagion " practised by the lower yogis is the stimulation of "possessions," a trick accomplished by a wild and whirling dance which is alleged, rightly or wrongly, to gather up into the limbs and nerves of the executant the baleful forces of the nether-worlds.

The particular usefulness of this accomplishment does not usually transpire. But it rarely fails to astonish and impress, and may, if genuine and not a shallow attempt to hoodwink the unsuspecting, be viewed like the balletomaniac exploits of the Dervishes, as a lesson in the undoubted vitality which can be drawn from the elements of the soil.

It is to be noted that the yogi magician has flourished since the days of the indigenous Bön religion of Tibet. Even Tsong-kha-pa, the decorous founder of the Reformed Sect was unable to curtail either the activities or the appeal of these prestidigitators of the spirit.

It would appear that among orthodox Buddhist sects there is deference paid to the propitiatory accomplishments of sorcerers. For, according to the Paritta Rite of Exorcism in use among the Southern Buddhist schools, certain passages have for long past been assigned for delivery to those skilled in the black arts. A typical extract goes as follows: " Therefore hear me, all ye spirits here assembled ! Be friendly to the race of men, for every day and night, they bring you offerings. For this cause keep scrupulous watch over them."

In Tibet itself, as was the case at the University of Salamanca in Renaissance Spain, a few centres are set apart for the study of necromancy by those suitably equipped. The famous cloister at Lhasa is filled with yogi aspirants to this branch of esoteric knowledge. This foundation dates from the seventeenth century, when the fifth Grand Lama Nag-wan organised " study-groups " of the most varied kinds and degrees. It is possible that the measure was taken *faute de mieux*; for it has been a hopeless task to suppress the deeper curiosity among the intelligentsia of Tibet. On the other hand, it can be argued that the more intelligent among the Lamas have always kept a completely open mind on the subject of the mechanics of the mind, and have sponsored any kind of research which may throw further light on the nature of the springs and releases of psychic control. Needless to say there are some protesting voices; but these are smothered in the unmistakable appetite of nearly all Tibetans for the elucidation of occult riddles.

The chief yogi wizards are styled " Reverend Protectors of the Faith," and " Defenders of Religion." They are regarded as keepers of the balance between the agitated denizens of the nether-worlds and the more serene occupants of the inter-stellar spaces. They are said to be incarnations of a group of malevolent spirits known as " Kings," who are traced back to five brothers who once inhabited Northern Mongolia. To each of them is assigned a province of influence. The monarch who governs the North is called " He of the Deeds "; the Eastern director, " the Body "; the Western adjudicator, " the Speech," and the guardian of the South, " the Learning." The fifth brother dominates the centre and spins the web which knits opposites into one skein.

The Lamas, like the ancient Romans, have always realised the benefits to their own rule involved in the keeping of a tight check on government officials by means of a strong line of priestly " magicians." For this reason the highest of the established yogic wizards, called Na-ch'un, is employed as a greatly respected government oracle-in-chief. He it is who is consulted when things go wrong and when private individuals of sufficient cash and standing are worried about their future.

This very important state official traces his origin back to a god of the Turki tribe. His ancestor, introduced into the heart of the country by the illustrious Padma Sambhava, perhaps the greatest of Tibet's religious geniuses, was given the title of " The Religious Noble." He married and became the hereditary consultant on all matters of occult moment. His successor is guardian of the first established monastery at Sam-ya.

There is an interesting legend in connection with the original appointment of this dignitary. The story goes that the possessed spirit, eager for the experience of life, hit upon an ingenious method for attaining his objective. He selected a holy and unsuspecting Lama for his purpose. Walking in meditation one day, this good man was startled to hear a spirit addressing his inner ear. The ghost was beseeching him to use his good offices so that he could be transported in correct and seemly manner to Udyana, the city of Padma Sambhava, and there takes up his rest. But the Lama, horrified to think that his reveries had been disturbed by a spirit of ambiguous antecedents, shut up the essence of the supplicant in a box which he flung into the River Kyi.

The affair was not to be ended quite so easily. The Abbot of the monastery at De-pang at this moment received a " hunch." Following up the intimation, he gave out to his disciples that " a box will float down the river." An assembled company waited patiently on the bank for the prophecy to be fulfilled. They did not wait long. Very shortly there came bobbing down the stream a receptacle similar to that which conveyed Voltaire's Irish Saint to the shores of France. The imprisoned spirit manifested itself in a flame of fire which disappeared into a tree. The Abbot, skilled in these matters, re-transferred the soul to the body, and, on opening the box a very alert ex-corpse was discovered who begged to be given a " small dwelling " (hence the name Na-ch'un) where he could settle down to a life of useful service. The request was granted, and an infallible guide to correct magical procedure was forthwith instituted in the land.

The appointment proved to be thoroughly justified. On numerous occasions the mediation of the Government Oracle was extremely effective. Once, in the seventeenth century, a band of Nepalese merchants, impelled by motives of jealousy, attempted to poison the tea at the Grand Lama's court. In the nick of time the plot was frustrated by the assiduous Oracle, who divined trouble afoot and took appropriate steps to foil the conspirators.

At the present day the Oracle is invested with considerable wealth, an entourage of a hundred and one monks and a palace which houses an extraordinary collection of stuffed birds, leopards and other occult paraphernalia. He is regarded with infinite respect by the Chinese, and could claim to be surrounded by an indubitable odour of sanctity, if it were not for the reputation attached to himself and his myrmidons of an excessive indulgence in Indian hemp.

This charge happens to be true and it is noteworthy that the warlocks of Sam-ya nearly all die an early death. A word may be said here concerning the connection between occult development and the taking of noxious drugs. It is, unhappily, only too true that many members of alleged occult fraternities resort to this mode of communication with the overself as the shortest cut to a pathway normally difficult enough of access to the uninitiated. When the individual is not ready or unfit for the high discipline of the spirit it is sometimes argued that the Kingdom of Heaven can be taken by storm, with the help of stimulating physical inter-mediaries. We all know that we can induce minor states of ecstasy in ourselves by the consumption of comparatively harmless kinds of food and drink, for instance strong Indian tea of the baser sort, or the resumption of the banished cigarette which brings the sensation of "port after stormy seas." How much more, it can be argued, may the psyche be elated by stimulants of a more hectic flavour ?

But the essential point to realise is that this " gate-crashing " mode of ingress is from all points of view thoroughly undesirable. One can hardly expect to be welcomed as a visitor, still less as a resident, when the usual formalities of introduction are not observed. To land, like the late-lamented Mrs. Guppy without warning, in the midst of the congregation of Saints is to run the risk of being ushered out rather more speedily than one had come.

There is no cheating permitted along the road of mental and spiritual development. There are many frontiers to be crossed and the passport examination is meticulous and searching in the extreme. Certainly there is no chance of deceiving the Guardians of the Gates as regards one's moral character and credentials. They may at times appear to wink an indulgent eye and to allow the rash spirit to rush in where only the pure of heart can take up their stance; but their latitude is calculated and purposive, and they know that the temerarious soul will issue from his sensational adventure not with the keys of the Kingdom in his pocket, but with the traditional flea in his ear. Thus can certain lessons be learned by those who have gathered enough wisdom to see that it is not always the bull who storms the fence, but (granted it is strong and safe enough) the fence which storms the bull !

But the Tibetan public have in the main no unfavourable criticisms to pass on the tonics which inspire the Oracle with his most sublime utterances. They are far too interested in the results of his prognostications to disturb themselves about theories of their origin. Everyone in Lhasa looks forward to the festival on the second day of the first month of every year, when the Oracle, clad in red robes and wearing a lotus-shaped hat, sallies forth through the streets of the city to a temple specially prepared for the occasion, where he takes his seat on his throne and proceeds to deal with probabilities for the coming year.   It is a spectacle which should turn our flourishing daily newspaper astrologers green with envy !   The Dalai Lama himself and the highest state officials testify their approbation of his occult standing by sending representatives.   Occupied as they are with questions of possible war, national sickness and invasion, they are glad to have recourse to an established mouthpiece of the chthonian gods who can foretell which way various winds are blowing, and suggest appropriate arts, if necessity demands, to change their direction.   Forewarned is forearmed !   It should be pointed out here that Tibet, in spite of its pacific philosophy, has been by no means free from militarisation.   This can hardly be wondered at considering the large part played in the national occultism by ideas involving ab-reaction to contending concepts of Force.   The Eastern province of Khan is notorious for the breeding of a particularly truculent type of marauding desperado.

The application to the Oracle is always made in writing. Normally, the applicant prostrates himself before the potentate and utters the following supplication: " To the all-powerful footstool, made of the dead bodies of the infidels on which rest the feet of the Great Defender of Religion, the soul incarnate of the Almighty Conqueror of the Enemies in the Three Worlds, the Receptacle of Wisdom! "   The script containing the request is thrown at the great man's feet.

An extraordinary scene follows.   The augur rises to his feet and summons to his aid a formidable demon from the nether-world, who is to possess his body for the time being.   Several Tibetans testify to having seen this grisly apparition with the naked eye.   It is described as a fearsome white monster, with three heads and six hands, the whole form enveloped in flickering flames.   In a few seconds the Oracle is writhing on the ground, the demon speaking through his foaming lips.

The declarations garnered in this way are apocalyptic in the extreme.   Only those used to the symbolical and analytical mentality of the East could honestly claim to find them a good guide to the unravelling of life's thorny problems.   Here are a few typical examples.   " Father wolf seizes sweet flesh while sister fox gets blamed."   (This is intended as a warning against over-siyness).   " The prancing steed thinking only of himself falls over cliff.   The fox will become greater than a huge elephant."   (A prognostication of the rise to influence of a careful, insinuating person).

TS'ON-K'A-PA

Northern Buddhist reformer founder of the Ge-lug-pa sect (yellow caps)
seated in lotus asana, with hands in ' teaching ' mudra.

Picture on left:

GROUP OF PRAYER WHEELS

Note roll of prayers extracted from and supporting prayer wheel on left. In front is a vajra (thunderbolt).

●

Picture below:

Left—Amitayus (Buddha of Eternal Life).

Centre—Yama (God of Death)

Right—Maitreya (The Coming Buddha—The Compassionate One).

Left to right—Green Tara (The Saviouress—Symbol of the Divine Energy); Hayagriva (The Horse-necked One); O-Mi-T'o-Fo Chinese Buddha of Boundless Light (Form of Amitabha) — *Note:* base removed showing roll of prayers as usually contained in images; Yamantaka (Conqueror of Death).

The State Oracle is run pretty close in popular favour by his brother-necromancer, known as the *Karma-s'an*, who functions at the Sera Monastery during the seventh month of each year. This sorcerer claims to be possessed by the spirit of the demon-king, Pe-har. Rather less theatrical in his mode of procedure than his rival, his utterances have a corresponding clarity of meaning. He it is who foretells where the successor of the Dalai Lama shall see the light. Before the Younghusband Expedition in 1904 he gave out this inspired sentence :" The English are like the ripples on water; here to-day and gone to-morrow! "

In Western Tibet flourish a sect of professional yogic experts popularly known as " God's Mouthpieces," whose special province it is to control and harness these specific devils and elementals to the underworlds indigenous to Tibet. These beings who would otherwise make themselves a considerable nuisance to godly and ungodly alike, can be distracted from their dirty work and made to serve a useful purpose by being drawn up through the vehicles of the " Mouthpieces," and their energies transformed into healing-power and sage advice. By a process analogous to snake-charming or broncho-busting, the demons are first placated and then used.

The " Mouthpieces," although not always manifesting the ordinary forms of grey matter, take their job extremely seriously. It is by no means uncommon to find a candidate for this distinction immuring himself for as many as five years in some desert fastness, shut off from all human contacts, training his capacities for the domination of the demonic world. And although these enthusiasts are more often than not of a very primitive grade of culture, yet they make up in devotion to their cause what they may lack in discrimation regarding its morality.

Women figure largely in the ranks of the " Mouthpieces." When developed they live together in small colonies presided over by an elected " General " who directs operations both spiritual and temporal. One of their specialities is " The tapping of energy at a distance " and there are some nasty stories current of their prowess in this particular pursuit. They definitely claim to be able to use the activities of unbridled, licentious males as a channel for the propagation of psychic force, and there are cases on record where they have seized some hapless and unsuspecting Don Juan ; and, keeping him in strict captivity, have animated his body with subtle varieties of vitalism, so that they can draw on it for their sustenance, just as the water-carrier draws from the well. It would not be proper here to dwell on this appalling type of vampirism; but it is as well to know that " such things do happen " and that the battlefield of erotic relationship is strewn with the débris of psychic slaughter.

The more respectable of these dubious " Béguines " devote themselves to the arts of healing. They are, indeed, much sought after by the Tibetan peasantry in cases of disease and distress and undoubtedly possess great hypnotic gifts; for they can usually allay symptoms even when they do not remove causes. At times they have visited the capital and have been consulted by the highest in the land.

The calling up of the earth devils for the purpose of medical aid is a complicated business. A large drum and cymbals are again brought into requisition, presumably to deafen the sensibilities of the spirits and to intimate that psychic " dinner is served." (The judicious may here recall the fanfare of trumpets which heralded the approach of Miss Aimee Macpherson into the arena). The five bats of fortune; incense, which, like blood, collects in large quantities of ectoplasm; the magic mirror which is placed on the head; the silk girdle and the offerings of cakes and wine—all these accessories are calculated to stir up some special function in the demon's being.

At last a divining-arrow is taken from a plate of flour and the blunted point placed on the affected area of the patient's body. The " mouthpiece " puts his or her mouth half-way down the shaft and sucks hard. On this a drop of blood shows itself over the painful part without any breaking of the skin. This is a sign that the disease-demon has been forced to repent of his malevolence and is either put out of action or is transferred to pastures new.

An important part of this ceremony is the correct invocation of the demon's name. Here Tibetan occultism joins up with the major schools of magic all the world over. Little control can be exerted over the denizens of the Underworlds unless the exact vibrations of the syllables which form their names are intoned so that projection affiliates itself with substance. Generally speaking, they are put into some kind of marching order before they appear on the scene: they are not permitted to fight their way in with any undisciplined, unregimental confusion. First, the tutelary demon of the countryside heads the rout, exerting as he does a coercive precedence over the " lesser representatives of the Law." It is only when he is held firm and fast that his esquires are allowed to issue from their dens in order of merit. The Dragon Demi-Gods, who are enveloped in a certain torpidity, give way to the Dré, the most malignant and hostile of those who seek to devour, only to be entrapped by the strongest conjurations.

While on the subject of invocation something should be said concerning the part played in Tibetan occultism by talismans and charms. In case any misconception should prevail it must be pointed out that these symbols are by no means always sentimental in character. Accustomed as we are to seeing these things manufactured by the gross for the delectation of those who have not sufficient confidence in their own charms to secure what they want, we may be tempted to relegate all such " superstitions " to the old-wives' paradises and sewing-bees to which they appear by right to belong.

Actually, the Tibetans put great faith in these aids to magical practice. Trained as they are in the perception of psychic facts, they know that force can, if desired, be constrained into the smallest compass. One of the supreme technical achievements of the ancient Egyptian magi was built on these lines. By the magnetisation of *ushabtis* and other images they protected their dead against desecration. Or, at least, they raised a rampart round sacred things which could only be stormed with the direst results to the foolhardy materialist who sought to explore the mystery without the requisite equipment of reverence and godly fear. It is all very well to attribute the calamities which have overtaken these people to mere chance and coincidence ; but we know in our hearts that these results have arrived inevitably from the taking of too perilous risks. What the gods have put together let no man try to break asunder. The same procedure is adopted by Tibetan yogis. They pour the energies of deities into small objects, and in this manner secure immunity for themselves and a certain clutch-hold on the actions of the gods.

The construction of these emblems is a delicate and exact business on which we do not propose to dwell here. Sufficient to say that some of the charms have a great popularity and are much used by the professional yogi healers as adjuncts to their work.

Talismans against plague and diseases are naturally in great demand. Perhaps the most widely used is a figure of Garuda, King of the Birds, holding a snake in his mouth. To each of the feathered plumes is attached the text: " Vouchsafe to the wearer of this talisman that he be saved from all manner of evil spirits, from injuries and diseases, contagious and otherwise, including rheumatism, cough, sore-throat and all plagues of the body, speech and mind."

Another favourite charm is made in the shape of a scorpion, its mouth tipped with flames. The demon against whom special protection is desired is perched on its shoulder. The recitation of several hypnotic syllables makes the emblem incandescent and effective.

On occasion, extreme measures are taken to ensure the full efficacy of the charm. The commonest of these is the eating of the paper on which the spell is written. Another mode involves the washing of the reflection made by the writing in a mirror: this is accomplished according to time-honoured custom with beer or grain-brandy. Afterwards the liquid is consumed in nine sips.

The most revered prophylactic in Tibet, however, is not a figure of a god or a demon, but an arrangement of objects in a diagram which is held to be both fool-proof and singularly efficient as a universal provider. This drawing, known as " The Assembly of Hearts of Lamas," comprises a series of concentric circles of spells edged with flames. In the four corners are representations of the thunderbolt *dorje*, the three-cleft jewel, the lotus flower and the flaming dagger with the *dorje* hilt. In the middle we see an eight-petalled lotus flower, each petal carrying the appropriate mystic syllables. According to instructions laid down in the Manuals which deal with the correct manufacture of these charms the design is finished off by a circular space, one inch in diameter, in the centre of the lotus, in which is written a secret talisman, originating in the fourth or fifth centuries.

The services of yogic wizards are employed not only for calling up demons " from the vasty deep " and harnessing their forces for the relief of pain and the conquest of lust, but for the reverse function of keeping the troublesome blades of the underworld " in their proper place." More often than not, this locality is anywhere out of the world.

The Tibetans are convinced that a country is troubled in proportion to the measure of unpoliced freedom attained by the malicious sprites, *yidags* and other *mi-ma-yins* which attach themselves to natural objects and speak with the voices of some of the most accepted phenomena of inorganic life. When these disturbers of the psychic peace get into their full swing there is no telling to what red hell of disruption their activities may not lead. For this reason the Tibetans argue that their country, and indeed, for that matter, the entire world cannot be in a healthy condition until some sort of damper is put on the " Earth-Masters " who infest rivers and streams, rocks and trees.

For the developed yogi such conceptions belong, not to the domain of academic folklore but to the province of actual fact. He knows that the discreet mind must be much more wary of the powers and presences which are wafted through the etheric world than of any of the more obvious gorgons visible to the untrained eye. Given full rein, and employing suitable persons as their media, these unscruplous entities can overturn the whole mental, spiritual, social and political life of the country which gives them house-room, and substitute for sanity and balanced vision an hysterical collapse of the mill-dams of force which may easily give the impression of inevitable strength.

The ceremony for " Barring the Door against Earth-Demons" is conducted by a competent sorcerer with the aim of shackling this type of malevolence. From the earliest times the Tibetans have regarded the Earth-Demons as living under the immediate domination of a beldame known colloquially as the " Old Mother." A witch of the deepest dye, she is represented as wrinkled and scowling of visage, riding on a ram, and attired in robes of a golden-yellow colour. It is she who must be contacted before the operation can take effect. The opening move of " Closing the Door of the Earth " consists of an invocation addressed specifically to her.

Next, the skull of a ram is taken from the altar and pointed downwards in the direction of the earth. This is no ordinary piece of symbolical apparatus, but has been specially prepared to suit the occasion. On its forehead are painted in ochre (the earth-colour) the signs of the sun and the moon, while a large geomantic emblem is affixed to the centre of the head. A number of threads in geometrical patterns complete the decorations. Inside the head objects of gold, silver, turquoise as well as portions of wheat and rice are jumbled together in a profusion not so much wild, as illuminating to the student of esoteric relationships.

Now the sorcerer takes up his chant. " You are known through all the nine planes of the Earth as ' The Old Mother.' To you is assigned the guardianship of the Gates of the Earth. Attentive to your desires, we offer you herewith the white skull of a ram. On its right cheek shines the burning sun; on its left, the gleaming moon. By this symbol we conjure you to keep far away from us any evil act of those who are your servants. Let the Gates of the Earth be closed." Here the sorcerer performs a subtle breathing-exercise on the head of the ram in order to charge it with a very powerful spell which will " put the stopper on " the machinations of the irrepressible fiends.

This ceremony is very often performed in order to counteract distress which has befallen some particular family or clan, or to protect intending partners to any contract, such as marriage, from the disruption which comes from the evil kinds of outside psychic influence. The usual conclusion is for the magician to clap his hands, emit the "banishing" *mantra* "Svaha" and say "Let all Evil be annihilated! "

The Demons of the Sky, that is to say, bad elementals, discarnate humans or fallen angels, are under the guidance of a being called the " Old Father ": he has snow-white hair, carries a wand of cystal and rides on "the Dog of the Sky." These entities too can be placated and harnessed by a knowledge of the requisite ceremony. But in this case, even greater forces are set in motion, and the planets with all their astrological and chemical implications are brought to the help of suppliant man. In particular the aid of Saturn is solicited; for his grave melancholy can lead the soul into pleasant pastures.

During this intercession, the skull of a dog is used after the manner described in the Earth ceremony. " Pray grant us your favours so that your emissaries work for our benefit; send forth the planet Saturn as a kindly mediator," chants the magician. To a certain extent the two conjurations, pointing to Earth and heaven respectively, may be regarded as complementary. The first allays, the second calls down something which may be equivalent to virtue. In the eyes of Tibetans, and for that matter according to established Buddhist theology, devils are not entirely and irremediably bad; certainly not as bad as they are painted. The pictorial arts in Tibet are exhortatory rather than decisive : a warning is not to be regarded as a sentence. It follows that devils can inhabit purgatories as well as earth-planes, the astral and psychic worlds, and, mayhap, the very heavens themselves. These creatures, like ourselves, make and have made their own destiny. As they think, so they are : if they endeavour to free themselves from corruption by the obvious and inevitable method of legitimate moral aspiration, they may shoot by the marvellous efficacy of constructive thought from bottomless pit to starry spaces. The mind is its own place !

It is for this reason that the pious Tibetans pray unceasingly for the " damned," for those " drowned in the deepest sea." Their love can go down to the most abject example of the crystallisation of man's baser impulses, and up to the beings who shadow forth his aptitude for his highest home. In a religion where all things will find peace at the last, there is no room for dogmatic departmentalisation of souls. We cannot condemn or ensky anybody: they can merely condemn or ensky themselves. "The Closing of the Doors of the Sky" should perhaps more logically be termed the Acceptance of the Lesson of Goodness from whatever quarter it may come. Even the partially arrived can help.

The human dead, in Tibet as elsewhere, frequently make themselves something of a nuisance to those sufficiently susceptible to their influence. Manifesting in the form of ghosts or in the still more gruesome aspect of vampires, werewolves and *poltergeister* they roam around places of ill repute and seek at times to replace themselves in a most disturbing manner in situations they have inhabited in life. It does not follow that "when the brains are out" the man will die. It is customary, therefore, in Tibet to employ the services of a wizard to ensure that the "dead" keep to their own part of the building and do not accentuate the woes of humanity by performing any impish or malevolent tricks from the vantage-point of "the other side."

The technique of ghost-laying is elaborate. For its successful completion it requires a full complement of lamas, observers and the usual officiating warlock. The person, spurred on by the solemnity of the occasion, exerts himself to the utmost to prove himself worthy of his reputation. In the dead of night with no landscape except that of the silent stars to divert the attention of the spectators from the matter in hand, the exorcism is enacted amid the flickering lights of torches and the remote cries of solitary jackals.

First a magic circle is traced on a rude mud-altar erected for the occasion. Inside this a triangle symbolises the circumscription of energy. Slowly, and with the correct conjurations, twigs are laid along the outline of the triangle, one piled above the other until a pyramid is formed. Then, after a kind of circumambulatory dance to safeguard any attempt at escape by the ghost, the structure is set alight. When the pile is blazing merrily various kinds of ingredients, similar to those employed in the medieval witches' cauldron, are cast into the flames. As a final precaution a piece of paper on which is inscribed the name of the recalcitrant spectre adds its weight to the occult armoury. The ghost, convinced by now that his presence is regarded as undesirable, stands not upon the order of his going, but vanishes forthwith in an appropriate rush of wind.

It would be impossible to convince a Tibetan that he could ignore the dwellers in the shades. Life, which for him assumes the inevitable complexion of a struggle between the powers of light and darkness, is only to be realised to the full when the soul has come to grips with the beings who menace its safety as well as with the angels that promise its release. It may be difficult for a European to follow the rules of this conflict, involving as it does such a delicate balancing of the axis of the psyche; but until he sees and feels that the battles worked out in what may seem at first sight a piece of obscene and crude symbology, is nothing more or less than the persistent contest enacted on the boards of his own inner senses, he will never understand even the surface of a psychism so profound as that of the Tibetans.

It may be for him "folk-lore," "primitive religion" and probably abracadabra. It may amuse his leisure hours as the vehicle of a new kind of thrill. But it is none of these things. It is the full-hearted and full-blooded attempt to conquer the only demon which really counts in this life or any other—the demon of *fear*. And this same bogey, even if he does not admit it, is at least as constant a visitor with the Westerner as with the oriental, and, in the former case, more insidious in its workings.

The Tibetans, wiser in this respect than ourselves, give a great deal of thought to the methods necessary for conquering the incubus of terror attendant on the perception of the proximity of spirits of the more malign and mischievous caste. He knows that the most effective way to attract evil is to run away from it. He is not going to waste his time by burying his head in the sand; for that way ignorance and ultimate disaster lies. He prefers to face his enemy in the open field where he can gauge distances and measure steel on steel.

Far from denying the existence of the personifications of evil, the Tibetan yogi trains himself to meet these dangers in the full light of day. There are many practices current to destroy fear of the spirits that deny. Encounters with demons are deliberately sought in order that familiarity shall breed, if not contempt, at least an asseveration of the natural supremacy of good. Sometimes devils are summoned so that they may be given alms or regaled with a short sermon on the error of their ways. It is the constant endeavour of every pious Tibetan to do all in his power to allay the lot of the temporarily damned by promising them a fairer future through good works and repentance.

On a par with our intrepid ghost-hunters who volunteer to stay alone in haunted houses, there are students in Tibet who truss themselves up for long periods, leaving themselves open to the attacks of marauding *yidags*. By this means they hope to conquer all fear of what the malignant hosts can inflict on them. In the will of the Buddha is their safety. Evil shall not prevail over good. No matter how helpless they may be in the body, they cannot be mastered on the plains of the soul.

But it is time to call a halt in this description of occult marvels. Otherwise the reader may lose himself in a fog of phenomena, and will miss the point of all the illustrations quoted. The whole purport of such a dissertation is to link up the known with the unknown by a series of implications. These implications will now be restated in a more tangible form.

The sounding-board of all magical operations lies within the territory of the subtle self. The constructive power of the " holy wand of direction," the obverse power of the evil eye and the relentless malevolent will, owe any efficacy they may possess to a knowledge of the subtle differentiation of the *chakras* which are the mainstays of our vitality. As suggested earlier, a skilful application of the laws of ordinary psychology, of elementary suggestion and auto-suggestion, may well look like the workings of the deeper " magic " to an observer untutored in analysis.

To a large extent such an observer would be right. But he would be perceiving only half the truth. An intelligent apperception of other peoples' moves will show us what is the extent of their knowledge of the mechanism of the surface sheeting of the mind ; but it is only by deep study of the foci of force which send out, maybe, only the faintest of tappings to the hull, that we can repair or enlarge these chance breaches made in the wall of the secondary, etheric body.

For it is this etheric, " psychic," body which gives us our real life. Without its agency we could function neither as men nor as gods. It directs all our operations, mental, nervous and muscular : through this channel flow the forces that feed our tissues. To study Yoga without allowing for this subtle vehicle would be to waste one's time ; for the miracles of Yoga occur not at all in the physical sheath, but entirely in the ectoplasmic body of force which uses the sheath as its temporary home.

It is the first business of the magician to isolate this subtle body (which is *positive* to the physical envelope below or around it) and see, not the material shape before him, but its projection in etheric terms. Actually this is a feat which can be accomplished by any trained clairvoyant, although such a person may not always know what he is doing. Once this first step is taken and the whole map of the psyche (with the *chakras* occupying the position of the plexuses and the endocrine glands in the physical body) visible before him, he can get to work on any experiment he may care to make.

Very few human beings exhibit in their subtle bodies a healthy and equable functioning of all the *chakras*. In most people a marked unbalance manifests itself in the size, shape and condition of these centres of radiation. From excess or disuse the *chakras* appear to the clairvoyant eye of very varying degrees of density and vigour. Some are atrophied almost to the point of extinction ; others are flaming with an excessive, inordinate fire. It is only in the being healthy and co-ordinated in body, mind, emotion and will that these beacons will be observed gleaming with an equal luminosity and working with a regulated rhythm.

It is only when the wheels begin to rotate that their mechanism can be said to be in functioning order. Before this rotation commences, the clairvoyant will observe a filament of light rush round the petals of the lotus and concentrate after the fashion of a vortex in the heart of the flower. When this happens, we are safe in assuming that the capacities associated with this particular lotus are in potential action : their outpost is primed for the reception and transmission of certain aspects of force.

Normally, in the average human being the lower *chakras* function at the expense of the higher. That is to say, the lower, more earthy nature has assumed a predominance over the possibilities of higher development. It is, for instance, very rare to see the centre between the eyes in a vital, emergent condition. Representing as it does the loftier reaches of the soul and spirit, it requires for its full " production-power " the capacity to live more energetically than most, in " the good, the beautiful, the true." Very often it is dried and gnarled in appearance, manifesting every sign of degeneration. It is interesting to note that a genuine transport of spiritual love in a nature which has accustomed itself for the most part to existence on the lower levels, will effect a remarkable transformation in the atrophied *chakra*.

We are not one body, but seven. And these various extensions of our being converge on the same ground. It is customary among occultists to describe the vehicles as rising in order of progression from the body of the flesh, through the psychic, emotional and mental manifestations to the body of the spirit which is free from division. On this reasoning a rather top-heavy structure is formed conveying a hint of Atlas bearing too many worlds on his shoulders. A more satisfactory image, we suggest, would be that of a series of concentric boxes of the Chinese pattern, ranging from large to small and finishing their course at the heart of the human anatomy. It is within ourselves that we discover the highest truth, not in the teeming world without us. The supreme spiritual realisation waits on our will ; when illusion and false seeking are for ever cast off, then, and not till then shall we recognise our marvellous heritage.

The chakras of the separate bodies interpenetrate. Our ordinary concepts of spatial division must be abolished here. Each vehicle has its *chakras,* and the exterior edge of each of these rests at the surface of the body it serves. In one sense all the bodies function together at one place. It is the correct alignment of these extended and extensible forces which gives poise, vitality and health.

What the sorcerer does is to separate either temporarily or permanently one of the lower bodies from the rest, and play on it with the full force of the rays of his thought-power. The process is analogous to the technique of " bewilderment " resorted to by the worldly-wise when they wish to subjugate anyone to their point of view. These practical psychologists, realising the lack of conviction and self-confidence in the individual they seek to gull, play a rapid game of battledore and shuttlecock with the wits of their victim. Just when he feels himself on solid ground they pull his chair from under him by suddenly changing the subject and returning to it when he is least prepared for its re-emergence. Thus, self-confidence is undermined and anyone is welcome to the wreckage.

If we are sufficiently developed we can live in any of our bodies at will, and this is the best safeguard against the rape of a large part of ourselves by persons accomplished enough to attempt the task. There are few burglaries when the householder is at home. To be forewarned is, in this, as in any other case, to be forearmed. To be sure of our stance in our own territory is to be able to ignore the most cunning machinations of any diabolist and to snap our fingers at those would-be figures of evil who know enough to trade on the weakness of others, but who are insufficiently schooled in occult common-sense to realise that they, and not their dupes, are the losers.

In Tibet is written, both in practice and parable, the history of those undertones and overtones of life which beset us and reassure us in our own daily round. If we can bring ourselves to see continuity and coherence where we have formerly, perhaps, imagined no interest in "that nonsense" on one side, and "archæology and anthropology" on the other, we shall have advanced some distance along that necessary intellectual path which cuts a way through misconception and folly to the land where the spirit enjoys a safe, abiding peace.

CHAPTER VIII

The Rites of Tibetan Yoga.

THIS SUBJECT should be of singular interest to all those interested in the inner meaning of Yoga. For under this title are grouped a number of rituals, theories, and practices which have remained practically a closed book to the Western student.

The reasons for this ignorance are complicated. In the first place, there is the obvious discretion exercised by Eastern pundits and scholars who hesitate to put into the hands of the uninitiated information and sources of reference which may do little more than make confusion worse confounded. And there are those ill-equipped enough to cry "Danger" where their powers of comprehension fail. Misunderstanding is particularly apt to follow on the heels of prejudice. It must be frankly admitted that our whole system of philosophical thought has prepared us most inadequately for the understanding of a code of mysticism which is based not on the division, but on the unity of all things, "good" and "evil" alike. Secondly, the highly concentrated nature of the practices and the energetic discipline needed to make them effective stipulates a brew of a decidedly major strength. It is not desirable to offer people journeys for which they are not yet prepared; better to lead up by degrees from the foothills whose paths may continue to the peaks than to damp the religious ardour at the start by asking too much of the hesitant novice. Again, some things are so sacred that it is incumbent on the devotee not to divulge the deeper secrets of systems which may be woefully perverted and misused by those who have no understanding of symbolism, and to whom the technique of reverence is likely to remain, for this incarnation at least, a completely alien territory.

The *asanas* and *mudras*, the postures and gestures of Yoga, will never be understood if they are regarded as an end in themselves. They are rather, the narrow gate which leads into the large open space, the preparation for the infinitely stimulating festival. Without the correct discipline and preparation, there can be no delight; but it is the most dismal of errors to confuse the entrance-porch with the full glamour of the land of heart's desire across the threshold.

Tibetan Yoga is not a simple matter. It is a syncretic canon based on the experience of many centuries and the unending application of the principle of trial and error to the cultivation of the powers of the soul. It is not even a completely indigenous product. Receiving some of its deepest impulses from Shamanism, probably the oldest cult in the world (and which has left marked traces on the whole field of Russian occultism), reinforcing the good things in this creed with recipes of its own, inspired by the regenerating influx of Buddhist principles, it has become the quintessential product of "the best that has been thought and known" in the world of religious practice and speculation.

A proof of this assertion can be found in the fact that the yogic rites analysed in this chapter are not necessarily Tibetan in origin. Indeed, some of the most striking of them were born on the other side of the Himalayas, in Bengal, Sikkim and Bhutan. It should be noted here that the very greatest Tibetan religious leaders were not Tibetans at all, but missionaries from Upper India. Padma Sambhava and Asanga in particular were "foreigners" of great expertness in the subtleties of Buddhist philosophy who were sufficiently enflamed with the zeal of their cause to wish to transplant its worshipping-ground to an air in which it could breathe with the greatest freedom. Hence they brought into Tibet, in the seventh century of our era, beliefs and doctrines which were eventually built up into the magnificent and gorgeous *Tantric* rituals, which are such a stumbling-block to the incurable misinterpreting faculty of the average Western mind.

These rites, practically unexplored by European scholars, are very gold-mines of the most exact and subtle knowledge concerning worship, occult chemistry, the processes of the mind, profound psychology and a medical and curative lore of unexampled efficacy and economy. It can safely be said that a right understanding of the Tantric Texts would be the best palliative to the unbalance and one-sidedness which endanger our world to such a marked degree at the present day. But before this understanding can come about there will have to be a firmer approximation than exists at present between the ideals of East and West—a "seeing eye to eye" on fundamental problems of human welfare, a clear-sighted envisagement of a common goal. The art of happiness is very largely the art of meeting our fellow-men on humane and generous terms; and it is this wide tolerance and disinterested benevolence which form the grounds on which the essential and concentrated religious spirit of the Tantras stake their claim to our respectful attention.

Without mysticism there can be no real understanding. It is the subtle underground language between human beings which tells them the truth about each other. The province of Yoga is to make possible such a training of the senses and the will that we shall be deceived no more, either about the right principles of living or the necessity for taking our souls in hand. A discipline in the art of religion is the best insurance for a happy and contented life. And the study of age-old scriptural texts which have stood the test of generations of intelligent and searching criticism and verification, is no bad introduction to the unification of mind and body which is the aim of every thoughtful trekker in the paths of the spirit.

These priceless writings date for the most part from about A.D. 500, although there is ample evidence to prove that the principles which they formulate were part and parcel of the higher speculative life before they were committed to paper. There are no translations available of the most important of these works in any European language except that of the late Sir John Woodroffe, Judge of the High Courts at Calcutta, of the *Mahanirvana* (Great Liberation) Tantra—a work of the eighteenth century. The present writer has made his own version of some of the more inaccessible of these Texts and hopes at some future date to give them to the world.

They may be regarded, very simply, as agglomerations of esoteric knowledge, tapping the deepest strata of religion and magic, and having as their basis and fulcrum the acknowledgment and worship of the Creative Principle in life. This Principle is regarded as feminine in character, and it follows therefrom that the idea of a Goddess came to oust in importance the idea of a God. This is not to say that women are in any superficial sense "more important" than men, but that their function is, in the very nature of the case, more dynamic and psychically active.

It is most interesting to trace through the course of Hindu literature influences and tendencies bearing in this direction. It would seem that from earliest times the minds of the builders of religions had been impelled by the force of acute observation to the recognition of certain fundamental facts regarding the constitution of the human (which is the divine) problem. Out of an endless mass of theological and philosophical research we can see this conviction, at first tentatively, then openly and unashamedly, rearing its head towards its fulfilment. Even in the Rig-Veda, the most ancient of ascertainable Hindu scriptures, the theory is finding its feet. The figure of Usha, the Goddess of the Dawn, gradually assumes a vigour and a relevance which betokens a balanced insight on the part of the anonymous author. Rather later, in the Atharva-Veda, a collection of hymns originating about 600 B.C., we find, among a corpus of herbal and mineral lore, the Earth-Goddess Prithivi, looming large over her husband, the venerable monarch of the sky. It is obvious that the Female Principle was fighting its way to the fore even in works not specifically drawn up with the intention of ranging the heavenly residents in order of priority.

The *Mahabarata,* that glorious epic of spiritual and psychical gallantry, is noteworthy for the fact that it contains a beautiful address to Durga, later to become one of the chief representatives of the Creative idea.

" Thou art ever followed by Brahma and other Devas,
By those who call upon Thee to lighten their burden."

Again, in the *Upanishads*, pre-eminent among the holy writ of India, there is visible the beginnings of that ranging of Gods alongside their counterparts or " energies " which comes so near to the heart of occult truth. Vishnu and Lakshmi, Brahma and Sarasvati, Kartikeya (God of War) and Kartikeyi, Siva and Devi —here is the eternal juxtaposition of apparent " opposites " which provides the key to the realisation of unity.

Turning to literature proper, as distinguished from canonic and mythological texts, we can find several examples of the Goddess-idea prominent in popularity throughout the whole of modern Indian civilisation. Particularly is this true of the period of the Gupta Empire, which was at its height in the period known in Europe as the Renaissance. Kalidasa, the most accomplished poet of this epoch, devotes some of his most exquisite pages to recounting the love of Siva for Devi (Parvati). We will not burden the reader with further references which can be chosen, if desired, from almost every field of Oriental literature—secular as well as religious.

Mention may be made here of a theory which is hinted at in many places and which has done much to reinforce the predisposition of so many Hindus towards some form of Shakta (Female Force) worship. This to the effect that a Goddess is generally formed out of the special " energies " of all the other

THE LIGHT OF ASIA

Gautama Buddha (The Happy One) enters Nirvana. *To the left* He calls
the earth to witness that He has resisted temptation. *Top right* is Kshiti-
garbha (Essence of the Earth). *Below centre* is Amida Nyorai (Buddha of
Infinite Light). *Right* an assembly of Buddhas. In the plaque the Happy
One sits encircled by the mystic phrase

Aum mane padme hum.

T'hanka (temple banner); Samantabhadra (Buddha of ...) Vairocarra (Buddha of Supreme

L to R Ghanta (bell) Kapala (skull cup); stupa (shrine);

deities. In other words, She is concentrated strength, unconquerable essence, which is compact of fire and force.

These concepts can be transposed into Tibetan terms without doing much harm either to chronology or to religious consistency. It is our special task in this chapter to give an exposition of a *Tantra* or Yogic Ritual of a specifically Tibetan character; but the reader must remember that the substructure and the seed of these rites are as common to Northern India as to the land of the Lost Horizon. National temperament and expediency will of course furnish points of difference to those interested in searching for such things; but, for all practical purposes, the *Tantras* may be viewed as a common ground and forcing-house for all subtle Asiatic modes of higher thought.

Once and for all we propose to answer any prospective critic who may come forward with specious objection that the *Tantras* are "primitive," "fetichistic," "an excuse for self-gratification," and all the other vituperative stock-in-trade of the scholiast. I have personally taken rather impish delight in collecting a number of these judgments from diverse quarters, scholarly and otherwise, only to find (as one frankly expected) that in each and every case, not a single line of the Texts under discussion had ever been read, let alone critically appreciated! Hearsay, to say the least of it, is an inadequate weapon with which to demolish an edifice housing the most sacred religious sentiments of a people much more quick in the uptake than ourselves in matters which concern the soul of man. Far better had these reckless protesters taken the not unsurmountable trouble to verify their "findings" with apt quotation and reference. Then a battle-royal could indeed begin! Meanwhile the hungry sheep look up, and are not only not fed, but are denied entrance into fields of mystical speculation where they might conceivably find something to fit their needs.

On the more positive side, critics of the *Tantras* have for the most part approached the subject with minds already made up Some express a tolerant condescension: others read, and fly with averted gaze. From a sheaf of adverse reports we select the following as an example of what a certain type of Western reviewer is capable of when he is given his head. It is from the pen of one Reverend Graham Sandberg, and the italics are ours. " As is *invariably* the case in Buddhist philosophical statements, were we to quote here (as we do later) these enunciations, *they would be found to contain no real recondite wisdom*, nor *even any scheme*

*of metaphysics and morality which could be dignified with the title
of an ethical system.* . . . There is *nothing ennobling to the
individual,* or calculated to make the world better; or even, in the
Buddhist sense, less steeped in misery, in the doctrine of sublime
vacuity and indifference to all earthly claims to which Buddhism,
whether Indian or Tibetan, occupies itself'' [*Tibet and the
Tibetans,* p. 152]. *Gegen die Dummheit streben die Götter
selbst* ! If ever any enterprising journalist, wishing to do well
what has not been done before, decides to compile a volume of
''The World's Worst Criticisms'' it would be tragic if he overlooked this veritable gem of impercipience.

That there *is* a bad side to the practice of the *Tantras* no one
with the least acquaintance with India would deny. One seems to
have heard at times of the misuse even of Christian churches, and
there is little reason to expect that a faith which can lay claim to a
much longer and much more consistent history than Christianity
should be able to show a completely clean sheet on the score of
perversion and iconoclasm. But it is surely admitted to-day that
the tenets of a religion are to be judged on what they say, not
what their more stupid and reckless adherents *think* they say.
Otherwise it would be impossible to believe in any system of faith ;
for there will always be those who, wilfully or through ignorance,
mistake the letter for the spirit, the trappings for the reality. All
that can be hoped is that these misguided ones will one day see
the light and repay to Brahma in expiation what they have robbed
Him of in misconception.

One of the most common charges levelled against the *Tantras*
is that in places the worshipper is recommended to ask for earthly
boons as well as heavenly. Could any accusation be more
hypocritical ! It is not only understandable, but thoroughly right
and natural that people should choose a religion which promises
them happiness in this as well as in any or all other worlds.
Masochism is not necessarily a cardinal virtue. One glance at the
pious and homiletic handbook which sought to call our Victorian
forefathers to God will convince the most sceptical that the bait
of prosperity was dangled in no uncertain manner before the noses
of the most conventionally godly. The *Self-Help* of Samuel
Smiles is an object-lesson in this style.

There *are Tantras* of the Left-Hand Path just as there are and
will always be persons who make use of pseudo-religion to justify
the indulgence of their baser impulses. These things are best left
alone, pandering as they do to a dangerous stratum in the

composition of aspirants without a great degree of balance and discrimination. The population of the East is not without its degenerates. The lawless temperament seeks always for companionship in any illicit enterprise which makes for apparent power.

What more natural than that recourse should be had to a time-honoured mode of worship so that the vitality arising from its performance can be "drawn off" for the bolstering and imposition of unworthy aims? It is an indisputable psychological fact that any group working consistently in one direction, produces what we may term a Group Soul* (that is a psychic reservoir) around itself, which gives it a varying measure of well-defined strength in whatever direction it may choose to operate. Religious worship, by its very nature, provides what may be regarded as a "ready-made" dynamism for those too lazy or too wicked to work their evil outside well-established centres of spiritual well-being.

A word should be said here on the much-vexed question of "progress" as applied to religious conceptions. It is highly flattering to ourselves to think that we are in a more flourishing condition of spiritual health than were our forbears; but these assumptions have to be proved, and when one looks round on the fret and fever of our day, our passion for cheap amusements, our incapacity to keep our attention fixed on one subject for more than two consecutive seconds, we may well ask ourselves whether we have any right to speak slightingly of faiths and concepts which have fallen for the most part into neglect and desuetude merely because they have been superseded by systems of a more popular (and possibly more flashy) appeal.

It is true that the elements of *Tantra* are to be found in the religious practices of the ancient Dravidians and Mongolians who were conquered and superseded by the Indo-Aryans as they swept their way across the Punjab to the meeting of the Jumna and the Ganges. Consequently, it has been the custom to sniff at the hapless "earliest inhabitants" as lacking in the ability to survive, and therefore below par. But the physical argument is, at the best, only a partial one. The ability to smite the other fellow on the jaw before he gets in first, *may* be a stirring and heroic virtue ; but it is certainly not the *only* one. The cultured Chinese have always treated the soldier with an amused contempt, and there is

---

* The author's use of the term " Group Soul " should not be confused with the sense in which it is used in works on Mythology or with its employment in Anthroposophy.

no reason to suppose that they are completely unjustified in their attitude. The "weakest" sometimes go to the wall voluntarily, being too detached to waste valuable energy in the primitive strife of arms. There is much hidden knowledge of enormous value in the archives of races who have "bowed low before the storm, and turned to thought again."

What, in more concrete detail, is a *Tantra*? The word itself has been variously interpreted as meaning a "weaving," a "ritual" and a "Way." Perhaps the first reading is the most helpful in the elucidation of the structure of these guides to worship and conduct. There are several variations in the Form assumed by the *Tantras*. Consider for practical purposes a typical *Tantra*, e.g., a Hindu. This has as its central nodus a conversation between Siva and his consort Parvati. This is philosophical and mystical in character, adumbrating some of the deepest concepts of human and divine thought. Pre-eminent among these is the doctrine of the *Shunya* or Void. Stated simply, this implies the constant need of the soul to aspire to a condition in which earthly standards of happiness do not apply, because they are transcended by a series of experiences infinitely more stable and exhilarating.

The word is used advisedly; for this most intense and concentrated expression of Hindu thought voices the sentiment that Release is in no way a state of nescience, but rather of a sublime and tremendously happy fulfilment for which our vocabulary and our modes of thought have no suitable terms and definitions. In this and other worlds, we are forced to employ ideas based on form, size, colour, weight and temperature; but there, we shall have sailed so far above what these words signify, that they will have ceased to serve any useful purpose. At the same time, we need the senses to guide us along the early stages of the Path; and it is permissible to argue that the delight we experience in the most refined and selective interplay of our psycho-physical apparatus, can give us some slight foretaste of the delirious spiritual exultation which will fill our entire horizon when we have attained to the summit of our Being. The organism is of one piece : sooner or later we shall develop in ourselves the requisite observatories and surveying instruments; and then, as we see the Divine Logic in all things, there will be no more impatience and complaining.

It is rightly said that the *Tantras* devote considerable space to the subject of "magic." But the word must not be construed in any narrow or denigatory sense. It implies here the notion of construction, not of any insidious and degenerate attack on the welfare of the world. Siva is the Lord of Magicians because He is the Lord of Creation. Out of Him comes progress, energy, and light. He makes the rough ways smooth ; and there is no human who can resist His beneficent wisdom. From this view-point He gives to His followers recipes which can be used to further the best interests of that within them which corresponds to the Spirit that Creates, and which offers the most effective antidote to the ruses of the Spirit that Denies.

The "magic" of the *Tantras* resides in their profound effect on the mind of the individual who follows the instructions embodied therein. Viewed from this angle they are probably the most wonder-working psychological documents the world has ever seen. It would be incxact to say that they state any categorical theory or interpretation of life. That is not their province or function. It would be much nearer the mark to say that the *Tantras* make it their business to *create a state of mind*. They do not assert that they can give any infallible intellectual or emotional answer to the manifold problems of life. What they *do* promise is something of much greater value than any mere dogmatism. Here, they say, are the difficulties and the means of combating the difficulties : we give you the never-failing technique for attaining spiritual and emotional balance. When you have reached this happy state, you will be able to work out the answers to your problems for yourself. And you will hunger and thirst no more.

Some of the finest *Tantras* allot many pages to the exposition of a number of ethical and sociological principles which are bound up with the whole structure of Oriental society. This fact alone should convince the sceptic that they are valid "human documents" and not mere hocus-pocus and mummery. Whoever was responsible for the best in Tantric literature knew, as every sane man must know, that the individual can only claim to be in a healthy condition of development when he acknowledges his duties to society as well as his responsibilities to himself. We cannot live completely alone : that way a dead and dispiriting selfishness lies. We must think always of others, regarding their distress as even more important than our own. Then our deliverance will slowly dawn upon us.

The sociological arguments of the *Tantras* avoid all senti-mentality and confusion. They take it for granted that men, by the very nature of the different endowments and circumstances of their lives, have different duties to perform. It behoves them, therefore, to take care not only of their souls, but also of their bodies ; to abandon all peevishness and false sense of injury, and apply themselves with all their might to the task which it seems to them most fit and virtuous to do. The structure of Eastern society, based on the wise Laws of Manu, is no temporary expedient, but the result of a wise provision for all the multifarious gifts and activities of men. There is a time for action and a time for seclusion, a time for founding a family and a time for forgetting and renouncing that tie in the attainment of the deeper peace of mind. Religious development, like Nature, is averse to making leaps. It is improbable that we shall find harmony before we have ransacked all the "lucky dips" of experience. A healthy disillusion comes slowly to the majority of beings. It would be unwise, in most cases, to hurry up the invaluable process of learning by mistakes, partial or complete. A graduation in the hard school of life is the best preparation for the dynamic tranquillity of the blesesd water-brooks of the spirit.

Another feature to be found in nearly all the *Tantras* is a great deal of meticulously-unfolded information on the art of ceremonial and liturgy. It may be difficult to convince an English reader of the value of this particular kind of approach, trained as he is in a very different set of conventions. Nevertheless, a fair study of this systematisation of thought and feeling will serve to show him that there *are* other instincts besides his own, and that the other man's meat is not necessarily poison, if an opportunity is granted of realising the concentrated vitamin-content of that food. The world would be in a much happier state if we would exercise the virtue of tolerance in a rather more far-flung fashion than has been our custom up to the present. There is no reason to doubt that an extraordinary degree of emotional and spiritual elevation can be induced by the meditation on objects and Beings around Whom has gathered a huge mass of psychic "attention." What is called in some communities "decent observance" is an unconscious tribute to those rules of law and order in which the Eastern genius for gorgeous symbology reposes as a monarch on his rightful throne.

The Buddhist *Tantra**, which we are now going to analyse, differs in many respects from the kind outlined above ; but the atmosphere and the philosophy expressed is sufficiently true to type to convey to the reader a correct estimate of the general scheme behind the individual differences.

* See *Acknowledgments.*   140

It is called in Tibetan, the *Demchog Tantra,* and the word means "Highest Bliss." By the proper performance of this devotion the student can free himself from all perils and threats implied in earthly existence. The famous " Blue Records," which give the history of the various Buddhist schools of thought, ascribe the authorship to a *guru* of the Tartar Empress of China, and those alive to these matters will get a faint whiff of Chinese analogy and association from these pages.

As usual the practicant is sternly advised to put himself in the correct attitude of mind and body before he sets out on this journey among realities. When going to sleep, on the night before the ceremony, he must ensure perfect tranquility of mind and spirit. He must be perfect in virtue, and must fix his thoughts along the main lines of Buddhist ideology. No jarring note must enter his life. He should imagine his body to be that of the Buddha of Power; and finally, he must banish all reflection, and lapse to the best of his ability into the happy state of the Void in which all things are resolved into Peace.

When he awakes he will feel himself in a healthy, elated and receptive condition. His mind will be primed to receive the best that the Gods can bestow. But now he himself will be of the Godlike company; for his arising will see him transformed mentally and volitionally into the figure of the Buddha of Power.

It is important that all phenomena should be envisaged as the product of sound. In the ears of the devotee will resound the noise of double-drums, the reverberation of the entire orchestra of Heaven. This is the signal that the twenty great Yogic Heroes of yore are at hand to encourage and sustain with their sacred *mantras.*

Once the aspirant has prepared his mind, he must see to it that there is no waste in his bodily movements. He will assume that yogic posture with which he is most familiar and in which he is most competent. He will be well schooled in the formation of *mudras* with hands and fingers. He should take up his position in a place facing South, and he must be thoroughly clean of body and garb. He may sanctify himself mentally by tasting on the tip of his ring-finger a drop of *amritsa,* the blessed nectar of the Gods, which dispels all illusion.

Next, he will repeat to himself the well-known Refuge Formula of the Buddhist faith. "I take refuge in the Buddha, the Law and the Assembly." This should be followed up by a repetition of the Good Wishes formula, always an admirable moral disinfectant. " May all sentient beings enjoy happiness and be granted the cause thereof . . . . May all beings feel completely equable."

Then, like a desert blossoming with roses, will come an amazing illumination of every sense of the body. A deep and organic pleasure will be experienced with every fibre of the being. This is the union of the Self with the Self which is the daily bread of the souls in Paradise. To retain this ecstasy it is necessary to conjure up a picture of the Goddess Heruka. This is accomplished by a gradual process of accretion.

First, the *mantra* is imagined as glittering in the heart of the supplicant. From this centre spring rays of blue, green, red and yellow : out of their light is shaped the figure of the Goddess, resplendent in beauty and power. At this juncture the worshipper ejaculates : " May all beings be free from attachment and hatred, and may they have all their worldly wishes, name, fame and wealth, granted to them without delay."

In the next step all the outward-going rays are re-absorbed and drawn inwards. The Goddess inhabits the mansion of decay There follows a meditation on the five senses, first as applied to a female Deity, then a male. After these possibilities have been explored, the worshipper, by a clever philosophical twist, co-relates each organ of the body, which in the last resort is doomed to dissolution, with some defect—that is, a vice. The eye stands for delusion, the ears for anger, and the mouth for greed.

In like manner, the five elements of the body, which it shares with the world around it, are contemplated as various aspects of the Goddess. The Earth represents, "She who strikes the unwary"; Water, "She who kills"; Fire, "She who calls to judgment"; Air, "Lady of Creative Force," and the Ether, "She who sits on the Lotus of Deliverance." Hereby is effected a great purification of the gross deposit or residue of matter which we inherit in the imperfect earthly condition.

The next meditation is on the line of *gurus*, or emancipated teachers. These are visualised, too, as forming out of the beams of light, and are grouped in order of ascendance, from the instructor on earth to the supreme initiator in Heaven. The worshipper should think here that he is multiplied innumerably, and that he can wander at will in the fields of asphodel which these twice-born inhabit. He offers to the denizens flowers, water, incense, lights, perfume, food and music. In fact, every imaginable object which has ever been associated with beauty or worth can be laid at the feet of the heavenly choir. The creative imagination can be exercised here in the manufacture of composite mental objects which will be found worthy in the sight of the celestial hierarchy.

All this time there has been erected around the suppliant an altar formed and consecrated by his own thoughts. Sitting in the midst of this vantage-ground, he generates an atmosphere in which spiritual things can live. Freed from hate and lust he can legitimately invite into his circle the ever-gentle Gods and adepts of compassion. At this point he calls upon these wise ones to further his cause. " OM, all-knowing one fulfil my hopes. Come forward. Manifest your presence to me. Homage to all the holy Buddhas . . . ."

Then comes confession and prostration. The devotee reviews his past life and seeks to " wash away all tears " by analysing his defects and seeing them for the limitations and obstacles they are. " I seek forgiveness for the faults I have committed or attempted to commit, by body, speech or intention. Also for those committed by others, which I have condoned." A firm resolution is made never again to fall into these traps of the flesh.

Instead of wasting his activities in the pursuit of the paltry delights of the flesh, he will henceforth repose in the everlasting arms of the Buddha. " From this moment I will to attain Bliss, pure and undefiled." A vow is made to persevere in all virtue and to consecrate the mind as often as possible to the contemplation of those holy men who have won Buddhahood on this earth.

A tremendous resolution is taken. The supreme task of the suppliant's life, once he has found his spiritual feet, will be to concentrate his vigour on the emancipation of those fellow-humans who still walk in darkness. He will do all in his power to give courage and hope to the desolate, succour to the needy. Above all, he will never cease to help others to attain Nirvana, and, by so doing, will ensure his own peace and prosperity. His constant prayer to the Buddhas of the Ten Directions will be for them to set their wheels of truth in motion, so that " the sorry scheme of things entire " will not seem so tragic, after all. He will entreat those holy ones who have already obtained deliverance from this life to come back again so that their example will shine before others as a beacon and a star.

A double interrogatory is performed here. The penitent imagines that the Gods hear his plea and answer it in their turn.

In his inward ear sounds the ultimate response: "O child of goodwill, well have you decided. If you persevere in your quest you will undoubtedly climb to the topmost rung of the ladder. Be of good cheer."

The worshipper again meditates on the syllable *Hum*, and again, from the region of the heart, the creative rays shine forth. This time the ten female "Keepers of the Doors" in the varying compass directions appear, equipped with their respective adornments. It is their duty to clear the ground of all the prying elementals and perverse fiends who would disturb a good man's colloquy with the Gods. To aid them, the devotee makes the Threatening Gesture. This is achieved by placing the thumb on the bent middle finger and raising the index.

An armament race is run against intruders. The suppliant now creates from the heart centre an arsenal of imaginary weapons which protect the mind from assault and fear. Chief among these are clubs and the *Dorje* daggers, described earlier. In some meditations these instruments are multiplied until they form a kind of pavilion in which the worshipper can well imagine himself free from interruption from agencies, human or divine. This is the Defence Line which no assault can break; for the elements of which these weapons are compounded are made from concentrated will.

It is usual at this stage of the proceedings to perform a multiplication process. In order to escape from egotism, and to strengthen his confidence, the "architect" projects himself in as many forms as he can manage, visualising these reduplications of himself as being also engaged in the summoning of spirits. Again he interjects a short prayer. "May there be brought about a dispersal of the dense mass of delusion. May all misery and sin be banished from the worlds. Cause all my enemies to be brought to nought."

For a few moments the worshipper devotes his thought to the absolution of the sins of the mischievous spirits who would seek to hinder his course. They too will inherit peace at the last.

Meanwhile, the "Guardians of the Gates," the formidable matrons who help good men to perfect their forces, have been silently taking up their positions at the angles of the mental armoury erected out of the will of the suppliant. Until he attains Nirvana they will be with him in every hour of need. To make friends with these stalwart supporters is to acquire considerable merit.

144

Once he has made certain of the proximity of these allies, the worshipper offers up a vow of complete purity. He will never again allow his mind to be warped by unsatisfying desires and unprogressive activities. "I am the symbol of the Pure, which is the secret of the reality of all things." Unless the mind is clean there can be no real perception of Truth.

Stone by stone the edifice is raised. Both the tempo and the intensity of the rite increases perceptibly. The devotee girds up his loins. He is going to pass from the laying of single slabs to the building of an entire temple, complete in every occult particular.

Mention has been made earlier of the function of the *mandala,* or altar, in yogic meditation. In this ceremony the symbol plays a large part. It is given colour and significant shape, and we learn that there are *mandalas* to correspond to each of the five elements. That of fire is triangular in form and has in its centre a flaming gem. The *water* altar is round, white of colour, and a pot is placed upon it. The *earth mandala,* coloured yellow, is square, with a three-edged *Dorje* dagger at each of its four angles. That of Air has the curious shape of a bent bow with banners at each end. Ether is represented by summoning up a picture of the fabled Mount Meru, on which dwell so many of the Gods.

First, the resting-place, then the Deity. On top of this last-named *mandala* is imagined one of the minor Gods of Power. It can. be said that all these preparations are in the nature of a working-up to a terrific climax. But still more of the flood has to be loosed before the high-water mark is reached.

It is necessary to make a slight diversion here. It is impossible to comprehend the full significance of a *Tantra* without knowing something of the part played in it by the Sanscrit alphabet. To put it as simply as possible these letters are no mere aid to intellectual understanding. They have a far deeper purpose to serve. When the vibrations of each single letter are understood aright, then there can be no more waste of energy and thought ; for these queer-looking counters have one and all their key-position in the etheric body. Fifty in number, the characters stand at once for part of our subtle organism and for the deities who preside over these parts. In *Tantric* parlance we have a Male and Female Armoury within our own systems. The former auxiliaries include twenty-five Gods who take up their stand like sentries in their " boxes " among our network of bones, nerves and blood :

the latter signify Goddesses who have different but no less valuable services to render to other sections of our frame. The trained *Tantric* clairvoyant sees each body blazing with this esoteric Neon lighting, and he is not deceived in his estimate of what each separate rallying-ground can show in power and effectiveness.

The never-failing efficacy of *mantrams,* or Words of Power, is held to be due to the apt combinations of the syllables. When it is realised that each deity has one of these syllables inalienably associated with his or her presence, there will be little difficulty in seeing that a correct appreciation of the philosophy behind the creation of the alphabet is a *sine qua non* for an understanding of the *Tantric* hypothesis.

The powers of the deities which are always "on tap" (if one may be permitted the expression) for those skilled in extracting essences, manifest themselves by the projection of *mantras* of differing appearance and movement. When it is desired to call on the Gods with peaceful intent, the resultant letters will appear to the inner eye as of a glittering white, leaping out with the speed of an arrow. It is to be noted that they are not flat, as in written characters, but upright, "endwise," so to speak.

When, on the other hand, one wishes a more passionate response, when, for instance, the aid of the God is sought to achieve some feat of fascination or success, then the phenomenon is reflected as red in colour and the shape is like a chain. (For it is by secret links of warm, controlled emotion that we bind the world and others to ourselves.) Again, if by chance the full destructive blast of a deity is needed, with the possibly excusable aim of counteracting some vile social conspiracy or some sore on the body politic, then the letters scintillate in black with a quick spinning motion.

To resume our analysis of the *Demchog Tantra.* Here the syllables are employed with the specific intention of making the body and mind more virile, more sure of itself in all respects. The oriental intelligence, contrary to current prejudice, is thoroughly alive to the necessity for the cultivation of as much physical perfection as we can muster. Many minds can only function efficiently when they are allowed action in a physique freed from the handicap of nervous and muscular disability. There is a purely physical rapture which finds its expression in abounding love of physical experiment and action. It is good, particularly for the young, that they should enjoy to the full the expansiveness which life has given them in the realm of the elementary senses. We can never see the sun and taste the dew of the morning as it should be tasted, until we

are strong of wind and limb.   The gospel of jubilant physical
vitality is no mean ambition for the beginner in soul-training.

With this end in view, the devotee inserts around the *mandala*
of the deity in the centre of an imagined ring the following Sanscrit
vowels, ranged from right to left: a, a, i, i, u, u, ri, ri, lri, lri,
e, ai, o, au, am, ah.   Meditating on these, he sees them as promises
of perfection in the sphere of the perfect conditioning, of eyes,
teeth, tongue, skin, larynx, hair, and so on.   He determines so to
control his appetites that the force, otherwise expended in gluttony
and excess will be used to contribute to the essential value which
comes from the absorption of necessary vitamins.   Henceforth
careful mastication, a pondering on the chemical constituents of
which our bodies are composed and the chemical elements among
which it moves and lives and has its being, will obviate any mistaken
moves in the direction of deceptive stimulants and unworthy
soporifics.   The Temple of the Holy Spirit will not be defiled with
ingredients which are not part and parcel of its well-being.

With the other letters the aspirant concentrates on the motor
functions of the body.   This time he dwells on those interior
supports which if properly managed, conduce to bodily balance and
symmetry, grace of walk and demeanour, ability to get the
maximum of effect with the minimum of effort in every movement
and gesture.   This is in very truth the field of Yoga proper—the
elimination of all stress and strain which is not essential to the
perfect synchronism of body, mind and will.   The right perspective
is so necessary here: it is hopeless to attempt any such exercise as
this until a very definite inner tranquillity is attained.   One must
not put the cart before the horse: meditation on all the symbols
under the sun will be quite fruitless unless the psyche is firm in
virtue and the senses located in a high and charitable ideal. Actually
yogic breathing only becomes automatic and easy when there is
no desire to work any kind of ill: beneficence, in the subtle world
as in the gross, acts not only as its own reward, but as the only
propeller of the machine.   We can only advance in goodness: any
attempt to cultivate strength for the purposes of selfishness or
malignity immediately slides the structure back on its runners.

After the meditations on the alphabet, the powers of application are rested by being centred on a new object.   The devotee
imagines himself surrounded by walls of flame.   Those readers
acquainted with the esoteric training of the ancient Egyptian
priests will recognise here a similar hint of a great cleansing process.
Indeed one could devote a volume to the recondite allegory and

the powerful antiseptics embedded in the central esoteric "Doctrine of Fire." As in the famous passage on "the Destruction of the World," in the *Book of the Dead,* fire is the grand purifier and regenerator. And merely to envisage that element in all its variants of colour and smoke is to breathe in some of the power attendant on its worship. Zoroaster did not err when he called a flame " the spirit of God."

But all this is by way of preparation for the central vision of this mystical feast in which there arises an edifice glowing with all the creation of which the worshipper's mind and heart are capable. In this building not made with hands the walls are strong with all the awe that a disciplined imagination and a steadfast will can produce. All the previous plans are woven together and fashioned so that in any possible mood of doubt or dejection the suppliant can find in the recesses of his own being " an island in a green sea " whose sustaining and invigorating beauty will never fail. The stones used for the construction of this paradise are made from the devotee's capacity for seeing and feeling the unity in all things, even the most ugly and "unimportant." As a Tibetan would put it, one is sufficiently expert in meditation at this juncture that every sentient thing is seen to be equally vivid and important in the end ; every sound has the ineffable beauty of a Word of Power and every actual and potential thought of the mind an invaluable portion of the Divine Wisdom.

In case the reader should be sceptical on the value of this difficult and carefully engineered imagery (and we repeat, if he has been brought up in a Northern European religious convention he may well find himself nonplussed and even startled to find that the concrete mind has its own laws of activity) he can be assured that the effort is attended by very real rewards.

Pre-eminent among these is the experience of Cosmic Consciousness, or an intensely increased perception of the fathomless beauty inherent in quite "ordinary" people and things. This in itself should be a sufficient enticement to a world grown old in the vices of cynicism and disillusion. (Cynicism is not a small or even an "amusing" quality: it betokens the death of a soul. For, when trust in life has gone, there are very few harbours which seem worthy for anchorage.)

It is a very difficult experience to describe to those who "do not speak the language." One can inherit a touch of it by contact with an eminent spiritual personality, and it is possible that everybody knows the state at occasional moments of their lives when the normal limitations and prejudices are in abeyance.

It is frankly impossible to produce this condition at a moment's notice in the rush and tumble of the ordinary economic round. That is, if a technique of self-illumination has not been learned and practised. Even in those not infrequent cases where the soul has been prepared by abominable suffering or a long, persistent tutelage in stumbling, indomitable little feats of virtue, there is no telling when the manna from heaven will fall. It may come during sleep, at any unsuspected place or in any apparently unproductive set of circumstances. It may take us by surprise when we have given up all hope, or when we think we have come to the end of our tether. It can, on the other hand, never come when the mind refuses to make an experiment in humility and when we are fostering the habit of indulging in resentment for its own sake.

What the creative worship of the imagination promises to those sufficiently adept in its performance is an entry into the "blissful self" which can be timed and calculated to a nicety. Just as a favourite delicacy can sometimes produce a condition of superficial nervous contentment, so a retreat into the imaginative sanctuary we have made for ourselves by the honest concentration we have put into the construction of new avenues for the unimpeded progress of the soul, can act as a key which turns, with an ease unequalled by anything made by Brahmah or Yale, the lock that is affixed to the golden gate that leads to peace, happiness, and prosperity.

The puritan and stoic need have no hesitation. The cultivation of mystic virtuosity is not an end in itself. If viewed aright there is no danger that the student will linger, like the lotus-eaters, in any *Paradis artificiel*. He may rest content that he is not slackening in any necessary fibre, not relapsing into any mere and decadent æstheticism. For those who care to search for evidence, there is abundant material to prove that the mystical life is far more energetic and vitalised, far more "practical" and realistic than the existence of the scoffer and the sceptic. The mystic is at least convinced that there is a central truth at the heart of things; and the knowledge removes from his path any lures which may pull him in contrary directions and so neutralise his activities. To see one's way clear is to know in one's heart of hearts that there is no difficulty that cannot be surmounted, no pain that cannot be borne, if the goal is clear and the will steadfast in humility and veneration. This standpoint it is which makes even the really successful business-man, organiser, or actor.   Mystics are not of necessity confined to monasteries or convents.   They do not inevitably yearn for Himalayan heights or jungle clearings.   Indeed, they may at times flourish in the market-place or dominate the forum.   The attitude is all.   The quality, to put the matter in a nutshell, is no hindrance, but, when well managed, a decided help to competent transactions of the business of the world.

But to return to our muttons (or rather to the fortress of our soul).   The central tableau which the aspirant has now succeeded in erecting, has as its basis " a house built on a hill."   Like that wonderful canvas of El Greco, now in the Chicago Art Gallery, in which the town of Toledo, majestic in its sombre destiny, cries defiance and a strange companionship to the storms and winds which throw their weight against the indomitable security of her passionate steeple and green-embodied plains, the *Vihara* or Temple rises as a memento and climax of all the aspirant has done to clear his mind of everything that may endanger the completeness of its functioning.

It is to be remarked that this Mansion is placed at the summit of a hill.   The parable should be clear: it is only by constantly lifting the soul aloft, only by living the life of diligent intercourse with the best and highest of which we are capable, that we can find strength and peace.   The essence of the well-regulated life is happiness; but it is also worship, veneration and aspiration.   Let us take the hint here.   An incarnatory experience is indeed "uphill all the way"; but there is nothing depressing in walking up hills when the ecstatic chant of all the voices of Nature is sounding in our ears, and the entire embassy of heaven waits on the ridge to welcome us home.

Below the Temple the worshippers imagine the " Eight Great Cemeteries."   These macabre localities represent the forces of earth from which we derive a parallel sustenance to that emitted from the highest heavens.   This vitality uses the *Muladhara Chakra* at the base of the spine as its channel and reservoir just as the benison from above rushes through the topmost *Chakra* of the Thousand-Petalled Lotus.   The cemeteries glimmer under the moon, because this orb collects and distributes the magnetic currents of the earth: the worshipper, in consequence, meditates profoundly on the second of the *Chakras,* the *Svadisthana,* and connects it mentally with the first.   Along this swept and garnered road march the hosts of the dead.

For the dead can help, even in their dissolution and decay.

There is, in the undertaker's sense, no death at all. If we could see " even as we are seen " we should recognise in the twinkling of an eye that coffins empty remarkably quickly and deposit their contents in a position of considerable vantage. To dissolve into the elements from which we came is not to " end our miserable existence " but to resume it in an indescribably heightened voltage. And with this sudden " rise in the world " goes an unending series of capabilities. This is why it is good to brood on the " country churchyard " with an interest and optimism never dreamt of by Gray. It is for this reason that the white-hot splendour of battlefields yield not only bones and the dim reverberation of vanished drums, but a power and a plenty which, treated rightly, are more than anxious to serve.

In the cemeteries one dwells yet again on the primeval elements. Following this revision, earth and air are peopled with some of their most typical features. A special stress is laid on the visualisation of the " eight gigantic trees " and every virtue of their sap and foliage is assimilated. The various shapes and kinds of clouds: the misty, the fog-bound, the enshrouding, and those which drift before the storm, are integrated in the worshipper's mind as etchings of the various subtilised forms of matter.

Similarly, the Eight Rivers and the Eight Fires are contemplated reverently as symbols of the spawning richness of phenomena. All the realised appearances are shifted up and down through the arcs of the seven worlds. In this manner the worshipper gets thoroughly accustomed to the climate of other planes. Among other benefits, he has acquired the facility of enjoying and observing his own experiences in sleep, when he will be able to travel astrally—that is, venture lightly-laden and adequately clothed into realms into which the heartfelt rapture of the night will give an added impetus to the energies of the waking day.

He will return too with an invaluable weapon for the forging of serenity and contentment. For to travel without a hitch in the elevator which serves the skyscraper of Perfect Being is to see very far ahead, and remember very far back. In a word, the recollection of past incarnations and the establishment of clairvoyant and clairaudient sensibilities are not the least of the guerdons promised to the virtuous apprentice in soul-climbing. An ounce of spiritual exaltation is worth a ton of arid academic information in the illumination and extension of the capacities.

The symbolic vocabulary for all this increase in the speed and tension of the faculties, consists in the drawing of five concentric circles around the base of the Temple to signify the spheres of life to which the good man may attune his intellect, emotions and will. In the innermost of these sit the God and Goddess carrying the secrets of existence, the promise of salvation: they are accompanied by the host of attendant deities always ready to fly to the aid of the virtuous and the distressed. The next circle is that of the *Mahasukha* or "Highest Bliss," where every instinct, emotion and effort are so delicately adjusted to the logic of spiritual fact that the hairspring of our mechanism calls for no change or renewal. The circle of Mind, which comes next, is no less necessary to completion. It is only in our part of the world that stupidity is regarded as the apex of virtue. To the philosophical oriental intelligence there is no inevitable connection between spirituality and cretinism. From the yogi's point of view the way to peace is rendered more easy of transit with a well-stocked and well-balanced mind to see things in Buddhist phrase "as they are"; and, like a wise judge, to distinguish evidence from camouflage. Here the "sweet child" of Kingsley's rather mawkish poem is assured that the possibility of "being good" does not by any means abrogate the possibility of "being clever." Rather, the mind works in harness with the sanctified instincts and will to expedite the progress of the soul. "There is no religion higher than truth" and the search for truth is not always so easy as it may appear to persons whose optimism exceeds their capacity.

The circle of Speech too is comprehensive and concentrated. "Hear no evil, think no evil, speak no evil." The good life is circumspect, free from spiteful criticism of others, looking always for the spark of the divine in the most "unpromising" human material. We must employ the phrases we use to help, guide, elucidate—never to injure or destroy. One kind word can change the current of a whole life, give it energy and hope, cause roses to bloom where thistles have flourished before. Lastly, the circle of "The Incomprehensible Mystery of the Body" collects all that the worshipper has thought, heard or hoped of the perfect disciplining of his "machine" so that acceleration, insight and the "Three Joys" (escape from the thraldom of the flesh, constructive control of the senses, the gift of godlike compassion) shall act as one. Above all, lust, the arch-anarchist and arch-deceiver, is hereby crushed and annihilated ; for its rude logic cannot persist when the true Light is seen.

Here the devotee uses the meditation on the *bindu* or point to consolidate his gains. A spark of light is envisaged as comprehending the essence of all experience, the concentration and control of all phenomena. This "point" is carried out into the actual world where it surveys the "hell-rook ranks" of sin and degeneration ; comprehends and absorbs even these slurs and renders them harmless. Then it enters into the *Chakra* of the heart, all doubt and passion spent.

The value of consistent meditation in this world is that it leads to stalwart action, when action is required. Purged of the root sins, Anger, Sloth and Lust, the aspirant sees himself as a magnifisent mechanism, more than sufficient to cope with all the wiles of the world. Projected from himself, he visualises his trained and fortified body-spirit, the habitation of the unconquerable Gods, winning its laurels in fields where adaptability, courage and intelligence are the symbols of an imperative moral resolution. The Four Modes of Action—the Peaceful, The Grand (involving decision, self-surrender and concentrated will), the Upholding (the support of all things virtuous and worth while), and the Productive (implying allegiance to legitimate progressive experiment) are all regarded as facets of the diamond of the integrated soul. And yet, unless all things are seen as an ultimate illusion, the true purpose of these rites remains unfulfilled. It is incumbent on the worshipper to bring the boat of his hopes and energies back to the landing-stage of a surety which has little truck with the standards of this world. This is not to say that the world is not to be loved. Nay, it is to be worshipped as an aspect of the Divine Intention. But this worship is not given to an actuality, but to a promise, a seed within a seed. This is why, in the penultimate stage of this "omnibus" meditation a skull looms up through all the strength and jubilation. And yet, within this death-mask, in which male and female, past and future become one, the gods once more take their cue, and stand out as the guardians of health, wealth and happiness in this and all the other worlds.

The rite ends with a purification and a blessing. Those who have arrived, the holy ones of the past, softly and delicately gather around and wash the devotee clean from all defilement with jars of ever-flowing water and oil.

This expedition into a very neglected field of religious architecture will not be in vain, if it has shown the existence of the never-failing fountain of *realism* behind the Tibetan philosophical mind. Thoughts are things, and much more important things than chance, hysterical actions. It is this truth which is at the basis of all effective worship.

And for those who can read between lines, we will make an ending with a quotation from a poem by a Hindu writer of the sixteenth century.

> " You may give your sun-dried rice, you may give your
> sweetmeats,
> But do not think that with these you can gratify the Mother.
> Light the lamp of knowledge, offer the incense of an earnest
> spirit ;
> Then only will one who is divine fulfil all your desires.
> If you would offer sacrifice, then slay your selfishness,
> And lay your love of self upon the altar."

There are many ways to Wisdom. Some are made out of the blood and tears of a thousand mistakes and misadventures: others go slowly through wastes of clogging sand. May not something be said for one which leads to the sea through the lock-gates of Energy, Love and Detachment?

CHAPTER IX

TIBETAN YOGA AND ART.

ONE OF THE MOST GRATIFYING SIGNS of the intellectual emancipation of our day is the rapidly increasing interest in all those phenomena that link up with the problems of art. This is no mere mental relaxation, but a groping out to something which is essential to a fully-rounded existence. Without the solace afforded by the best things in art we are bound to remain incomplete. We tend, unless we are saints, to become egotistic and limited in vision unless we take the trouble to make some acquaintance with the best that has been known and thought in the world in the realm of music, poetry, painting, sculpture. And furthermore, a proper appreciation of art is the best introduction to the world of philosophy in the larger sense. For it is only when we have trained our senses to react to the beauty of the universe around us, and become capable of the ecstasy which is the reward of the cultivated intelligence, that we can begin to ask the larger questions and prepare our receptive apparatus for the essential truths of religion.

The secret of all great art lies in its immediate proximity to the laws of scientific truth. The real poets are not only the " world-losers and world-forsakers " but, much more, the prophets of a divine revelation. They prepare us, by their inspired utterance for the first glimmerings of the true romance which lies behind the veil. They are in very truth, the unacknowledged legislators of the world; for they are, in their best moments the harbingers and heralds of that comprehensive loving-kindness which is the one sure basis of any civilisation; and without an ethical civilisation laws cannot exist.

The word poet is used here as a symbol. Everything that uplifts the heart of man has something in it of the poetic impulse. And the East, always more alert than we to the undertones and overtones of the spirit, has never failed to pay all possible respect to Art as the great adjunct to Religion. Furthermore, Yoga can be linked up very logically with artistic expression in the high sense, because of its inalienable affinity with formalistic design. To treat the body as a vehicle for the delineation of the yearnings of the spirit, is to bring the problems of art very near home.

In Tibet, where Yoga is studied in its multifarious ramifications, and where its philosophy is part of the air breathed by great

155

and small alike, art has always held a very secure position in the affections of the people. It has never suffered from the degeneration attendant on its creation and practice in the more "utilitarian" air of Europe, because it has never been severed, at least in theory, from the major issues which confront the human soul in its journey to its fulfilment.

At first sight, this statement may seem excessive to those who have never bothered to extend their mental horizon beyond the purlieus of the accepted conventions which blind and bind just as surely in matters of this kind as in the more obvious world of social convention. There are at present very few Westerners who adorn their homes with the rich trappings of the East: they are repelled rather than attracted by a style which paints gods in the seeming disguise of men, and which is not in the least afraid of subjects and themes which tax the imagination to its furthermost limits. They are not usually disposed to surround themselves with tapestries and frescoes which are remarkable for their infusion into the atmosphere, of those lofty fundamental issues which pass far beyond the province of mere æsthetics to the statement of eternal mystical facts.

Most of us are as yet too hidebound by preconceived ideas instilled into us from our earliest " cultured " adolescence concerning perspective, " apt treatment of subject " and all the rest of the academic stock-in-trade, to appreciate an artistic outlook which breaks all the long-established rules in favour of a tropical wealth of line and colour which may well prove too strong a potion for heads wrapped in a narrow conservative tradition.

In innumerable Tibetan monasteries and anchorites' cells there are depicted on the walls scenes which at first sight seem to defy our ideas of what good art should be. Here, we may be tempted to say, the canvas is too loaded: the painter has maddened himself in the frenzy of his own over-exuberant imagination. The " vice " of the oriental imagination, it will be remembered, is a jungle-like exuberance which defeats its own ends by satiating the eye with a great deal more than it can take in. Also, it may be argued, there is too much concentration on the forceful or even the terrifying to suit the taste of our culture, which tends to regard art as a refinement rather than a consolidation of the powers of the soul.

The present writer has in his possession a number of hangings of a *Tantric* nature which embody the very spirit of Tibetan conception of art. On one of these is depicted the figure of Kali, the Goddess of Destruction, trampling on the Demon Vinataka. The description may seem to be a contradiction in terms; for why should two such apparently friendly forces agree to annihilate each other ? It is not until one has brooded for long on this picture that its profound symbolism asserts itself, and one realises that the Goddess of Destruction is, in effect, the symbol of that cleansing and sifting process which makes all things new, which echoes the very voice of Nature, whose laws are compounded of light and darkness, the passing from one form of existence to another.

The colouring, too, is not so much decorative as functional. That is to say, the colours on these canvases, although gloriously effective merely as stimulating combinations of the possibilities of the spectrum, have much more to say to us when we fathom their connotations. In this *genre* colours have a significance which cannot be fully defined in the scope of this short chapter, but of which it is sufficient to say that they provide the sensitive mind with a key to a code of mystical learning which our civilisation has yet to re-discover. This kind of art definitely *does something* to the emotions of an infinitely healing and integrating nature. Some of us have suspected it for time past; but very few have tracked the phenomenon down to its deeper reaches. To put it as simply as possible, the apt conjunction of colours calls into being something which answers to them in the very depths of our being; and, in consequence, we are inspired to new resolutions and incited to the exploration of new paths of the spirit. This fillip to the mainspring of the emotional life has a marked effect on the intelligence; for it is necessary to point out to our generation that the reason, in many cases, cannot function properly unless the generators of feeling are doing their work with the maximum of efficiency and the minimum of waste.

Another painted scroll in the author's possession, this time from one of the great Tibetan monasteries, has as its subject the depiction of a very different branch of mystical faith. Here, to all intents and purposes, are arrayed a group of Lamas, one and all engaged in the contemplation of that Nirvana to reach which is their life's highest goal. They sit in the famous "Lotus" Posture (incidentally one of the most appropriate to perform) and on their faces is an expression of rapt contemplation. There is no movement in this picture, and indeed, no perspective, in our sense of that word; for the heavens and hells which set off their serene beatitude are filled in with a complete disregard for anything that we could term verisimilitude. The boundaries of these widely-contrasted realms are too near to each other to please our conception of propriety; and the ordinary rules of dimension are suspended in favour of an intensity which does not hesitate to drive its point home by overcrowding each separate section with a paraphernalia of " business " of a character too specific for a taste which prefers to take its allegory in small doses.

But the central idea is defined with an unmistakable distinction. It is a picture of men of great spiritual discernment ensconced in yogic postures ; and it crystallises for all who can read, that rare capacity for what may be called " suspended movement " which is one of the prerogatives of the Eastern artist at his best. And here again we come to one of the essential *motifs* of the type of art with which we are concerned. This is interested primarily in a kind of suggestion which demands of the critic that he treat the surface as a point of departure for the interpretation of what lies behind it. Once one has penetrated the extreme formalism of the outward figuration one can enter intellectually and emotionally into a world in which the causes of action are seen in their slow progress towards their fulfilment.

It is the same in actual life. It is always the contained, unagitated person who conveys the greatest suggestion of power: the fidget can never really command attention. All he can do is to communicate to others some of his own instability, and so create an atmosphere around him which is prejudicial both to his own happiness and to the self-confidence and serenity of others. It is not entirely by accident that the most " gaga " exploits of our more exaggerated neo-impressionists have been accompanied by a slackness and viciousness of character in the artists concerned. It takes a stabilised soul to be a really first-class artist: it is the second-raters who fill the gossip-columns with accounts of their feckless inanities.

The contemplation of these " tapestries " is morally as well as artistically good. It disciplines the intelligence because it brings the mind back to first principles, and it invigorates the emotions because of its subtle hints of what to concentrate on in the world of form and colour.

Even more is this fact brought home to one if one secures a number or even one of those little statuettes of the gods which can be picked up without much trouble in the junk-shops of Europe and America. It is surprising that there is not a bigger public for these most intriguing examples of the carvers' and moulders' work. Is it because they are " supposed to bring bad luck " (a thoroughly exploded fallacy) or is it that the essential severity of the figures depicted repels a generation accustomed to the " repository art " of our chapels of meditation ?   It is difficult to say.   But anyone who has lived for a short time with images of the Buddha and his attendant deities will testify to the atmosphere of fortified calm which these things bring in their train.

Those found in our part of the world are brought here frequently enough by casual travellers who little reck of the spiritual treasure they are amassing under an æsthetic guise. They fetch no high figure; and it is easy to find a bargain among objects of real art which have never suffered the taint of a cheap popularity. Even the cheaply-cast Buddhas which come into the market as an attempt to foist the " precious " on the small public which wishes for " something different " can bestow an extraordinary distinction on any attic which sees fit to give them house-room.

Most of these statuettes are about the same size as our *Tanagras*.   They occupy very little space, and they are ideal as ornaments, if only because they represent the acme of taste. This is due to the fact that the figures are moulded according to a long-tried established æsthetic pattern in which there is no room for pointless divagation. This is to say, that from time immemorial, they have acquired their own proportion and perspective; and so the mind is already prepared for the assimilation of the religious principles embodied behind the elaborately conventional facade. Every deity has his or her correct delineation (with certain variants) and the " ornamentation " employed is strictly in keeping with the subject

For instance, the ferocious goddess Lha-Mo, the protector of the Dalai Lama of Lhasa is never depicted without her mule on which she rides in triumphant state.   Gautama, the Buddha, postures his hands within a strictly delimited æsthetic field, and his legs are crossed at an angle which bears witness to a certain esoteric tradition.   In another conception he is depicted in a reclining position; but the pose is controlled by considerations deeper than the merely pictorial.

It is reserved for the very greatest artists to show what can be done with the inexorable laws of form.   In our own tradition, creators like Bach and Fra Angelico approximate most nearly to the Eastern outlook in this respect.   It is also the reason why a hysterical " modern " appetite finds these philosophers in the school of serenity " dull," lacking in the superficial appeal which distinguishes even the least gifted of the romantics.   There is far more skill and insight needed to work according to a set theme than to splash and splurge on the largest romantic canvas. It has been said that "the classic is health, the romantic disease": the discerning will see at once what is implied in this definition. The nature of life is, in the last resort, simple enough. It is only the person who seeks to spend his days in chasing his own shadow, that is, neglecting major issues in favour of the evanescent glitter of phenomena, who will afford to cavil at the strong and severe sense of line which is inseparable from the Easterner's philosophic conception of art.

It is significant that these little images are often the receptacles for small rolls of parchment on which are inscribed suitable invocations and prayers. Without any taint of the smugly pietistic, a lesson in the rules of form is thus combined with an exhortation to the chief duty of man on this earth, which is to praise and obey his inspiration, and so carve out his path in pleasant and lasting places. One can see in any well-equipped museum the appropriate blocks for the turning-out of these charming religious reminders. They provide a silent testimony to the combination of religious "instruction" with the appeal of high art which is the best guarantee of the durability of both.

Of Tibetan music it is difficult to speak in terms which will convey much to readers unaccustomed to the practice of acute æsthetic analysis. Two Japanese gentlemen were noticed at a pre-war performance of the B Minor Mass at Queen's Hall convulsed with helpless mirth. One can criticise their manners; but at the same time it should be easy to understand their reaction. Their ears were being assailed with sounds of a character for which they were completely unprepared. What would strike us as the very acme of harmony seemed to them a cacophony which approached near enough to gibberish to arouse a feeling of illogical contrast which is supposed to be the main constituent of laughter. Many of us would react in the same way to a first hearing of oriental music. We should be unable to trace any why and wherefore in a combination of sounds which would give the lie to all that we have been brought up to believe is the requisite of melody.

The main reason for this acute disparity of appreciation is a technical one. The use of the very ancient pentatonic scale is part and parcel of the systematisation of Tibetan musical modes. And to those interested in such matters, it may be pointed out that some of the more searching contemporary musical researchers are groping their way towards a re-understanding of how this old medium can serve the æsthetic needs of modern times. But deeper than this technical argument is the insistence of the cultivated oriental that music should be ancillary to the religious consciousness. Or, to put it another way, music is only one of the many methods of that auto-hypnosis which vivifies and integrates the faculties to a condition where they can deploy their energy towards a fulfilment of the entire being.

" Even that vulgar and tavern music which makes one man merry and another mad, does inspire in me a profound reverence and a contemplation of the First Creator." This confession of an old-time lover of beauty may be taken as a hint on the enormous value of sound as a consolidator of certain nerves of action and meditation. And when one has tired of the first fine careless rapture which is the concomitant of an early love of the musical art, a new start can be inaugurated by a realisation of sound not as a soporific, but as an opener of occult doors.

Even writers of jazz know how nerves can be worked on by the conjunction of a set of primitive tones and timbres. It is a very moot point whether this application of cheap ointment to ragged susceptibility-centres is a boon or something resembling a poison; but extreme examples prove the existence of a mean; and the influence of the phenomenon is widespread enough for us to treat it as an instance of what can be done in far higher planes of musical endeavour.

For example, instead of reducing æsthetic discrimination to a vague and childish dither, the skilful " occult " musician could employ his energies in bringing into submission the more respectable constituents of the subconscious. This has in effect been achieved by those medieval connoisseurs of the psyche who gave us the form known as Plain Chant. Anyone who is able to watch the works of his reactionary apparatus in action has only to enter a church and listen for half an hour to the sung " Office," to feel that a very subtle magic is acting on his nerves. He is being " tuned in," as it were, to a sphere where much of the normal sense of striving and insecurity is being eliminated in favour of an intense mental and emotional reverberation which, if he react against it, may well seem to " take the reason captive."

This is a good enough introduction to what the music of the yogis of Tibet endeavours to achieve in its own peculiar fashion. The whole country teems with folk-songs which testify to a music which it not only an emotional outlet, but, much more important, a spiritual stimulus. The best-known of the ballads of the country recount the exploits of heroes who were also saints, and the music moves accordingly. Here is a verse from a poem very popular among the Lepchas, a hill tribe whose chanting is rich in a special " cachet " of its own.

" O Joy ! In the olden time the Head-Father-Spirit made the earth,
He the Sky-Existing-One made this paradise,
He clothed the hard bosom of this tearful earth with fertile fields.
When the men were made and the jointed bamboos and the trees,
At that same time were we, the sons of the one-mother-flesh
Exalted into life."

This popular expression of a cosmic consciousness is sung to the reiterated accompaniment of small drums and reed instruments. The general effect is almost minatory: it instils in the mind of the listener a salutary memento of the inevitability of destiny: the auditory nerves are riveted with a memory of " time's chariots " ever drawing near. We are reminded that our friends are exultations, agonies and man's unconquerable mind. It is a music which brings serenity in its train; for its starkness leaves no room for illusion; and he who only hears these strains is set thinking for the rest of his life on this earth.

But it is perhaps in its theatrical entertainment that Tibet may appeal the most strongly to the unprejudiced Western observer. The word must not be misunderstood. As with the ancient Greeks, the " theatre " of Tibet is not so much a relaxation as a *catharsis*—a means of ridding the mind and will of their dross, putting them through the mill of pity and terror; a religious ceremony, in fact. Our own notion of a " National Theatre "— a place set apart for the production of the best in a country's dramatic literature, has something of the same religious tinge, but its implications do not carry us anywhere near so far as the motive which prompted Æschylus to write his tragedies and Aristophanes his comedies. It is to old national celebrations and customs that we must look if we would seek to appreciate what the Tibetan stage means to the Tibetans. Perhaps also to those Mystery Plays of the Middle Ages which embodied so much of the soul's aspiration in a guise which could be understood by the multitude. Those time-honoured May rites and festivals of harvest which are still retained as a quaint survival of the past, are, in fact, to the percipient mind, rich in suggestions of a sacrificial sense which can be traced as a constant throughout the whole history of civilised peoples. It were well if our antiquarians gave rather more thought than is their wont to the reality under these trappings, the underlying spirit under the surface charm. Then some information could be obtained as to the "oversoul" of a people which finds expression in a communal linking of instincts and words and gestures.

Some years ago, under the ægis of Mr. C. B. Cochran, a troupe of Japanese Players was brought to London and enchanted the Town with an exhibition of a virtuosity of a very different kind to the *ersatz* orientalism to which we had been introduced by the more flamboyant Russian Ballets and those rococo artists among us who had been seduced by an early reading of *Omar Khayyam*. It was a revelation of what can be achieved by an extreme economy of action and movement, combined with an elaboration of costume and accessories which had its own peculiar function to perform as a stimulus to the understanding of a tradition richer than most in a concrete realisation, in the large sense, of religious fact. Anyone who was lucky enough to see any of these performances gained thereby a liberal education in the attitude of mind necessary to adopt when confronted by a dramatic tradition as rich and evocative as that which we are about to consider.

Such a student will not be bewildered by any superficial complexity of themes; for the Tibetan theatre has a very limited repertoire. This is confined to about a dozen Buddhist Mystery plays each with its own "moral" to impart. It is not story nor incident that matters in these pieces; but representation of the great moral issues which activate and determine the stormy life of man. If the student had no access to any source of information on the subject of Buddhist philosophy other than these plays he would possess at least a good working idea of the general bearing of the theme.

They belong in origin and practice to the monasteries, just as did Moralities like *Everyman* and *The Castle of Perseverance* in the Europe of the Middle Ages. They are acted by monks, although lay persons are occasionally introduced to play women's parts. Some of the monasteries have their own especial play, and the regular repetition of the same performance leads to an extremely high standard of acting and production.

Something should be said here on the extraordinary subtlety of the Tibetan language as a medium for the "conveyancing" of this type of art. It is particularly rich in expressions of elaborate courtesy, and the present writer holds that when strict attention is given to manners there tends to be very little wrong with morals. "Manners makyth man," and there is a very traceable connection between a gracious exterior formality and the right training of those instincts which subserve the needs of our highest being. Furthermore, the acting in these plays consists very largely of a series of set gestures and movements which carry the same moral and psychological implications. It is in this respect that they can be regarded as a genuine extension of the cultivation of personal Yoga; for they speak the same language, and their technique is related to the same source.

In the very nature of the case, a certain emphasis has to be laid in these works on the obvious. They are written partially at least, for delectation and entertainment, and doubtless it is not every Tibetan spectator who is sufficiently equipped to extract the essence from the lines which he hears. There is an appeal both to those within and those without the veil. To the more simple-minded an attendance at these performances will involve little more than the viewing of a panorama in which the virtues and vices are personified in a homely human form: the initiate, on the other hand, will recognise through the allegory the pillars and struts on which the whole world rests. But even to the frivolous there will be nothing which cannot be turned, if so desired, to a very real edification.

There is much talk nowadays on the relative merits of the different kinds of suggestional and " photographic " stage *décor*. The Tibetan monks, like the Chinese and Japanese, solved the problem long ago by concentrating on giving the greatest play to the imagination of the spectator by suppressing as much as possible cheap adventitious aids to verisimilitude, and putting in its stead a highly simplified background, whose only purpose is to throw into relief the significant byplay and expressions of the players. In our sense of the term there is no " scenery " on the Tibetan stage. The plays can be performed at short notice in any fit spot where an audience is gathered together. Frequently enough, they are given in the open air, with nothing but the vault of heaven for covering. Here too the student will call to mind the medieval market-places, which provided the setting for so much that was fine and valuable in the dramatic fare of the Middle Ages (a period, by the way, more attuned than ours to the pre-eminent need for philosophy in human affairs).

It is perhaps inexact to call these Mysteries plays in the usual sense; for they consist of a curious mixture of dialogue and narrative which may convey to the beginner a certain impression of scrappiness. Unless he happens to be conversant with the

structure of the ancient Greek drama, where the introduction of
the chorus as commentator and interpreter of the action will give
him some clue to the functioning of the narrator in the Tibetan
ceremonies; for the " hunter," as he is frequently called, has, in
his own peculiar way, the same duties to perform.   He is the
unprejudiced witness to the implications of the action: he stands
for an impartial wisdom, points out the ways of gods with men.
Without his intervention the play might swerve from its intention in
the excitement of action: he calls it back to its purpose as an
æsthetico-religious tract.

Very often the " hunter " is multiplied by several of his kin.
When this happens the resemblance to the ancient Greek play
becomes even more obvious.   For when two or three " hunters "
are gathered together in one play they extend the province of their
functions and sometimes dance a ballet in between the sections of
the action.   Invariably they wear masks.   There is a very definite
reason for this custom.   In contradistinction to our taste in drama,
the Tibetans seek to eliminate from their plays the personal and
the narrowly " realistic " and to substitute instead a vision of life
in which man is envisaged as a unit in a huge scheme of salvation.
Therefore it is not essential to concentrate on any personal
characteristics, but to bring into focus as much as possible those
elements in the human situation which link up with the Buddhist
conception of the inseparable unity of all things.

Most of the plays take a long time to perform, as impatience
has never been a characteristic of the Tibetan people.   An element
of comic relief is often inserted in order to satisfy the cravings of
the groundlings for variety; but as the interpolations have no
particular bearings on the subject we do not propose to bother the
reader with descriptions of this side of the proceedings.   In any
case, they have no value either as ceremony or literature, and are
inserted cynically enough as a makeweight and padding for those
whose brains are not strong enough to endure unrelieved truth
without an admixture of the irrelevant.   Like the comic scenes in
Marlowe's great play, *Dr. Faustus,* they can be omitted with perfect
safety as an excrescence on the main body of the text.   The more
subtly-minded will smell a larger and richer humour (a " world-
laughter " in Jean Paul Richter's sense) between the lines of the
dialogue as it winds its way to its conclusion.

The first piece we choose for analysis is entitled *Tchrimekundan*.   It is of exceptional interest to students of Buddhism, as
it recounts the story of one of the incarnations of the saint who was

to be reborn later as Sakya Muni, the founder of the Buddhist creed. It takes us through a landscape of the most harrowing trials; for, like Job, the good man is tried in the fire and is tested in the furnace of adversity.

The scene is laid in remote Nepal, and the theme is illuminated by a poignant charity and simplicity which conveys an atmosphere of extraordinary charm. In the centre of the picture is the young prince who chooses virtue as other men choose comfort and safety; around him are grouped, in a scheme which leaps to the eye, the forces of good and evil, which carry on their eternal struggle for possession of the soul of man.

The prince is aided in his instinct for charity by his father who opens the royal coffers to his son so that he can dispense largesse. He is prompted, too, by a chief minister who is also of a large and benevolent disposition. But there is also a chief minister who is devoted to evil. Between these two advisers the prince's lot is cast. The latter, in order to circumvent the good works of the Buddha, hurries him into a marriage with Princess Mendezanmo. As it happens the lady is herself of virtuous quality, and instead of hindering the activities of her husband, she supports them wholeheartedly.

In the possession of the king is the famous Cintamani Gem which grants all desires. It chances one day that a Brahmin appears unannounced at the court. He has been sent by a king of a neighbouring country to enveigle from the holy prince this treasure of his father's collection. The youth, unable to resist any appeal for charity, parts with the jewel. The die is cast. He and his wife are tried before hostile judges, and it is only by the hair of their heads that they escape punishment by torture. Instead, they are condemned to wander forth to a destination called " The Mountain of the Demons," where they will be subjected to all manner of trials. The exile is to be for twelve years.

The two set forth, provided with a modest retinue for the carriage of their necessaries. Hardly have they started on their way, when they encounter three Brahmins who beg alms. Tchrimekundan immediately parts with his three elephants which carry food for the journey. A little further on, he gives away his horses and waggons. Further tests follow when beggars demand of him his children; but he relinquishes this bond too. He hesitates a little when he is asked to surrender his wife; but such is his passion for sacrifice that he consents even to this severance. But it is not required of him: Indra had appeared in the habiliments of a mendicant in order to test his fortitude. His wife is restored to him and husband and wife arrive together at the Mountain of the Demons.

Here they take up their rest in separate huts and pass their time in mystic contemplation. The sorrows of life gradually take on a relevance and a meaning. In the silence of the hills a deep philosophy is born: they are strengthened in their determination to keep up their spirits to the end. They need their stoicism; for the return journey is as full of trials as were the days of exile. A short time after they have turned their steps towards home, the prince comes across a beggar who asks of him the gift of his eyes. Tchrimekundan complies with the request and continues his journey blinded. But out of suffering comes good; for the beggar goes before them and announces to the king the marvellous bounty of his son. The monarch, heavy with remorse, comes to meet his child who, by a divine miracle, has had his sight restored.

All ends happily. The Cintamani Jewel is restored to its original owner. All parties are reconciled. The Buddha, freed by his love and detachment from the chain of existence, is transported to heaven in the form of a lotus: justice has been done.

This legend, in its dramatic form the most frequently performed of all Tibetan plays, has its counterpart in all Asiatic tongues. It points an obvious moral, and adorns a tale filled with romantic incident and an atmosphere of high places. The Tibetan public never tire of its profound pathos and the picture of lofty morality which it portrays. In this respect they are superior to ourselves. For they are not bored with the representation of superhuman virtue which is the ground-plan and justification of this story of a soul. Indeed, there is a very strong connection between the popularity of such a piece and the native idealism of the Tibetan temperament, which, however imperfect an expression it may assume in action, is always ready to kindle itself at the flame of things above it. There is no talk in these quarters of virtue being " outside the reach of average men." On the other hand average men are constantly inspired to new endeavour by the example of the saints who have hewed and laid the common road.

It may interest the reader to quote a few examples of the lovely verse which carries the play along. We take these passages from the lucid translation by Jacques Bacot. Even at a second remove it is hoped that the quality of the thought will come through. The following extract describes the birth of the Buddha.

" As soon as he was born, before any other word he said:
'*Om mani padme hum.*'
Then, having said these words, he wept.
He showed to all beings a mercy like to the love of a mother for
an only son.''*

The simple nature of the medium will be noticed, its chaste
quality, its freedom from all frills and affectation.   It is the kind
of narrative which Maeterlinck sought to achieve; but it springs
from a stronger and purer tradition than that inherited by the
Belgian mystic.   It is the very voice of sincerity without self-
consciousness and hesitation.

And this is how the mother of Tchrimekundan beseeches " the
four potent Protectors of the world " to comfort her son in exile:

" Lead him by paths free from danger
While he swiftly crosses mountains and plains,
Let him not be exhausted by sorrow and weariness.
Let him find a divine house.
When he eateth the frozen fruits of the earth,
Let them be changed into exquisite foods and nectar."†

It can be imagined what an effect the chanting of these
poignant and starkly economical lines has on the imagination of
the spectators.   They feel themselves to be participators in the
play.   As the piece winds its slow length along, they too are
transported out of themselves by the subtle intermingling of
miming, chant and verbal suggestion into a plane of existence where
yogi principles of concentration and inundating charity are the
accepted counters of thought.

The play ends with the simple adjuration: " Be happy.''   The
lesson of all that the audience has heard and seen is contained in
these two words.   The way of virtue is the way of contentment:
although the action has told of suffering and endurance, the outcome
is more than sufficient compensation for the price paid.   Our trials
and tribulations will seem a very small matter when we have passed
beyond and through them to the place where they will be seen in
their true proportion.

Djroazanmo, another play very popular in Tibet, partakes in
its subject more of the nature of a fairy-tale rather than of a record
of saintly action.   It has the charm of the best things in Hans
Andersen, and the same underlying morality.   But it must be

*† v. *Three Tibetan Mysteries* [translation by H. I. Woolf, pp. 21 & 54].

remembered that fairies are endemic enough to the climate of Tibet and are not relegated to any mere realm of folklore. They are the minor inhabitants of a spirit-world whose chief denizens are the major gods and goddesses, and there is enough pantheism in the national temperament to give mental house-room to a multitude of these elusive beings who flit, sometimes inconsequently between the confines of heavens and hells.

Djroazanmo is the story of the adventures of two children. At first sight it may call to mind memories of Snow White and the Babes in the Wood, until one realises that it implies a deeper allegory than do these charming *jeux d'esprit*. In fact, it is once again a parable of the struggle between good and evil, a philosophic study of the relative powers inherent in the constructive and destructive elements in life.

It commences with a scene depicting two aged Brahmins who bemoan the fact that they have never known the joys of father-hood. They cannot see their lives as complete until they experience the solace of childish voices in their homes. Their desire is miraculously granted. '' When the five goddesses Who Fly in Space had seen and understood this, each sent forth a ray of light. And these lights together took the form of a little golden man as big as the thumb. And he went into the Brahmin mother's bosom through the top of her head with the sound of music. She had a dream like this. She saw the sun and the moon rise out of her own heart, and shed light on the four continents and the little islands. From the top of the highest mountains resounded the preaching of religion. The son and daughter of a God having cleansed her of all ill and of evil spirits, her body was like a *stupa* of crystal.''

So a daughter is born. An incarnation of the all-beneficent Goddess Tara, she grows up in grace and beauty. The shadows darken when some fairies foretell that a king and queen will work her much harm, and that she will eventually fly away into the sky. The prediction comes true in the following manner. The King Kalaombo, who has a passion for the chase, one day sights the Brahmin's house among the trees. He visits the place, falls in love with the maiden, and carries her off to his palace. He has children by her, and it is some little time before the situation is discovered by the queen, who is an ogress.

Wild with rage, the queen decides to revenge herself. The king she renders mad with a poisoned drink: the children she seeks to destroy as she is unable to wreak her hate on their mother, who, as foretold, has flown away into the sky. " I, without tarrying, am going to the abode of the Taras. Ye too, brother and sister, go confide your destiny to the king your father." After saying that, she disappears into the blue sky.

But the children are protected. Do what she will, the queen is unable to work her will with them. The spirit of Djroazanmo, who has flown away " for the good of creatures," looks down benignly on the innocents she loves. They pass securely through all. Fishermen are ordered to drown them; but their hearts are touched, and they allow their victims to fly into India. Assassins are sent after them; but here again they experience a change of heart when about to execute their dreadful task, and the little boy is allowed to escape to the Land of the Lotus. He is guided there by a sacred parrot who, like many oriental birds, is gifted with far-seeing wisdom.

The parrot turns round and says: "We are from the Land of the Lotus where we adore the Great Compassionate.

" And we invoke him by the prayer in six words.

" The power of this prayer hath stopped our rebirths and the royal line is extinct.

" This is why it would be excellent for thee to become King of the Land of the Lotus."

Thus he speaks, and Lhaze cries: " Shall I be King? "

And the parrot saluting in its fashion the four directions, bows each time three times its head. Lhaze also salutes the four directions. And at the same moment a brown monk's habit falls from the sky as well as some white monk's sandals and a linen turban. Then the parrot clothes Lhaze's body with the habit, he shoes his feet with the sandals and he coils the linen turban on his head. Lhaze says then:

" Now shall I be King of the Land of the Lotus? "

And the parrot answers:

" Thou shalt be indeed."

The little girl, sorrowing for the absence of her brother, wanders too into the Land of the Lotus, and while begging near the palace recognises her Lhaze. Amidst great joy the two are united and they rule together over this realm where the heart takes its fill of rest. The ministers sprinkle them with sandal-water and call them back to glorious life. And they bathe Lhazikuzan in a piscina. And they dress her again in a garment of silk and panteli. And they adorn her with diamond jewels. Then the brother and sister sit down on a throne of precious gold and on a throne of turquoise, and they rule over the Kingdom of the Lotus. . . .*

With this scene, reminiscent of the gorgeous ending to Stravinsky's *Firebird*, the play virtually ends. All that is left to narrate is the overthrow and death of the wicked queen and the freeing of the subjugated king. The usual device of fairy-tale technique rounds off a story with implications far beyond the province of fantasy.

In the first place the play is equilibrated early on in its course by a transposition to the atmosphere of a heavenly realm. It is to the fact that Djroazanmo has " flown away " that is to be ascribed the safe passage of her children (who represent each one of us) through the perils and vicissitudes of life. She acquires in her new abode a great strength, and is able to wield the weapons of virtue for the protection of the right running of the earthly world below. One of the most unmistakable charms of this type of Tibetan " mystery " lies in the creation of a world in which material and immaterial intersect: in this way is produced an enchanting fairyland which lulls the senses to sleep while raising the mind to courage and high resolution. But it is not, in any superficial sense, " a land of faery ": it is rather a transference to a delicately-etched allegory of the symbols and compensations which live below the water-lilies of the subconscious. Again, it is a study in high patience. It would be impossible to find another work in which, in such soft insidious stages, is traced the conviction that good must ultimately prevail over evil because good has all the cards of beauty in its hands, and beauty is the standing and unconquerable proof of virtue.

This play is of an immense antiquity. How old it is is impossible to say, as the original manuscript hails from Darjeeling in Northern India and there is no means of tracing how it reached this district. There is every reason to suppose that this "original" is itself a transcription; for there are certain variations in tone and expression which suggest that more recent hands had filled in gaps due to parts being missing or undecipherable through age. The whole thing can be taken as an illustration that the " primitive," whether in art or religion, has much more to give us than is commonly thought.

* *Three Tibetan Mysteries* [p.192].

The last play we shall consider is of a very different calibre to the preceding. It is much later in origin, and, as we should say, more sophisticated. Its main appeal to modern readers lies in the picture it draws of Tibetan manners and customs and the philosophy upon which these are based. It can be regarded from one angle as a work of edification, insisting as it does on right modes of thought and behaviour in this temporal world. From the strict Buddhist point of view, the play of *Nansal* presents a curious anomaly; for it suggest in several of its lines that only once can the soul be born as man. Whether this point of view represents an incursion of Western thought it is difficult to say ; but the divergence implied from rigid Buddhist orthodoxy is sufficiently marked to merit notice.

Nansal is a maiden of sensitive and pious disposition, who has an aptitude for the life of meditation and retirement. But her leanings are frustrated by her parents who are unwilling that their daughter shall immure herself from the activities of the world. They force her to frequent places of public amusement, and one day at the theatre she is admired by a governor of the country who seeks her hand in marriage. She weds him ; but the union turns out unhappily, largely owing to the fact that she is hated and envied by the women of her husband's family. Unable to endure the situation she returns to the home of her parents. Her husband follows in pursuit ; but, on finding that she is not built for the married state, leaves her respectfully to her solitude. It is interesting here to note that the Tibetan marriage laws give full liberty to the woman to leave her husband if she finds the bond alien to her spiritual peace. There is, in fact, something like a trial marriage for two years : within this period the woman has a practically complete freedom of decision with regard to her future fate.

But Nansal does not find what she wants at home. Her mother is a conventional woman, and does not understand the desire of her daughter for the religious life. She attempts to draw her towards the pleasures of the world, and points out how she is "wasting her life" as an old maid. Nansal acknowledges the blessings she has received, but still yearns for her ideal. At this moment there comes by a daughter of the chief, named Rich in Happiness. And she says:

"Elder sister, to-day thy face is sad. Have thy father and mother scolded thee, causing thy tears? Is thy little child dead? "

Hundred-thousand Light answers:

" Daughter Rich in Happiness, hear me. My father and mother have not scolded me. My son is not dead. But all these ephemeral things, at the moment of death, are not useful like religion. The world of transmigration filleth me with sadness. I cannot endure the suffering of the Three Damnations. When one doth remember the holy doctrine of our origin, there is no subject for tears."

Nansal has to fulfil her destiny. She wanders, first to a convent, and then, searching a further solitude, into the desert, where she finds the peace for which her nature has called. From this vantage-point she sees life as it really is, and is able to point out the path to others. Her heart-broken mother comes in search of her daughter, and finds her deep in meditation in a solitary glade. Nansal is touched by her parent's grief and endeavours to console her. But in this case her efforts do not meet with much success, as the mother is not ready for the revelation to which Nansal has attained.

" My daughter, let us stay together a month, or only a half-month, or for the least ten days."

But Nansal sings these stanzas: "Father and mother, I pray you. Father and mother full of grace, hear me. Our fragile life is like the flower of autumn. The flower, drooping from the morning, is parched at night. The world is ephemeral as the growling of thunder in space. The strongest growling of the thunder is only an empty noise. The ephemeral soul is like the clouds in the sky. |

With a homily on the unsatisfactory nature of life in this world and a diatribe against monks who turn their " call " into an excuse for luxury and wantonness the play *Nansal* ends. A trite statement, it may be remarked, of a boring theme. The same critics will feel that we have enough of such exhortations to piety in our own civilisation without going to Tibet to discover its analogues.

In one sense they will be right. There is nothing particularly original about the " message " promulgated by this simple and guileless piece. And it has, at a first reading, a certain suggestion of smugness which will repel those who like their religion doled out with a more definite fervour. Indeed the chief intelligent critical objection to the play will lie in what may be regarded as the coldness of Nansal's temperament. She treats ordinary life and its inhabitants as a panorama which is best forgotten; and the Buddhism which she expounds has a strong tincture of the

† Ibid [p.260].

puritanic variety which is associated with the " Reformed " Sect instituted in the fourteenth century.

But the charm of the play lies, in this case, by no means entirely in the virtues given to the main character. The minor parts, the men and women of varied types and professions who fill out the delicately-coloured canvas on which the story is painted, are drawn with a rare understanding of the merits of a more average humanity. It is, in fact, this careful delineation of minor characters so sympathetically realised and executed, which gives the play a kind of balance. The whole work is, so to speak, a compromise between extremes—on the one side the exhalted and rather fanatical temperament of Nansal; on the other the picture of the types of ordinary people with ordinary virtues who keep the world going. It is at least arguable that the latter class are more valuable in helping to further the slow progress of humanity towards the light : they understand average problems far better than do many of the mystical virtuosi (like Nansal), and they often possess in contradistinction to the " elect " a saving gift of humour which sees very deeply into the heart of many mysteries.

Experts in mystical training are extremely suspicious of sudden flights of virtuous fervour. They know that such extremes of feeling tend more often than not to be of very short duration, and to leave the person who has experienced them in a distintegrated and overwrought condition. Pope Leo X once told a nun who pestered him with stories of having seen visions, to "take something for it." The episode has a cynical flavour ; but it bears witness to the claims of common sense over the flights of hystérical fancy; and Leo X probably knew a great deal about the habits of mystics.

The Lama in *Nansal* who is entrusted with the education of the girl has an eye on the possible extravagances of his charge. He tells her that in this world, at least, the highest merit often consists more in doing those humble tasks which go against the grain rather than in coaxing exalted aspirations which frequently have a basis in a morbid kind of camouflaged selfishness.

The advice in this particular case is unnecessary, as Nansal seems quite capable of taking care of herself in spiritual matters; but it can be taken to apply to a large number of persons who fancy quite wrongly that they yearn for solitude and sanctification, when, in reality, they crave for things much more material and tangible.

The three plays discussed represent, in their respective manners, different facets of the same almost obsessional belief on the part of the Tibetans in the fact of ultimate spiritual victory and the rules by which it is attained. In the first the concentration is on a man, the future Buddha ; in the second, on the creative innocence and virtue of childhood, and in the third on the innate saintliness of a woman. Thus the whole human gamut is sounded in order to show the accessibility of revelation to anyone who desires it with heart and soul.

As a tail-piece to this description of the characteristics and essentials of the Tibetan theatre, it will not be amiss to say something about what may be called the specific Tibetan "National Play." We have already made some mention of the connection between folk-festivals and the religious background of the finest type of drama. Now we shall give as detailed an account as our space permits of the great Mystery-play known as *The Dance of the Red-Tiger Devil* because it deals like other and better-known Mysteries with the eternal changes of the seasons and their repercussions in the hearts and lives of man. Also because it is attended by rich and poor alike, who come to it as to a place of pilgrimage, inspired by the same feeling that used to prompt international vistors to visit Oberammagau. A further inducement too ; for, according to the Tibetans, there is no better way of assuring good luck for the ensuing year than an attendance at this performance.

For it is a ceremony which says good-bye to the old year and ushers in the new. It expels in allegorical guise all that has made life difficult and hard to bear. With the host of demons who have conspired to upset the balance of men disappear, it is hoped, all those bad psychic " directions " which harass and distort the tenor of our days. Everyone participating in this play, even as a spectator, has the consolation of feeling that he is adding something to the power behind the general desire that the bad shall be left behind and the good consolidated and reinforced. And indeed there is every reason to suppose that the tug-of-war between good and evil is won more surely for the former, when the whole voice of the people is raised in its favour. This is an aspect of mass emotion which has not been sufficiently stressed by our critics : when a crowd of people are gathered together to support a spectacle which has as its theme the triumph of good over ill they can give the good a " shove forward " as it were in the direction of its goal.

As well as the ceremonies of expulsion there are rites of propitiation. The guardian spirits, the war-gods, the countless host of beings who haunt the confines of our etheric being — all these entities receive their share of homage and respect. Thus a balance is established between the hatred of the bad forces which might set up a condition of stultification in the spectator, and the proper fear of the good.

The National Play is also acted on the birthday of Padma Sambhava, the revered missionary-saint who founded the institution of Lamaism. This falls on the tenth day of the fifth Tibetan month, and is the occasion for a general reunion of families and clans, officials and Lamas, who come from all over the country, very often taking as much as a week for the journey, in order to pay their respects to the saint.

The play is given in the open air outside the precincts of a large monastery. As at Bayreuth the orchestra is hidden from view. The actors are housed in tents of yak-hair, and there are intervals in which singers oblige with songs from the country's large repertory of semi-religious music.

The prelude consists of an " orchestral " introduction which takes the shape of a piercing wail set up by a trumpet made from a human thigh-bone. Gongs and shawms help to swell this " subject " ; this is followed by a low chant consisting of the reiteration of certain esoteric vowel-combinations. The play actually commences with a procession of black-mitred pre-Lama priests who, dressed in robes of the most elaborate Chinese brocade, enter preceded by boys swinging censers. All of them make the sign of the Trident (a gesture signifying the possession of great power) and set up a slow and (to Western eyes) rather sinister dance.

This consists of a series of mass movements which suggests an experiment in the more advanced eurhythmics. Stretching out the right and left hands alternately, they turn now to the left, now to the right. They advance and retire to and from each other several times. After these sallies they re-form in a circle, straighten out in single file and take their exit.

The next episode is of a more exciting nature. The man-eating demons who are held to infest earth, air, fire and water, show themselves in visible shape. For some time they have it all their own way: they rush round in a wild bacchanal, seeking whom they can devour. Occasionally their progress is impeded by a holy Lama who faces them armed with his sacred symbols. He reads a rite of exorcism ; but even this is not enough to vanquish their evil energy. There ensues a frenzied fight between the hosts of good and evil respectively.

The evil hordes wear hoods. One by one their cloaks fall back to reveal the countenances of satyrs and devils : these masks are painted with the object of conveying the extremes of villainy. In contrast the masks of the good spirits represent static calm. At last the armies of righteousness prevail: the Lamas have subdued the forces that menace human safety, and peace is preserved for the days to come. It is the parable of the subjugation of early superstitions by the regenerating power of Buddhism.

Next comes a real *danse macabre*. This is executed by a group who represent those souls of the dead who have as yet found no abiding home. These half-naked figures recoil from each other in horror ; they keep up a piercing wail which adds to the general confusion. Their sufferings are complicated by the incursion of a troupe of animal-headed demons who attack with violence these only "half-arrived." A terrible combat ensues which, in its turn, is ended by the intervention of good Lamas, anxious to succour the helpless. After the victory holy water is sprinkled in all directions and mustard-seed is thrown into the air as a propitiatory offering to the leaders of the ghostly bands.

The final tableau brings on to the scene Padma Sambhava himself, accompanied by a retinue of disciples and servers. The saint descends the scaffolding erected on the scene of the play while acolytes and abbots prostrate themselves before him. From now he takes command of the situation. He is the protector of the nation, the defender and consolidator of the country's faith. It is through his agency that a group of men have been formed who will for ever, by the enacting of this play, help to preserve the land from evil.

Drawn up in square formation are heroes and deified beings who pay homage to a religious genius. Prominent among these are conquered demons who have yielded to the superior forces of Padma Sambhava's virtues. Now, as we would say, these are "ready to eat out of his hand." The scene is set for the final episode which has some relation to magical practices described earlier.

In the centre of the square is erected a raised platform on which is placed the image of a male figure constructed usually out of dough or some other malleable substance. Inside the body are inserted exact reproductions of the various internal organs, heart, kidneys and the rest. These are filled with a red liquid to represent blood. The whole figure stands for the essence of the evil which must be destroyed if men are to go on their way cleansed of fear and self-induced mishap. It is the agglomeration of the refuse of sin and error left behind in the old year. Its demolition ensures safety and the clean start in the future.

With a wild cry, the actors hurl themselves on this image of decay. They slash with their knives at the monument of ill, leaving it an inert mass of pulp. The " four cemetery ghosts " who haunt the confines of mortality are also symbolically sacrificed to the just rage of the Lamas and their myrmidons. Padma Sambhava now reigns supreme over his faithful subjects: the land has been purged of woe.

So ends a lurid piece of theatrical ritual which will give hints to several of our symbolists of the future. They will admire the rise and fall of its momentous rhythms, the allegorical figuration of an ever-present strife. Taken out of its setting it will always seem to lack some of its primitive vigour ; but the lesson it teaches is for all men, great and small. Eat not your heart : kill the desolation of the past with the resolution and discipline of the future, and all will be well. Never look back : man is built for a happy and strenuous life.

It would be unfair to end this chapter without some reference to the tribute paid by a modern artist to the magic of Tibet. For there are still intrepid travellers, with more artistic perception than most of their ilk who, braving all kinds of dangers, concealed and overt, venture into the country determined to reproduce and interpret what they have seen for the delectation of their less fortunate and gifted brethren. This is not strictly Tibetan art in the narrow sense; but as such experiments invariably bear the imprint of their place of origin, the unmistakable contagion of high places, little violence will be done to consistency by saying something about the greatest of these spiritual adventurers, the painter and man-of-letters, Nicholas Roerich.

This very distinguished Russian, who lived for a time in America, has achieved fame as philosopher, scientist and artist. He undoubtedly possessed that type of universal intelligence which has become more and more rare in our day owing to the system of specialisation under which learning inevitably labours. He is near enough in blood to the East to interpret its atmosphere with a sympathy born of intuition ; and intense study and affection have done the rest. For some years Roerich was Secretary of the Society for the Encouragement of the Arts in Russia. In this capacity he amassed the knowledge and experience which was to produce his conception of an integrated art which will unite men.

The Urusvati Himalayan Research Institute is only one of the memorials set up through his agency to a courageous attempt to unite the ideals of East and West. Here researches in medicine, botany, biology, geology, astrophysics and archæology were carried on with this end constantly in view. It is little wonder that Roerich should have found himself approaching ever nearer to the ideals which have always guided Tibetan philosophers and artists. From 1924 to 1928 he headed an expedition which travelled through India, Tibet, Turkestan and Siberia. In his book *Alt Himalaya* he gives an account of these wanderings, and, what is even more *à propos* for our purpose here, he illustrates these pages with mystical paintings which reach a very high standard of accomplishment in their particular field.

For a full understanding of the spirit which prompted the execution of these paintings, a reading of Roerich's other book, *The Heart of Asia*, provides the key. The account he gives of his conception of the New Era tells us much concerning his general outlook. " In the Temple of Ghum Monastery, not far from the Nepalese frontier, instead of the usual central figure of Buddha, you see a huge image of the Buddha Maitreya, the coming Saviour and Ruler of Humanity. . . . The teaching of Shambhala is a true teaching of Life. As in Hindu Yogas, this teaching indicates the use of the finest energies, which fill the macrocosm (universe) and which are as finely manifested in our microcosm (man). It expresses not a mere Messianic creed, but a New Era of mighty approaching energies and possibilities. . . . The epoch of Shambhala will be attended by a great evolutionary momentum. The teaching of Life by the Mahatmas of the Himalayas speak definitely of it. That which but recently was commonly known as the teaching of will power and concentration has now been evolved by Agni Yoga into a system of mastering the energies which surround us. Through an expansion of consciousness and a training of spirit and body, without isolating ourselves from the conditions of the present day, this synthetic Yoga builds a happy future for humanity."

" Without isolating ourselves from the conditions of the present day " . . . this is the important truth that Roerich has seized upon to propagate his gospel. He saw that the great need of the modern world is to fill its conduits and pipes with the healing and revivifying waters of the ancient cultural traditions which are far less perverted than our own with irrelevant matter. It follows that his paintings are all illuminated in a fashion hard to describe, by this uplifting hope to which he had grown to cling with all his heart and soul. Perhaps the old Latin tag which promises such a wealth for the future expresses as well as anything the source and conviction from which this gifted Russian drew is inspiration. *Igne Natura Renovatur integra*—(All Nature is renovated by Fire) : could any sentence define more adequately the secret of jubilant sacrifice which it is the privilege of the higher occultism to impart ?

Roerich's pictures become all the more remarkable when it is realised that they were painted practically " in the saddle." On his constant journeys in what is perhaps the most difficult travelling country in the world, he found time to create these " impressions " of what he saw and felt. Mukerji, the Hindu poet and novelist, characterised the spirit of these works when he remarked to a friend that if he wanted to know how the Himalayas struck a beholder he should take the earliest opportunity of acquainting himself with the paintings of Roerich, which, he said, gave not only a vivid reproduction of their form and colour, but, more important, conveyed a true impression of their mystical associations.

This indeed is but faint praise, as a close study of Roerich's achievements in art reveals something more than diligent intelligence. They belong to that class of creation in which the artist has so soaked himself in the fundamentals and spirit of his subject that it, so to speak, *paints itself* through him. The painter becomes a perfect mirror and medium for the spirit of the place which he has comprehended. One may call it the art of *obsession* ; for the soul of the medium has been seized to such an extent by the imperative demand of his theme that he is unable to resist the automatic responses which his faculties make to the suggestions of his engrossing passion.

The culmination of Roerich's life work is expressed in the series of canvases named by him "The Tibetan Path," " Himalaya " and " Banners of the East." These titles include a vast variety of subjects, but all are related to the same centre. Although profoundly mystical in feeling and outlook, none of them are in any real sense difficult to understand for anyone with the elements of a spiritual consciousness. Compared, for instance, with the more recondite works of Blake or Goya they have a fresh and spontaneous simplicity. Technically they belong to the school of

" formal design " whose praises have been sung in this country by Roger Fry and Clive Bell; their line is strong, integrated, decided. They are architectural rather than pictorial in conception ; the human element is subdued for the most part to the majesty of rocks and torrents.   One of the most typical portrays a titanic valley, somewhat like the Grand Canyon, rock-strewn, without flowers or trees to relieve the vast, stark simplicity.   In the foreground is a bridge over which passes a road, and on this road are a few human beings who bow in adoration before a great radiance which suffuses the background of the picture.   The symbolism refers to the coming of a Buddha who shall unite the scattered tribes of men.

This may be taken is the very core of Roerich's attitude towards Tibet.   It is yogic, clean, complete.   If further evidence is sought for, here is a quotation taken at random from his vastly exciting correspondence.   " Friends, it would have been far easier for me to have set down the entire journey in all its fairy-tale of fantasy, which colours every peak and every desert-space with unprecedented truth.   But then some will be incredulous, as he who sleeps in darkness does not believe in the sun.   Is it possible that the sun is already rising ? Facts are needed. . . . But even in facts, the Sunrise comes from the East."

CHAPTER X.

Tibetan Yoga and the Relation between Mind and Body.

THAT THERE IS a very strong connection between the processes of the mind and those of the body is one of the first postulates of any brand of Yoga. Indeed the word would mean very little unless it implied some attempt to unite the laws of spirit and flesh into one organic relationship. It can be affirmed without hesitation that the most advanced and effective Yoga philosophy is that which shows the greatest knowledge of the bodily foundation on which our mental and spiritual efforts are built.

This is not to say that the body is in any narrow and dogmatic sense the soul. To assert this would be to fall into the error which used to be known as " epiphenomenalism "—the assumption that, in some inexplicable way, the workings of the body actually produce the infinite variations of mentation. Such an assertion is as ridiculous as it is arrogant and is only made nowadays by the most callow type of materialist.

But what *is* true, is that without a minute study of the intricacies of our physical organism we shall find ourselves handicapped in our search for the secrets of the spirit. For there is no shadow of doubt that, in the course of our karmic development we are given that type of body which will best help our spiritual progress. Or, to view the situation from another angle, the limitation or the magnificence of our fleshly endowments travel hand in hand with the particular lessons we have to learn. To understand a person's physical characteristics is very largely to be able to make a very fair assessment of his character and disposition. This, even the empirical criminology and psychology of our day have been groping towards for some time past : it only needs now an infusion of the " mystical " sense into the brains of our latter-day detectives to put them on the scent of mysteries they had not suspected even in their wildest dreams. Even now there is a glimmer of suspicion in orthodox medical circles that the tracking down of bodily correlations promises deeper revelations than those which belong to the province of anatomy and physiology.

After all, we are anthropomorphic in our imaginings because we find it impossible to envisage the nature of the world and its government except in terms with which we are familiar. The great

Scots philosopher David Hume pointed out that, at the most, we can only be *certain* of the existence of our own physical frame with its automatic mental correlatives. We are by no means inclined to share the extreme intellectual scepticism of this gifted thinker ; but we *do* suggest that the apparently narrow radius within which a very sincere philosopher hemmed his conceptions is not such a handicap to clear occult thinking as may be at first supposed.

The habit of projecting our own bodily configuration into our ideas of the constitution of the whole cosmos has, therefore, a wider justification than that attributed to it by the cynically disposed. " God made man in his own image and man hastened to return the compliment " is a neat enough epigram, but Voltaire was lacking in the larger reverence and hence, in the larger understanding. It is probable, in the final working-out of transient symbols, that the hidden forces which drive the whole of the world will be seen to be shaped and moulded in the same way as the miniature systems on which is dependent the full functioning of our psycho-physical constitution. At any rate, the majority of the chief occult systems of the world have based their teachings on this supposition, and there is no reason to criticise the logic on which the teaching has arisen.

Orthodox religion, too, manifests the influence of this deep research into first causes. The doctrine of the Resurrection of the Dead, extravagant as it may seem to persons unused to visualisation, is not half so absurd as those reacting from childhood's instruction may conclude. The conception of the body, freed from all its imperfections, equipped with a new strength which comes from the elimination of wasteful activities, has haunted the imaginations of men of the highest type as far back as thought can travel.

Through all occult learning, through Kabbalism, through what may be called esoteric Catholicism, through the secrets of the Yezidis and the arcana of the Egyptians, we can trace this unfailing perception of the very real relationship which persists between the little world of the self which we call the Microcosm and the greater universe outside which is made out of the same component parts and which obeys the same eventual laws. It has come about that in all the main lines of ancient forgotten learning, in astrology, palmistry and the more recondite kinds of medical treatment, the illustrations portraying the human body are always connected with a system of correspondences which link it up with the plants and the solar system generally.

Mystically speaking, we are faced, as regards our study of the relationship aforesaid, with a nucleus and an extension. The nucleus is the body we all inhabit, the indisputable " I " which hopes and suffers and enjoys. The extension includes both the possibilities of this apparatus in other realms than this and the surrounding factors as well. This expression involves a number of considerations on which a fresh light has been thrown in our own day by researchers in the province of electro-dynamics. We live at the centre of many contending forces. These forces can be canalized for man's good or entangled for his ill. The direction and " fate " of our personal life are largely dependent on the way in which these quite predictable factors are "managed" by the intelligence and the will. A science, using the weapons of inductive logic and dynamic force has been brought into service to prove the laws of the architecture of the soul. The constant application of these discoveries to ever-widening knowledge of the self will be the task of the genuine intellectuals of the future. Although they will find their lives pretty full as regards observation and inference, they will nevertheless be in a happier position than were their brethren of an earlier date; for they will be buoyed up with a spiritual ardour which will be more than enough compensation for the gruelling to which they will subject their brains.

All this, a hypothetical reader will retort, is the veriest materialism: surely there is something else in life besides the observable. As a matter of fact there is not. If we had sufficiently developed faculties to apperceive all that already exists, we should cease to cavil at the dreary boundaries of our vision. It is only the circumscribed nature of the daily round that makes it, in bad moods, a tale told by an idiot, signifying nothing: if we were able to see further, hear more acutely, feel the nature of the gift of life more intensely with our nerves, we should soon change the nature of our reverence from a wilful obscurantism to an insatiable curiosity. There is nothing inimical to a truth in the fact of being able to perceive it. No harm is done to the highest " romance " by an acquaintance with its components.

The East has never known that give and take with convention which leads to a compromise with sheer ignorance. In Tibet, above all other places, there has been no end to the development of a rationalism of the sane and progressive sort. It has never been the fashion in yogic circles to call a halt to the march of pains-taking observation nor to the accumulation of any kind of existent or potentially existent facts, even if these do not throw a particularly flattering light on the constitution of the human animal. Much that we regard as the enlightenment of modern times was learned and forgotten by the East long before our history commenced. In many ways their wisdom begins where ours leaves off. But this is not to say that we have not to traverse again the paths of learning which once they trod, and without prejudice and *parti pris,* to accept in all humility the data which they patiently collected, and left behind as the larger vision dawned.

We must start regarding the human body as at once holy, and necessary for an understanding of the spirit. We must rid ourselves of any dislike for any part of Nature's handiwork : much of our endeavour should be given, at least to start with, to as meticulous a study as our opportunities permit of the complex systematisation and inter-relation of bodily parts. Only thus shall we be adequately prepared for that moral furtherance which depends on a sure-eyed perception of given volitional possibilities.

It is not easy to understand how the ancients attained to such an extensive knowledge of bodily functions. It is probable that the ancient seers opened human bodies in order to analyse their contents. There is a certain amount of evidence to show that what is now known as fractional anatomy was widely practised by the medical men of yore. That is to say, dissected parts were carried to lakes and rivers where they were submerged for a period until the skin and muscle decomposed. After the subsequent peeling, it was an easy matter to get in touch with the inner structure and study its composition and correlations.

While on this point, it is interesting to note that the *Kshatriya* or warrior caste were, in the ancient world, the class from which the best-known surgeons were chosen. Owing to the fact that they were chiefly engaged in war and destruction it was natural enough that the best opportunities for dissection should fall into their hands. One can imagine the bodies of enemies serving other purposes than the merely triumphal : their released selves had the pleasure of knowing that their mortal dust was being examined with a view to the profit of mankind at large.

But far more important than any surface observation of the constitution of the anatomy is the conviction, so strong among the ancient Tibetans, that the body is the dwelling-place of a whole multitude of deities. And not in the pious sense in which the physical organism is spoken of as the " Temple of the Holy Spirit," but in a more exact and organised manner. The Tibetan physicians and surgeons set out to show that each portion of the anatomy has its own attendant god, its protective guardians whose business it is to see that their particular section comes to no harm.*

The organism is not immune, of course, from the attacks of deities of a more injurious kind. A philosopher of these early days advises surgeons to take all possible precautions to protect the bodies of his patients from incursions from these invaders, before performing an operation. He adjures such a one to repeat the following incantation. " I am about to practise a spell to safeguard thy person against the malignant influence of demons and their attendant demonesses, and may the god Brahma be graciously pleased to approve of its performance. May the gods and ministers of grace put to flight and confound the armies of wrathful serpent-gods, Pisachas and Pitris that might be maliciously disposed to strike thee in thy sickly condition. May the spirits who roam about in the night and make their way about the sky and on earth defend thy person in recognition of thy heartfelt devotion. May Agni (Fire-God) guard thy tongue, Vayu (Wind-God), thy breath, Soma (the Moon) and Vidyat (the Lightning) preserve the healthy course of the vital airs about thy body. May Manu defend the two-sided tendons at the base of thy neck, Surya thy eyes, and Purushotthama thy dynamic action of purpose. . . .† We can take this list of dispositions as an intimation of the scheme of bodily architecture which researchers would seek to instil into the minds of the curious. From the first formulation of a Creative Principle to the exact accompaniment to the psychic power inherent in every limb, " architects " have mapped out a " mannikin " which is both complex and simple—for those who hold the key.

It will be necessary here to give the reader as clear an account as possible of those constituents of the human anatomy which provide the ground plan for a comprehension of the "housing arrangements" for the gods mentioned above. Firstly, let us start at the beginning by saying something of the way the human being comes into existence. " Before God is and God above all Gods " is *Hiranya-garba* the originator of all beings. This is a name for the ovum, which is quickened by the sperm, and so

* For further information on this subject, v. *Vedic Gods as Figures of Biology*, by Dr. V. G. Rele, F.C.P.S. He is the originator of the scheme of occult-physical " correspondences " outlined here. The Tibetans would approve !

† *Not* Tibetan, be it noted ! The Hindu form of an incantation has been cited deliberately, as a Tibetan version is too advanced for our immediate purpose.

The Hindu Gods and their attributes will doubtless spring more readily to the mind of the reader. Where necessary this substitution has likewise been adopted in other pages.

becomes fertilised. It must be remembered that the human organism consists of a whole community of cells, all of which spring, in the first place, from the single cell, that is, the fertilised ovum, spoken of in Tibet as "the Golden Egg."

All Buddhists believe that the germ cell passes through successive lives, learning as it goes and carrying over to one incarnation the tendencies of another. Man is made up partly of the characteristics derived from the germ-cell in which the self is embodied ; and for the rest, with the modifications he makes in these with the forces of his will.

The fertilised ovum divides and subdivides itself into innumerable cells which all together make up the structure of the body. The essential fact to note here is that the nervous system of the individual is one of the first things to form from these embryos. Man's dominance over the lower creation depends entirely on this central nervous endowment which houses all that he has of intelligence and capacity for expansion. This nervous " backbone " can be compared to a tree, the leaves and branches of which are grown by the impetuosity of the forces dormant in the trunk. And this tree corresponds to a systematisation of the world within, which corresponds to the natural architecture of the world without.

The evidence goes to show that, at a very early age in the development of the embryo, a groove was formed which was destined to play a most important part in the growth of the nervous structure. Nowadays this is known as the *medullary groove*, the two sides of which rise to form the medullary canal. In time this became the central canal of the spinal cord, and the walls of this eventually formed the spinal cord and the brain. The narrow lower part went to form the spinal cord and the upper part the brain.

The brain itself is a complicated instrument. The two constrictions which appear at intervals in the wide upper portion of the cord divide it into three distinct vesicles. From the lowest of these grow the small brain, the Cerebellum, the Medulla Oblongata and the Pons—that is, the parts that constitute the hind-brain. The middle vesicle develops in its turn into the mid-brain, which is composed of stems and the four circular masses which are commonly called the Quadrigeminate Bodies. The top ventricle finally develops into the fore-brain by a process of folding and compression. This consists of two cerebral hemispheres as well as a quantity of grey matter, called the Corpus Striatum.

It may be of use to call a halt here and point out that the world, according to Eastern cosmology, is composed of two halves as is the cerebrum. Each half has its own heaven and earth and hell. Each can be subdivided into further divisions. The mighty god Indra is stated to have kept the edifice together by keeping the elements in their allotted places, and not allowing them to overflow their boundaries. Savitri, the representative of Cosmic Ecstasy, also does her part in integrating the structure by causing the sun to dispense its light through all the sections.

Illustrations of this chart of the world which is the chart of the body show the brain-structure as bearing a remarkable resemblance in its configuration to that of a horse. *Hiranya-garba,* the originator of the gods, is sometimes known as the Horse-God, and those with an eye for these things will recall that this figure occurs in some of the most formidable *Tantric* statuettes, notably among those in the fine collection at the Indian Museum, London. Certainly, the figure has a most sinister significance in some of the darker aspects of occultism, where power is collected and re-distributed for amoral ends. Some readers will call to mind that remarkable painting by Goya in which a Spanish priest is depicted as busied in his study of the hellish arts. Behind the furtive shape of the cleric looms, clearly outlined, the limbs of a titanic horse.

Other portions of the nervous system, too, have a certain resemblance to other animal shapes, dogs, cows, bulls and sows. Attached to these are certain ideas of sacrifice, in which the lower is offered up to the higher. In the case of the horse itself, an association can be made which symbolises the abandonment of the mid-brain, where all the centres of the organs of sense are located, in favour of the medium of the highest intellectual transcendence. Similarly, the same eliminative process can be adopted with the other animal forms ; the forces of nature, which can carry us so far and no further, are to be superseded by the infinitely expanded light of spiritual emancipation.

A relic of this old-time " superstition " can be found in modern medicine where we find the elevations surrounding the horse-shaped area is called the Hippocampus or Sea-Horse. And if we bisect the brain vertically we bring to light the horse-shaped appearance of the mid-brain and the *medulla oblongata.*

This horse in the mid-brain has for its outer boundary what is formed by the cerebrum or upper brain which circumscribes it. The chest of the horse which can be correlated with the front portions of the *medulla* is said to " rest on earth " : that is, on the bones, the part of the body which most nearly corresponds with the element earth. The substratum of the air and water, which are woven inseparably into the structure of the middle sections of the body is earthy matter in the form of nerve tissue: this surrounds the brain and the spinal cord. According to Eastern anatomical teaching, the chief motor centre in the brain which is symbolised by the sun, supports this mass of tissue. The moon too is brought into this picture as representative of the sensory centres which line the ventricular cavities, and this in its turn is reinforced by the world of the stars which, in physical actuality, are the fibres from the sympathetic ganglia of the sympathetic nervous system.

It will be seen from this sketch that a knowledge of cosmic laws is ineradicably bound up with the first principles of embryology. It is the patient investigator of the beginnings of the crystallisation of matter who is the best equipped for trailing the secrets of the higher will. Here is an all-important science in which it is particularly incumbent upon the student to begin at the beginning. Otherwise, truth may dissolve along deceptive *cul-de-sacs* and concrete commonsense vanish in mists of dubious speculation.

Before going on to describe the departmentalisation of the psychic body into the nesting-grounds of deities, we would remind the reader that the human system is divided up, as medieval physicians knew so well, into the elements, earth, air, fire and water. To the province of earth belong our muscles, bones, hair, glands, nails and skin. Water, in its turn, encompasses the various secretions of the system—the bile, the lymph, the components of the blood. Fire comprehends our desires, the primitive fighting impulses within us which keep us going, and which have their specific physical " primings." Air also plays its part in our personal scheme of things: it entraps the various vital essences which have their existence in the unseen universe around us, and enslaves them for our well-being.

Anyone who has done any reading in works of an occult import (for example that magnificent achievement *Anthony Adverse,* which combined the virtues of a best-seller with the subtle consideration of many of the most important constituents of our psychic being) will have been found to have come across references to the " Body of Light " which suffuses our being at certain stages in our experience. This " Light," according to Tibetan Yoga, is an aspect of cosmic energy, which enters our body at birth and excites the gaseous elements of the constitution into constructive activity.

The nervous system, the horse-dominated *Hiranya-garba* of the ancients, has its own separate heaven, atmosphere and earth. Its heaven can be taken to be that section of the cerebral hemisphere commonly called the brain; the atmosphere lives in the hind-brain, the *medulla oblongata* and the cavities of the four ventricles; finally, the Earth includes the whole length of the spinal cord which, with its psychic centres is so fraught with import for the strengthening or dislocation of the organism.

Strictly speaking there are two kinds of nervous system—the cerebro-spinal, and the automatic. The two are interdependent. Neither could persist without the proper functioning of the other. The chief use of the latter is to supply the nerve-force for the transmission of thoughts and emotions to the discriminating brain. Also to work the interplay of preservation and destruction, the building-up and pulling-down which is the necessary condition of our vitality. The grey matter of the brain links up this energy through its cortical layers, in which are enmeshed innumerable nerve fibres that carry impulses to and from these layers. The two cavities in the hemisphere of the brain, known to medical men as the *thalamus* and the *corpus striatum* also have their part to play in providing an outer mechanism for the exact interconnections between the spheres of the automatic and the utilitarian activity of the cerebro-spinal organisation.

The first god to be considered as an inhabitant of the ordered tenements of the body is *Tvastri*. This hefty deity, who is concerned with the incipient beginnings of our life is behind the workings of the embryo. He can be said to be the dweller in the fertilised ovum, for from his activity spreads the whole formation of the human system. To follow his course in the body is to trace the development of the embryo from a mulberry-like mass, through ectoderm and neuroderm to the fully-evolved anatomy. In occult mythology he is represented as carrying a hatchet; by the aid of this weapon he carves his way forwards by a series of bends, constrictions and loops, until the whole of the spine and brain is fashioned (that is to say, evolved). In this reading the brain cavities above mentioned can, without straining a point, be regarded as sacrificial cups which are made to hold the divine nectar of the triumphant god.

But the story goes that *Tvastri*, for all his skilled and crafty workmanship, was defeated eventually by the wiles of those that came after him—or, if it be preferred, overcome by the riotous abundance of his own creation. His sons, Agni and Surya, who carry on his work after he has taken refuge in the harem of the gods, govern the subsidiary sensory and motor centres; they have subtilised and orientated the direction of the main psycho-physical forces of the system.

Perhaps the most far-reaching achievement of *Tvastri* is his manipulation of the afferent (ingoing) and efferent (outgoing) nerve-fibres connecting the spinal cord with the brain. These he gathers into two thick bundles and spaces their parts with a due regard for pitch and tuning.

The *Ribhus*, the next deified forces to be considered, amplify the work inaugurated by *Tvastri*. Known as " the Genii of the Seasons " these governors of winds and storms satisfy the desires of the other gods by sending impulses to the organs of sense and activity. In a word, they charge the circuit laid down by their predecessors with the necessary dynamism to effect the smooth running of the machine. The spinal cord is their domain, and they know every twist and turn of its intricate mechanism. Without the agency of the Ribhus there could be no life; for it is the song of the energies which reside in the backbone, the motivator of all of abiding value in thought, desire and will. The all-important psychic centres lie in this vicinity and can only be set in action when the physical superstructure is thoroughly sensitized, and charged with dynamism.

Savitri, on the other hand, reigns alone. This effulgent and joyous god moves in a majestic way his wonders to perform. He is envisaged as travelling in a golden car, his hair floating in the wind. Moving upward and downward along the whole length of the spinal cord, he carries the rays of the sun to all parts of our sentient apparatus. He confers their godhead on the Ribhus and raises them up to his own level of grace and splendour when he is so disposed. His especial activity is to develop the efferent or outgoing impulses which are such an essential part of the integrated will, the " extensions " of the force which we have made our own. The efferent fibres of the spinal cord radiate as they grow upwards in the shape of a fan to form the *corona radiata* which has been aptly called the " yellow hair " of Savitri. Savitri is said to extend his arms in a sweeping gesture in two directions : upwards, in the direction of the heavens (the brain) and downwards towards earth (the spinal column). Savitri is not so much an architect as an influence; he belongs to the primordial group of Energisers who breathe over the waters of our spirit the running fire of cosmic force.

The *Asvins* go in pairs. They are divinities who preside over the powers inherent in light. They are essentially benevolent in their characteristics, as they take it upon themselves to cure the maimed, the halt and the blind. They are drawn in a car manufactured for them by the *Ribhus* and it is to be noted that their conveyance has three seats and three wheels. They are sometimes spoken of as "the two pious kings" who are engaged in constant acts of salvation. They represent the transition from darkness into light, and, if he so desires, the reader can regard them as the conductors of mankind out of the sombre saturnian age which was superseded by the age of the sun when the slow evolution of mankind rolled along its course.

Technically speaking, they are the projection of the efferent nerve-fibres on the interior surface of the *medulla oblongata* at the top of the spine. These "strings of communication" start from the cerebral cortex, pass through the actual substance of the brain, and converge in two separate bundles. They manifest themselves as the two projections known as "pyramids" on the surface of the *medulla*. In one sense they are the barricades and bastions of the fortress of nervous controls. In the lower section of the *medulla,* the marrow of the bones, these efferent fibres cross each other to form the cross-tracts of the spinal cord.

The horses, that draw the car of the Asvins are an allegory of the impulses moving along the nerve fibres which are surrounded with a soft, jelly-like substance. It is for this reason that the Asvins are said to carry honey in their skin. That is to say, they stand for the protective sheath which covers the nerve-fibres. We know that no nerve-tract can function until all the fibres which compose it have been so encased and armoured right to their terminations. This is a process equivalent to lubrication and is an important factor both in a physical and psychic sense.

It may be stated here that it is only with the birth of the fœtus that the outgoing and incoming fibres become sufficiently developed to carry impulses. The growth of efferent impulses is dependent very largely on the force of habit. It will be observed that it takes about two years to educate the centres so that they carry efferent impulses to the extent of accomplishing voluntary actions. The Asvins find their opportunity during this period: all their energies are directed towards the task of forming connections between the dormant centres in the brain to effect their full functional activity. The first of these centres to be stimulated is that which controls the visual apparatus: the child, "muling and puking in its mother's arms," gets its first revelation of the miracle of the world through the help of his eyes. Later come the other senses which act on the pivot of the first.

We grow then, under the hammers and chisels of the gods. Our bodily texture is fashioned, forced into extensibility, sensitivity and motion by the vast underground activities which stone by stone and course by course are laid on each other by these workers in the unseen sheds of the spirit. Who, realising this unconquerable masonry, could ever relapse into any cynical under-appraisement of the body we carry and the laws which govern its control and preservation?

There are several amplifications of the legend of the Asvins which have their own place in the picture. There is the story of the sage *Cyavana*, who, deserted in his old age is rescued by the Asvins and taken under their protection. This personage is the cerebellum or small brain, and his abandonment is portrayed in the position and shape of this in the brain-structure. Another subsidiary figure is *Rebhu* who is stripped and left for dead by the wicked band of desperadoes (the nerves of the sense-organs). He stands out as the chief sensory ganglion which is situated at the base of the brain. He belongs to that order of beings who sustain and buttress rather than electrify and conduct.

To save risking the danger of bewildering the mind of the reader with too elaborate a summary of occult cosmology we will return for a moment to the main principles upon which yogic breathing is based. All that we have described of the correlation between the parts of the body and the gods of Eastern biology is nothing more nor less than a ground-basis for the raising up of peaks of power within the framework aforesaid. These power foci are, of course, the centres of the etheric body which have been described in a previous chapter.

What we have said of the " sacred " nature even of our physical frame (and the adjective is used in a double sense let it be noted) is by way of preliminary to the much more " advanced " degree of stability and effectiveness which attaches to the etheric. If the gods build the skeleton of the anatomy, how much more can they be said to have a hand in the evolution of those *chakras* on which we spin all that we know of ecstasy and power? The relationship between the mind and the body can indeed mean very little for the individual unless it infer at least some attempt to yoke the currents and the energies of the system to those nodal points which are in the nature of guiding-stars to the waggon of the soul.

But these must not be regarded, on the other hand, as the all-in-all of the etheric plan. They are in no way self-subsistent and self-determined, as some of the more gullible of us may be led to suppose. If we take our ideas of the *chakras* from the illustrations in the usual handbook on Yoga we shall be tempted to indulge in an over-simplification. The spectacle of a human form empty of everything except seven flaming sigils looks pretty enough to the eye of wonder, but has little relation to reality. It is essential to realise that the body, even of psychics, consists of something more than whirling wheels: it is also the repository of a huge number of muscular and neural reactions which all have their appropriate physical background. Also, of course, the coursing of various tides, digestive and otherwise, which have no immediate and obvious connection with the rotation and appearance of the *chakras*.

It is therefore eminently desirable to have at least a working knowledge of elementary anatomy and physiology before we attempt to grasp the profound truths behind the constitution of the etheric force-centres. Otherwise we may end up as the more insane type of spiritualist, the like of whom was never seen on sea or land. A wise mysticism is only fostered by a completely faithful devotion to facts, which are empirically observable by people like many honest, hardworking and altogether admirable surgeons and osteopaths who make no claim to mystical experience or intuition. Some day, by the grace of the gods, these labourers in the material vineyard will find their curiosity sufficiently stirred to follow facts into their mystical lair: then, once again, science and religion will join hands and the hopeless case of uninspired materialism will stand self-confessed as a vain and empty thing.

Kundalini, " the Serpent Power "* which lies coiled up at the base of the etheric spine, becomes a reality only when its connections are understood. It is, as all occultists agree, the prime instigator of the action, the force which sets the other forces in movement. But it is also more than this: it is the condenser of all the energy in the lower part of the body and at the same time the axis on which is balanced the clamant action of the creative desires and the cleansing function of the intestines which makes for freedom of the upper reaches of the system.

To speak anatomically, *Kundalini* guards the three important openings in the cerebro-spinal nervous system—the ventricular cavity in the brain, the channel in the spinal cord and the coccyx.

* v. also *The Serpent Power* (Avalon) and *The Mysterious Kundalini* (V. G. Rele).

In itself it can be regarded as the vagus nerve. For the benefit of those unused to medical definitions, this is one of the important cranial nerves which carry impulses to the various plexuses (or " glands " as a modern endocrinologist would put it). These cranial filaments are eleven in number, and one of the longest of them reaches the level of the navel, where it ends in the solar plexus. By a series of connections it establishes junctures with the other plexuses situated lower down. This pair of nerves is known as the " vagus " on account of its wandering nature, and it forms the bulk of the parasympathetic part of the automatic nervous system.

The reader should cling tenaciously to this point; for it is only by a complete understanding of this major nerve-twining that he will be able to prove to his satisfaction that *Kundalini*, viewed in visible operating-table form as the vagus nerve, supplies and controls all the main vital organs through the different plexuses of the sympathetic part of the antomatic nervous system. The student of Yoga is advised, and rightly so, to carry out his breathing exercises while keeping all the time before his mind the fact that he is awakening his centres into life according to a definite progression. This progression starts at the *Muladhara* or lower *chakram* where *Kundalini* lies coiled, and is continued in ratchet fashion through all the remaining six centres. This order of progress is not arbitrary. It bears witness to the fact that the centres are interdependent and that one cannot be cultivated satisfactorily at the expense of the others. The illumination of the main nerve of the system is only accomplished when the lower *chakram* is conducted through it consistently according to the law of ascent which states that the central cord must be vibrated before the lesser strings echo the tune.

There is nothing imaginary about these plexuses. They can be actually seen by clairvoyants and their shape and constituent parts analysed. It is very rarely that all the *chakras* are in full working order at the same time. Indeed, in many persons, only a small section of the *chakral* apparatus can be said to function with any degree of efficiency. To be in a condition in which the wheels whirl with an equal velocity and light up with the same pulsating glow would be to share the ecstasy of the delivered: it is not given to the majority of men to know their own mainsprings so well that they can forego those things which hamper their full resiliency.

The question of health and its preservation enters into consideration here. There are two ways of enjoying abounding physical health. The first way may be called the way of luck: that is to say, we have chosen our ancestors well; we have no obvious physical defects, and we possess a mind free from propensities towards carking cares. We all know persons who fall into this category; they are popular, " successful," and they seem to enjoy life. They are frequently held up as types to imitate, and they develop a certain conceit in consequence. The arrogance of " perfect health " of this type is not always particularly pretty: it savours too much of animalism; and at the same time it usually lacks the full-blooded honesty of the animal. Also, it is seldom connected with any especial endowment of brains. To this class belong the " muddied oafs " and " flannelled fools " of Kipling's rather acid stricture and some would add, a certain type of hockey enthusiast among the ladies !

The other type of fitness has altogether different concomitants. It is not loud and does not protest at all. Its chief sign is a quiet, imperative self-control ; and it does not have to worry overmuch about the frequently boring claims of the " correct " habits and attitudes. More than the first regiment of the healthy it can afford to *relax*, and it is not nearly so abjectly bound by the dreary menace of convention. This is the health founded on the mastery of the psychic centres. It can override defects of structure, and even people who start life handicapped by the most apparently hopeless physical limitations can improve their lot a thousandfold by concentrating on the invigoration of their centres of power. This is in a very real sense the victory of the mind over matter, the domination of spirit over flesh; for the life of the *chakras* has its being in a world in which the obvious anatomical and nervous mechanism has been encompassed and " surpassed " to lift the devotee into a higher and more trustworthy set of reactions.

This means that the practice of Tibetan yogi has for its reward something more than the establishment of a chain of connections between mental and emotional processes and what is generally regarded as the " body." Correctly achieved and consolidated it does in actual fact abolish the " body " in the ordinary sense and thereby relieves it from the wear and tear which is the primary cause of its decay. The reason why yogis live to such almost unbelievable ages is not so much that they " take care of themselves " in the popular use of the term, but that they are able by a reaction of their mental control to give the body what amounts to a very long holiday while they live their life in the etheric " extension " which knows no fatigue nor frustration.

A similar bond can be established between the higher capacities of our being; but we will leave the reader to work out for himself the respective rewards which can be gathered from these connections, and to judge whether he is fit enough to essay those further flights away from "normality" and its limitations, which a mastery of the mechanism of his will, plus a keen appreciation of the landscape of the astral, mental and spiritual worlds would imply. Sufficient to say here that there is no end to the application of the bodily facts of which we are cognisant here below, to the extension of the powers of the spirit. The wise man is he who labours constantly so to understand both his body and the extent of his spiritual range that equilibrium can be established between them.

The most "ignorant" intellectually, people quite unversed in the technicalities of medical lore, can help the body-mind relationship enormously by simply taking the trouble to make a very easy experiment. Let them notice what happens to their systems when they are unphilosophical enough to indulge in any of the negative emotions. There should be no difficulty here; for all of us are guilty at times of hatred, envy and all uncharitableness. And we inevitably pay the price! It has been proved in our day that some of the most malignant cases of cancer are caused by a soured and malevolent mentality: frustration, too, takes its toll in ways that can only be traced by persons trained to observe the interactions of flesh and spirit.

It is not always easy to alter this deplorable state of affairs. Life is full of injustice: there seem to be excuses in plenty for the innumerable victims of its callous and indifferent treatment. One has only to read any daily newspaper to realise that, on the surface evidence at least, there is much more to endure than to enjoy in human affairs. And to some the cup of misery must seem very full at this particular time! But even to these hapless ones, the same truth applies—sorrow can be turned into joy if certain measures are taken.

These measures consist simply of flooding the heart and spirit to the best of one's ability with the waters of affirmative charity. In case this may sound a vague and fruitless counsel, here are a few precepts which have a long tradition of usefulness behind them. Never criticise anything or anyone adversely. Refuse to let the mind dwell on any thought or image which has in it any tincture of malice, destructiveness and revenge. When analysing other people search always for the spark of the divine in them, for the contribution, often hidden, that they make to human evolution. This way a gate will be opened to let in certain kinds of force into the soul. And the first signs that this force is operating will be an increased activity of the glands and currents of the body. A high degree of well-being will be experienced; and the individual will feel himself capable of endless exertion and endowed with the confidence to extend his range of vision.

Charity and benevolence, like honesty, always " pay " a great deal better than their opposites, in spite of all that cynics may adduce to the contrary. Also, they put the mind in a condition in which it can have the maximum of constructive effect on the arteries and nerves of the physical envelope. This is a lesson in self-management which all, the untutored as well as the learned, may practise, and which will inevitably bring some degree of profit to whosoever adopts its principles.

Once the technique of the instrument has been learned, its response to varying stimuli, its intricate series of coils and adjustments, an ever-growing mastery can be obtained over both body and mind. All will find it necessary sooner or later to learn the rules of this particular art, if only because it is normally rather difficult to keep the mind in a sufficiently rigorous attitude of consistency for the affirmative virtues to bite themselves in.

When a person experiences the spiritual graces outlined above, when he lets himself be invaded by the purifying forces of love and benevolence, such a tonic is given to every part of his organism, physical, mental and emotional, that he frequently finds his head turned with the abounding bliss which turns out to be his. The awakening *Kundalini* stretches herself and yawns, and the whole of a man's being is filled with a rapture which is so strong that it can hardly be borne without the aid of the gift of joyous tears and the release that comes from some form of violent self-expression. Unfortunately such ebullitions of ecstasy tend not to last, unless due precautions are taken to ensure their permanence. These precautions consist very largely of a knowledge of the body-mind relationship outlined above. When it is realised that states of extreme happiness are largely dependent on a combination of good bodily functioning and correct mental and emotional balance, it will be easier to ensure the more frequent appearance of these most acceptable visitations, and Shelley's complaint about the Spirit of Delight which " comes so rarely " will be negatived by the spectacle of its common recurrence.

A certain type of mind will complain at this juncture that the mystical sense becomes tainted when it is "brought down," as the saying goes, to contact and union with the mother earth we all most indubitably see and recognise. Such an objection is as old as the hills and very difficult to combat in an atmosphere impregnated with the more foolish kinds of conservatism. It is based on the dangerous fallacy that the higher kinds of knowledge are to be shunned rather than wooed: for all practical purposes it affirms that there are certain kinds of two and two which it is iniquitous to put together, for the reason that by so doing, man begets a rather larger idea of his own possibilities than he has hitherto enjoyed. The present writer has no hesitation in asserting that most of the agony of our civilisation has been caused by this perverted passion for ignorance, this most cowardly ducking from the shafts of truth. In particular, the perilous divorce of flesh and spirit, the bane of all our religion and nearly all our philosophy still has to be atoned for in a thousand sociological mistakes and a couple of bloody wars.

The enormous help that Tibetan Yoga can give to the modern consciousness is just this insistence on the holiness of all truth and on our bounden duty to seek and ensue it. The body must never be regarded in the bad old pseudo-ascetic sense which has only been an excuse for masochism, but as the divine beginning of an evolutionary progress which leads us ultimately to the stars. Morality, under this argument, will be seen to be a matter of sense and expediency rather than of irrational taboo; and no clear-sighted critic will dispute which attitude has the greater claim to respect. Indeed, it can be categorically stated that the improvement in genuine humanitarianism in the last three hundred years, the development in humanity's sense of humour and sense of tolerance, is to be attributed to the fact that this truth has been recognised, and something like a beginning made of a systematised relationship between the guilt of the body which implies the guilt of the mind.

To return to *Kundalini*, which we have defined as the vagus nerve. This nerve, it is to be observed, is of especial importance to the functional system, as it is the only nerve which is composed of both motory and sensory fibres; that is to say, both outgoing and incoming potentialities. This nerve is at the heart of the two great rhythms of human physiology, the anabolism and katabolism —the building up and breaking down, which have their exact counterparts in the life of the planets and the recurring waves of the seasons.

The efferent (outgoing) fibres of the nerve are said by the Eastern specialists to be kept in action by the divine fluid (the cerebro-spinal fluid) which is secreted in the brain by the forces of the moon. These fibres exercise a controlling and restraining influence over the whole of that portion of the anatomy which includes the larynx, pharynx, lungs and heart. They will be seen to rule at the same time the upper psychic centres which have such profound affiliations with higher planes of being. The mention of the moon here is no mere piece of fancy, but refers to the lateral ventricles which bear a decided resemblance to the shape of the crescent moon. These analogies are all part and parcel of the general correlation of the physical with the divine which is the bedrock of Eastern philosophy and psychology.

The descending fibres of the vagus nerve work their way downwards and eventually make connection with the fibres of the sympathetic system in the solar plexus. In this important centre of energy the efferent or incoming fibres of the vagus have their source, and those who have any reservations with regard to the occult significance of this centre will do well to remark the vast intermeshing of psychic strands which takes place in a region usually associated with knock-out blows in the art of boxing.

This centre is indeed a concentration-area of some of the major forces in the human psyche. In India it is known as the *Manipura,* and artists endeavour to surpass themselves in their illustrations of the associations which have collected around this great reception depot for emotional energy.

For, in the last resort, this is what the centre roughly paralleled with the solar plexus is and does. It receives the influx of all that can be garnered from the potencies of the emotional life of the whole world: further, it sorts out these strengths into their proper voltages and groups them so that they are best trained to dispose themselves for coursing through the system in such a way that the maximum of invigoration may ensue. This may sound somewhat obscure to persons who have never realised that they possess a whole arsenal of defence and aggression within the compass of their own skin; but here again a little simple practice will reveal the truth in assertions which may strike the uninitiated as markedly esoteric.

There are many students who cannot find the time to carry out breathing exercises on a major scale: they feel themselves incapable of the necessary concentration, and the circumstances of their lives do not permit of their settling down to a complete investigation of the rights and wrongs of Yoga. The utmost they are prepared to concede to the subject is a rather grudging acknowledgement of the virtues of deep breathing, particularly when this is prompted by desire to excel in the accepted sports. But if they would combine this deep breathing with a little imagination and think not so much of the muscular health but of the spiritual vigour that will accrue therefrom, they would be wise.

We all carry in the region of the solar plexus a huge accumulator of occult power. At any moment of the day or night we can recharge this battery with very little difficulty, by concentrating on the area in our mind's eye and drawing into its centre all that we can muster of recreative energy from the spheres of emotion. By this phase is implied the capacity to raise ourselves into a fairly " high " dimension for the time being, and so entrap for our need the forces of another plane. It must be remembered that just as like calls unto like in the world of social relationships, so the same principle applies in the realm of psychic realities: when we think and act according to the flesh, we are circumscribed by the laws of the flesh; and we can only meet men and things in general on this comparatively low level. When, on the other hand, we transpose ourselves to the etheric level (that is, get nearer to the more essential self) we can exert more influence on those in whom we are interested, and our vision becomes correspondingly wider. But we are still far from our highest goal. When we rise to the astral, which is the emotional plane, we are on even surer ground. Now we can enrich our psyche with an ichor drawn from all that men and women experience of poetic impulse and ardent aspiration. This is by no means the highest type of human experience; but it is sufficiently removed from the cynical hurly-burly of the more aggressively materialistic modes of thought and action, that it deserves to be elevated to something like an ideal when considering the question of the possibilities of human reactions. Art, the law, the more civilised branches of orthodox religion, are not final values: it is probable that they will be far surpassed by the more integrated humanity of the future: they can be regarded as vague yearnings towards a state of more solid and intelligent harmony. But they represent the best that normal men and women can show for their advancement up to the present, and the world would be infinitely poorer without these inadequate but very signficant landmarks on the road towards the light.

One of the reasons why affirmative charity is such a stimulant to the entire system lies in the fact that, on this wave-length, the solar plexus centre is receiving constant streams of regenerating energy from the uplifting reservoir of aspirations and ideals to which all men at their best subscribe. It is fashionable in some cynical circles to sneer at those sometimes pathetic attempts at superiority which go under the name of "refinement." But the cynics are wrong. Any move in the direction of culture, no matter how effete, is far better than a brutal and dogmatic defeatism which argues that because the majority of men shy from perfection, they are therefore to be content to remain on a purely animal footing. Extreme courage is not common, and man is still backward enough to show an extreme diffidence when he is confronted at odd moments with his own higher self. All the more reason for conducting him as far as is possible along those vistas by which he may attain a *Pisgah* view of his own ultimate progress. To live in the solar plexus of *Manipura* is, then, to breathe in some of the best things of which man is capable and to be loved and love in consequence.

There are, of course, the attendant dangers. To enjoy too fully the refined language of the emotions is to be so sure of one's stance in this earthly paradise, that further progress is not even desired. One of the main objections to complete personal harmony (although one hesitates to make the point) is that the invaluable apprenticeship to suffering which is the lot of all men in varying degrees at the present, will have to be foregone. It would be unpleasant for a genuine mystical progress to develop into that boring mastery of material comforts foreshadowed by Mr. Aldous Huxley in his *Brave New World*. The great desideratum is that a continual aspiration shall be kept alive even when great happiness is secured by "going from the *Manipura* to the Heart."

Here again some definition is needful. To find one's way about the map of the psyche is enormously helped by a grounding in the chart of the anatomy. One must imagine that the system is divided up into a network of routes, each with their set of byways, and each bearing a double significance—the atmosphere of the city from which they start and the anticipation of the city to which they are bound. At the junctions (that is, the *chakras*) one loads up with oil and fuel for the journey. The direction taken is dependent on what we have called the "moral will." The student who was accustomed to live at ease in one of the higher *chakras* is wilfully perverting his energies if he elects to turn back on his traces and wend his way among the lower. He must of necessity absorb the "earth" forces through the main *Muladhara* centre at the base of the spine; but this once done, he should use the energy for the momentum behind his effective entry into higher spheres, and only for that purpose: otherwise he will run the appalling risk of entering the world of the Darker Magic from which no one emerges unscathed.

The passage from the solar plexus to the heart which can be easily followed in the superficial sense is, to speak more exactly, an adventure along a highway made by the arborisation of the nervous system. This quickening of nervous fibres is one of the most interesting manifestations of how the nerves live in a physical sense when prompted by some galvanism of the psyche. In the heart centre are gathered certain subtle kinds of esoteric strength which owe their efficacy to a physical as well as psychic aggregation. Not much is known as yet regarding the strict delineation of the currents within this network; but it is one of the great hopes of our modern psycho-therapy that one day the joins and cross-references of this psycho-physical traffic will be completely mastered and controlled so that anatomy will be in the position of giving hints to conduct.

What mystics *do* know is that the heart is the centre in which the faculties of clairvoyance and mystical intuition have their native hearth. Some suggestions can be tendered on the effect these gifts (or curses, if it be so desired) have on the bodily constitution. It is a commonplace of empirical observation that persons of psychic faculties strongly developed are more often than not, unbalanced, irresponsible and even slightly or wholly mad. These strictures, although frequently merely silly, deserve some consideration here as they happen sometimes to hit on truth as by a kind of accident.

Modern civilisation has for the most part been reared and fostered on the grossest form of cynical materialism. The plums and prizes of the earth have invariably gone to the most impercipient member of the community. Can it be wondered at that the seers and mystics, particularly when not born with an independent income, have been forced to wage a silent battle with the smug complacencies of the successful, which would have been enough to daunt the courage of archangels. The conflict has not been without its sad effect on nervous and mental balance. It is not to be expected that a minority should emerge unscathed from such a combat with tremendous odds. Naturally enough, neuroticism has been rife in the ranks of the " illuminated," and at times the habit has become catching among persons who are prepared for the neuroticism but not for the illumination.

It would seem that a new type of human being has been for long past struggling for self-expression. There is nothing hypothetical in asserting that this type is the salt of our present earth and the seed of another and fairer system. The genuine clairvoyants and " sensitives " of our time are the forerunners of this brave new world. Experiments in Europe and America have shown beyond any shadow of doubt that greater nervous sensitivity is becoming common among all classes of society and that a quality bearing some resemblance to positive transcendent vision is being discovered in the most unexpected quarters. The important thing to notice in these experiments of Rhine in America and Haldane in England is that a definite extension of consciousness or at least that " cryptaesthesia " which Myers discovered and classified in his classic, *Human Personality*, go with persons showing no trace of weakness or abnormality.

The truth of the matter is that as soon as experimental common sense becomes established in the classrooms and laboratories of our civilisation mysticism will " start looking up." That is to say, the forward-looking and forward-feeling members of the community will lose a great deal of their over-sensitiveness in a newly-acquired sense of social usefulness, and the various parts of their nature will adjust themselves into a more fruitful and efficacious balance. They will also prove that mystical knowledge does not deteriorate but, in fact, improves the physical constitution.

After all, we know by observation that even small doses of ecstasy or cosmic illumination are the best of all tonics for a tired set of reactions. Surely it should follow that the use of the ability to control and amplify this gift of the inflowing Spirit would produce not vacillation and unbalance, but an abiding sureness and resolution which would pull body and soul into indestructible economy and efficiency.

We must except here certain abnormal cases in which the vessel has proved itself too weak for the wine which it was destined to hold. The stigmatisation of Theresa Neumann, the sacred " possession " and holy rollings of a score of the elect seem to have occurred as instances of the substitution of one spirit by another, rather than as a desirable end for the spiritually ambitious to pursue. It is also very much open to doubt whether the persons who manifest the sort of ecstasy which goes with the transference of marks of suffering or dedication is so much a matter of virtue as of pathology. By a study of the evidence we are forced to the conviction that the experiences of these types of the " exalted " tend to illustrate the dangers attendant on giving oneself too much to the imitation and exaltation of another. Man was not intended to submerge himself in any morbid worship of suffering, but to improve his psycho-spiritual faculties so that he will be able to exert the maximum of good on his associates and surroundings before he passes on to higher climes. The best saints are they who cast the greatest fragrance, not those who have provided the most exciting problems for psychopathic wards.

There is one phenomenon connected with our subject on which it is difficult to be dogmatic in our present imperfect state of knowledge, but which is sufficiently common to merit suggestive consideration. This is the curious difference experienced in what may be called bodily proximity between individuals of varied moral development. Most of us are so content to like or be liked that we have neither the wish nor the patience to analyse the laws on which these reactions are based. But that they have causes behind them is evident to a little diligent scrutiny.

Consider the question of strong personality. Not a very common phenomenon in these machine-made days, but recognisable enough. Usually it either attracts very powerfully or repels after the same manner. Why is it that some feel aversion and some enthusiasm when confronted with the same individual. It is difficult to be sure of one's ground here ; but one is justified in saying that the reason must be instinctive ; and this in its turn must be due to some chemical affinity which persists between some persons of the same " wave-length " and which, when absent, has a contrary effect varying in strength according to the stature of the people concerned.

Certainly we shrink from some of our kind and go out with all our hearts to others. As humanity fortunately is more prone to grope after good than evil, it follows that decent virtuous people are on the whole more popular than those of an opposite ilk. But their virtue has produced some chemico-physical changes in blood, nerve and muscle which have their own very definite say in this matter. Just as the body of Alexander, according to Plutarch, smelt sweet even in death, so it is pretty certain that the practice of decent thoughts and decent conduct purifies the system in such a way that a subtle attractiveness is set up which acts as a magnet to all and sundry.

In that most exquisite book by Romain Rolland, *Prophets of the New India*, we are given some very striking instances of this reaction in the account of the extreme sensitivity of the mystic Vivekananda in contact with humanity. He is described in one passage as shrinking back involuntarily from one man who sought to hoodwink him with the plea that he was anxious to forsake the world, when he was merely seeking an outlet for vanity. The saint touched his flesh and knew in a moment that this was not the body of a "twice-born." "Not in this life, brother," he whispered, "will you receive liberation." This contagion of imperfection which seems to infect every particle of the anatomy of people devoted to selfishness and greed is in some degree felt by all who come in contact with them, although they may not have the discriminating wisdom of Vivekananda. There is undoubtedly a material background to this generated atmosphere. In the common phrase "something goes out of such people" and acts as the best index to their character: in most cases this "something" will be "picked up" by children and animals who are the best judges of the qualities of nervous voltages.

Among other benefits which a recognition of this fact has brought to the growth of applied psychology is a new offshoot of criminal investigation. A distinguished criminologist of my acquaintance, who combines a keen appetite for facts with the gifts that make a successful writer of detective fiction based on these same facts, refuses to subscribe to any views which may be regarded as "psychic" in tone or character, and indeed insists that such things are too much the preserve of the unbalanced for *her* taste. But she makes up for her intransigence in this respect by claiming for nervous reactions the value usually attributed to purely psychic "intuition."

According to her reading the faculty of suspicion which is such a help to this in unearthing various kinds of vilainy, is set up by factors by no means primarily intellectual (that is by observation, inference and deduction). It is much more set in action by a kind of *animal knowledge* which is in some way connected with the whirring-up of nerve fibres, the tingling in the system which betokens danger. This means to say that in the intercourse of every day, we are all exchanging a constant series of nervous impressions of each other which must frequently have a wearing effect on the system.

There is much to be said for the theory. Animals certainly exhibit these reactions; and it is natural and logical enough to infer that these centres of reference play their part in our more developed frames. Its weakness lies in the fact that it does not take into account the fact that man has not only one body but seven, and that it is impossible to erect a scheme of "sensational" deduction, which does not endeavour to trace the manifestations of the reactions we can see to their home in those departments of the psyche which are hidden from the normal gaze.

From the point of view of Yoga there is much to be learned from this revelation of possible influences. Half the battle in successful yogic practice consists in insulating oneself from the innumerable shafts and waves of nervous emotion directed toward us incessantly by the undisciplined traffic of the world. It is idle to imagine that we can avoid the toll for this membership of the madding crowd. For the happy life, a mean must be struck between that kind of insensitivity which spells selfishness and that galvanometric response to other people which is so automatic that it ceases to be of the least use as aid to the sufferings of our fellow-beings. A wise detachment is the only way to understanding.

Just consider for a moment what happens when we take a walk along a crowded street. Although we may not know it, and although the fact may not cause us any apprehension, we are being assaulted on every hand by volleys of psychic "influence" due on the one hand to the automatic casual interest we are taking in other people and, on the other, to the interest they are taking in us. This interest is hardly ever sufficiently controlled and detached to keep away the menace of exhaustion. Most of us look on all things and people with a certain amount of prejudice, due to our reaction to early experience. It is this prejudice which exacerbates so many of the impressions we receive and presents us with a bill for torn nerves and consequent depressed spirits for which we are at a loss to account.

The same thing is manifest in the unpleasant process of vampirism. This is not the place to discuss the more "romantic" aspects of the subject: we do not propose to entertain the reader with accounts of bloodsucking barons and sadistic sergeants of the Guards. But we do think some useful purpose may be served by suggesting that the obvious aspects of the matter which the lurid examples illustrate, are equalled in interest to the psychologist by their more subtle equivalents in the life of every day.

We have probably all had the unenviable experience of being "vamped" after the latter style. We all know the type of person a short intercourse with whom leaves us high and dry, our energy considerably depleted. If we are wise we shall fly with averted gaze from those among our acquaintance who have this deplorable effect on our spirits. At least unless we possess within ourselves the necessary prophylactic to counteract the bad influence. This can only come through the agency of a knowledge of the "Yoga of Detachment" which has at its command the art of beating off without any undue effort the waves of aggression which flow into us and weaken us from people who, consciously or unconsciously, actually do perform an evil kind of psychic invasion on others.

For this, in effect, is what constitutes the mechanism of the experience. There is a way of opening up the floodgates of the centres so that they receive in an unlawful fashion the wandering energies of another. Yoga teaches us so to adjust the balance of our own psychic tides that no " outside " agency can succeed in unleashing us from our own native moorings. All sorts of interesting questions arise here: the nature of the instinct of possessiveness: the reason why some people " get it all their own way " while others struggle against every manner of obstacles as far as the grave. But space forbids us to answer them in any detail. We must confine ourselves to saying that there is irrefutable evidence to show that behind all the apparent arbitrary play of fate, luck and chance, there is the combining and recombining of the nervous energies of the physical and subtle bodies, and that if we but knew (as we *can* know) the rules of this rhythm we could all put our lives in the direction of good luck and good order.

Perhaps the most hopeful sign for the future in the growth of knowledge of the interplay we have envisaged, is the progress of the art of healing. No longer do we trust entirely to phials and surgical implements in our treatment of the sick: we have discovered a better way—the righting of the balance of the spirit on which the health of the body depends. We know now that when we have ministered effectively to the " mind diseased " then a flourishing condition of the body will in most cases follow automatically.

The " laying-on of hands " practised so successfully by many healers in Europe and America is by no means only the sanctimonious suggestion that it is made out to be by observers with various kinds of prejudice to overcome. When it is " the real thing " and not an excuse for religious exhibitionism, it can work wonders in the readjustment of subtle forces which put even the achievements of chiropractors and osteopaths, in more obvious fields of therapy, to shame. It can only be accomplished successfully by persons in whom the gifts of the spirit are functioning to the expansion of the psyche and the priming of all its batteries with their full value of chemical and glandular voltage.

The difficult " theology of the body " which we have endeavoured to make clear at the beginning of this chapter is, in very truth, the symbol of the divinity which is inseparable from every particle of matter.   Tibetan Yoga insists above all on this point—that we do not go outside ourselves to see the miraculous element in the life we live.   Rather, this element becomes especially apparent when we take the trouble to contemplate the least workings of our own machine, the infinite complexity of that psychophysical endowment which our every thought can make or mar.

CHAPTER XI

Tibetan Yoga: The Way and Its Power.

IN THIS CONCLUDING CHAPTER it is time that strands should be gathered together and some attempt made to see our subject in as clear a perspective as understanding will permit. Also to venture certain opinions on the reason for the absorption of vast numbers of readers in Europe and the United States in a subject which at first sight may seem to savour of the sensational and the fantastic.

There is not the least doubt that interest in Yoga is advancing by leaps and bounds among people who take the trouble to think. And even if they are incapable of this effort, they are rapidly developing a state of mind and nerves which will drive them sooner or later into an attempt to solve their problems by attaching themselves to that larger life of which Yoga is the symbol and the expression. Modern civilisation is exacting a very heavy toll. What it gives with one hand it takes away with another. It has as yet been found impossible for the majority of men to reconcile with the obvious gains that have come their way in mechanical progress and comfort, the underground protests of the soul against submersion and extinction.

Our little systems have had their day and many of them look like passing pretty rapidly into a deep impenetrable night. The world has got no final satisfaction from the promises of its gods ; and the questions of the bewildered are even more poignant than the cries of the distressed. Faith seems to have fallen on a barren soil, and many have given up the hopeless fight against their own imperative doubts. If ever there was a time which needed a message it is this.

But not the usual sort! Not a mere appeal to wish-fulfilment and a sop to disordered emotions. What is wanted more than anything else in our unhappy era is a gospel of unity. We have had enough of division—of hatreds built on a false sense of superiority, of inconsistencies which have needed the vilest hypocrisy to keep them from becoming too apparent ; above all of that fatal severance between spirit and flesh which has been the very bane of all that we have sometimes flatteringly termed our "philosophy."

In the last resort our philosophy is the expression of our racial and national life. If our thinking is imperfect and corrupt it is not probable, but certain, that the individuals who form the flocks are having a time which can only inadequately be described as "thin." In a thoroughly harmonised state it is doubtful whether much energy would be spent in book-making. People would be so busy enjoying and realising themselves that there would be very little time available for substitutes. Life would be seen to be good and would need no buttressing from argument to support its claims on our respectful attention.

To express it another way : it is doubtful whether we have ever *had* a philosophy. At least one which takes into account all the parts of the machine, physical, mechanical, spiritual, and does not expire in a squelching bog of pessimism or scepticism. And in the present writer's opinion it is impossible to have a satisfactory religion until the nature of the physical world is thoroughly understood—its components and rewards estimated and analysed and a thorough justice done to the possibilities of self-development by any means which can prove justification by fruits. Spinoza came nearest to it with his doctrine of the evolutionary growth of natural processes, and the inter-relationship of all phenomena ; but his genius foresaw little possibility of an even moderately perfected mankind, and is thereby of little practical value to inheritors of a strong affirmative hope.

It can be said of Tibetan Yoga that it is the only spiritual system in the world which has at once "taken everything into account" and at the same time refused to clutter itself up with any theories which do not contribute to the perfectability of the developed human being for whom it caters. Viewed aright it is a panacea for all our ills ; for, contrary to common prejudice, the individual is in the last resort much more important than the group, and Tibetan Yoga teaches us that the individual can save and integrate himself even if all the cohorts of the world are ranged against him. Indeed, no flourishing group can exist unless it consists of a fair leavening of individuals who are sufficiently advanced to be able to stand on their own feet and divorce their interests from any merely ephemeral considerations. It is probable that the civilisation of the future will leave much more time and space than does ours for the fostering of the soul in solitude, realising, as it will, that the cultivation of psychic balance and psychic power is in no way hostile to the proper functioning of society but rather impels it along a sure and fortified path.

Within the last hundred years in particular there have appeared all over Europe symptoms of this renaissance of the individual soul. The inauguration of psychic research, the birth of the spiritualist movement, the public interest in the achievements of Anton Mesmer and the early and later hypnotists are evidence of a spirit of research hot on the trail of " things that matter " in the consolidation of human effort and the pursuit of human happiness. The tours undertaken by prominent oriental mystics, such as Ramacharaka and Vivekananda, the spreading of a gospel of unity and understanding are further evidence of a rediscovery which had to come. Slowly but surely the way was being prepared for the yogic standpoint which can be expressed in short as a declaration that once the Kingdom of Heaven is within you, then and not till then will it be possible for that type of co-operation which will lead the way to a fairer and above all a more rational state of society. It is only our disordered emotions which lead us into temptation and peril. Once these unruly tyrants are successfully taken in hand, there is no limit to the heights which we can reach in efficiency, stability and happiness. Yoga expressed *tout court* is the art of seeing straight : a simple enough procedure it may seem, but, in actual fact, only possible when we have gained some degree of transcendence.

It is necessary to warn the reader here that he must exercise some discrimination in his choice of literature on this engrossing subject. It is not foolproof, and there are many false guides whose interest in the subject is confined to what they can get out of it. But the presence of black sheep need not blind the novice to the magnificence of his view. He will soon find his perceptions growing, once he has got a whiff of the real air of the country, and, with an ever-increasing ease, he will be able to separate the white from the black.

The beginner who wishes to draw up a course of reading for himself and is not sufficiently equipped in oriental languages to go to original sources, cannot do better than start by acquainting himself with the work of Helena Petrovna Blavatsky, who spent an arduous and almost incredibly adventurous life in amassing a store of encyclopædic information on theories and certainties which are all directly or indirectly connected with the province of Tibetan Yoga. It is a stout novice who would tackle her major works, the monumental *Isis Unveiled* and *Secret Doctrine* ; but her tract on the subject of Raja Yoga will give much food for thought and will guard the student against the danger of probing too deeply into the more dubious aspects of the subject. There is no doubt that Blavatsky drew her own enormous personal power and fascination from the practice of elaborate systems of meditation in her youth ; also, she is the best of instructors, for she never commits the fatal error of putting the cart before the horse, and is never tired of pointing out that all the poses and postures in the world are worse than useless if they are not founded on a correct and all-embracing system of morality.

A perusual of the works of Rudolf Steiner will also provide a good groundwork for investigation, although in the present writer's opinion, the Austrian occultist had not the curiously subtle feeling for these things which the great Russian manifested. It may well be that the Russian temperament is peculiarly adapted for the pursuit of esoteric research standing as it does at the boundaries of East and West. Nevertheless, Steiner's *Knowledge* of *Higher Worlds* is as good as anything in classical occult literature as a guide to the patient, plodding application which must be undertaken by any novice in a science so voluminous and so full of traps for the unwary. Steiner's exposition is admirably clear ; and he always manifests the patience necessary to direct the steps of one not previously experienced in these fields. And he is of course, like Blavatsky, one of the great popularisers of occult knowledge in Europe.

But when we come to actual specialisation in Tibetan Yoga we are faced with a dearth of really reliable and first-class works. It is indeed difficult, unless one has had the good fortune to put in some time in an Eastern country among Eastern people of a religious cast, to develop the type of mentality needed to appreciate Eastern reactions at their true worth. Perhaps the most glaring fault in writers ambitious to try their hand at this theme is a lamentable lack of knowledge of the first principles of the subject, which can be best defined as a very subtle kind of humility. The Kingdom of Heaven does not come by standing on one's head, not even by amassing an encyclopædic knowledge of *mudras,* invocations and spells wherewith to smite the ungodly. Instead, this way sometimes madness lies ; and, which is even worse, the rapid growth of a galloping disease, commonly known as swollen head. It is not to be expected that there will be many people who are sufficient masters of their own environment to grow the intensity of perception and calm and curious reverence which is indispensable for setting up a stand in this sublimated spiritual commodity.

Some of the comparatively unvocal have had it, and have expressed in their conduct a steadfastness which the more glibly endowed have sought to commit to books. We refer to those solitary Europeans who have lived their lives on this earth with the decorum and dignity which are the hallmarks of the Eastern sage. The English race has supplied a full share of these transplanted ones, who have lived under the beneficent shadow of Eastern ideals and that quality which is rather inexactly known among us as "fatalism." The late Lord Kitchener (probably the greatest Viceroy India ever had) possessed the quality; so did Colonel Lawrence, when every allowance is made for his limitations and eccentricities. Even the stormy and reckless Sir Richard Burton, underneath the arrogance and the restlessness, was no stranger to this country; the shadows of these men will never grow less !

But alas, these have gone from among us, and we have fallen on what may seem to the impatient a somewhat barren generation. We must look to the travellers and to the professional scholars for some sparks of the information we need. Among the former there have been men of intrepid courage (and women too) who, not content with ransacking the sphere of the physical have returned with loot of a more durable and elevating kind. The diaries of Aurel Stein, and von Sternberg, the records of Desideri and Lady Hester Stanhope contain nuggets of precious gold for those willing to delve. There is a contagion in the mere acquaintance with an Eastern landscape which can leave an impression which colours and influences a whole life. The present writer's father, who as a young soldier spent some time in the East, was never tired of talking of the intangible but quite unmistakable "hold" which the experience had on affections and interests.

For the general reader, however, the most interesting of the travellers is that remarkable Frenchwoman Mde. Alexandra David-Neel, who unites to an intrepid personal courage and curiosity a deep sense of Tibetan mysteries. Although viewed purely as a writer she may seem to a purist a little patchy and scrappy, yet there is enough material in the many books she has written on the subject of Tibet and its mysteries to stock a hundred thrillers. She has sojourned for long periods in this land of her adoption, has made innumerable friends among the priests and people of the country and is remarkably free from that pernicious sense of "superiority" which so many peripatetic Europeans think fit to assume in contact with the sacred things of the East.

She has interpreted Tibet both from its secular and its religious side. For the beginner her *With Mystics and Magicians in Tibet* will contain a great deal of simply-described esoteric matter on which he can ruminate and map out his own "promised land." She is particularly good on that type of ceremony and ritual which abounds in colour and varied movement; and she has a *penchant* for describing the more lurid aspects of magic. Much of her time has been given to a study of Tibet's extremely rich epic literature ; and an acquaintance with her work will at least serve to point out that the country contains not only a religion, but a culture. In a word Mde. David-Neel, a member of what is perhaps the most intelligent race in Europe, has turned her gifts to excellent account by illuminating the secret places of the East with a lamp which burns with all that the Gallic mind can command of observation and inference. It is good to know that her books have won a wide popularity in Europe and America. That this can happen in the middle of this century is a sign of the way the wind is blowing: a wind that carries in its wake all kinds of promises for a more organised and intelligent future.

Turning to a more strict and meticulous scholarship, the present century has produced two men of a very decided eminence who have given their lives to the understanding and interpretation of the most profound truths that the religion of Tibet can be said to include. The first of these is the late Sir John Woodroffe, who wrote under the pseudonym of Arthur Avalon, and who won an equal eminence for his studies in Indian Law. This very learned scholar and most refined and kindly of men was for many years a judge of the High Courts in Calcutta, and there is a credible rumour which used to go the rounds, that the chief prize of his profession would have fallen to his lot if he had not shown such a profoundly sympathetic understanding with native malefactors who were brought before him. Fortunately for culture Woodroffe was all his life very comfortably off, and was able to devote a considerable leisure to the erection of a philosophy based on a thorough study of the principles of the *Tantras* which are the main approaches to Tibetan Yoga in its more complete and all-engrossing aspects.

It is interesting to note that Woodroffe was educated as a boy as a Roman Catholic (and indeed died in the bosom of that Faith); for there are numerous affinities which can be traced between ancient Tibetan rituals and the more recent edifice of Catholic æsthetico-religious consciousness. He had a fervid and indisputable sense of that mighty warmth which is at the heart of all true religion; and if ever there was an Englishman who understood the quest of the Eastern mind for truth it was this most tolerant and humble judge who was in the best sense of the word a solitary and a mystic.

But it must be said that Woodroffe is not for every student. His writing is for the most part compressed and difficult in the extreme ; and there is every reason to suppose that he was by no means anxious that all the truths he held dear should fall into the hands of the ungodly. For this reason it is probable that he quite deliberately employed a manner of writing that is at once baffling and intriguing. Moreover, to acquire any real intellectual or spiritual benefit from a perusal of these books, it is practically essential to have at least a nodding acquaintance with the ancient Sanscrit language. Now Sanscrit is not an easy tongue to learn even for those with a linguistic gift; and the problem is more complicated in the case of Woodroffe's works when it is realised that there is a kind of tacit understanding going on between the author and the hypothetical intelligent reader which is built on the assumption that words do not always mean what they say. Or, to put the matter more plainly, the Sanscrit words used by the author have in nearly every case a double meaning—the obvious one which is more often than not deceptive, and a more subtle one, a meaning within a meaning, in fact, which is hidden from the dilettante student.

The present writer has good cause to make this point. When he first came across *The Serpent Power* and *The Principles of Tantra,* and realised in a flash that this was what Henry James would have called " the real thing," he was compelled perforce to put in a certain amount of work as well as to enjoy a new and lasting thrill. It took some weeks to copy out and correlate all the Sanscrit terms " translated " by the great scholar, and a detective impulse was at last satisfied when it was found that a secret code had been set up for the enlightenment of persons who had some claim to call themselves initiates. The printed words were nothing more nor less than a card-index to their actual and exact meaning —an interesting illustration of the fact that words are given us not only to conceal our thoughts but also to guard the gates of an intense spiritual and emotional reality.

No, Woodroffe is not an easy writer, and it is perhaps pointless to recommend him to the novice. But we *do* recommend him, because we believe that the kind of truth which he tried to reveal by hint and implication is of inestimable benefit to all who can pick up even a few of the fragments which fall from the philosophic and religious table. Also because a first contact with Woodroffe, even when little is understood, is like sitting before a huge fire when all is cold outside, and having nerve and sinew heated to the point of ecstasy. With him the generosity and promise of faith is more apparent than its more formidable qualities: there can be fewer writers on major "mystical" themes who have been so imbued with the essence of their subject that they can be said to have sunk their own personality in the larger reality outside it.

If the reader is lucky enough to ride the exciting waves of the Sanscrit language, and is at the same time keyed up to feel the particular voltages that Woodroffe has to impart, he will have no more to wish for as regards a guide ; for he will be in the very heart of the Yoga country. And not the respectable watered-down *paysage* which is usually deployed for the benefit of the Western reader, but a landscape bursting with rarest flora and fauna of the most exotic and intriguing kind and full of every power to tonic and sustain.

In *The Serpent Power* in particular, there is given as complete a guide as is possible outside the cell of a teaching *guru* to the powers and capacities of the Centres. The illustrations which accompany the text are of a sumptuousness and completeness which give more than an approximate idea of the endless riches behind the elaborate and decorative facade. An excellent visual exercise is to study one of these diagrams blazing with all its colour, and then endeavour to reproduce in the mind's eye the main figures with their attendant satellites and trapping in the right order and juxtaposition. It becomes perfectly clear, once one has " got the hang " of Woodroffe, that each of the Centres has its own life, at once independent and impossible to appreciate without a full understanding of the functions of the others. Siva and Parvati, enwrapped in their ineffable ecstasy, assume different postures as their functions change. To each Centre is attached the powers and the abuse of the powers. There is a good and a bad "angel" standing side by side as guardians of the various thresholds. It is incumbent on the student to distinguish very carefully between these two occult personalities, the one, when well contacted, fortifying to a degreee that the man of the world cannot even imagine; the other the wielder of all the evil that disintegrates and destroys.

Woodroffe makes all this clear for those who can follow his argument.

Like Blavatsky, he propounds at times theories which seem casual enough, but which are of the profoundest import for the " placing " of occult phenomena. If one reads between the lines of many of the early articles in *Lucifer* and *The Theosophist* it becomes evident that the " priestess of Isis " was highly trained in some of those more esoteric aspects of mind- and will-control which she thought it inexpedient to give to the world at large. The hint is there for the initiated. Similarly the footnote of the *Mahanirvana Tantra* which Woodroffe edited with such rare discrimination and insight, contains information which boils down a great many facts into their essentials. The remark that all urgently important religious manifestations originated in the delta of the Nile is more than a theory: it is the key to the comprehension of many of the secret strands of occult research.

We have spoken of Woodroffe as an indifferent writer, on the grounds that he is too concerned with compression to allow his literary wings full flight. But it is necessary to qualify this criticism with the admission that there are " purple passages " in his work as fine as any to be found in any field of exalted literature. When he is caught up by the gorgeous richness of his theme, when he sings the praises of the all-loving and all-repairing goddess Kali, then Sir John Woodroffe joins the ranks of the great masters of prose.

The second of the great modern scholars is a personality of very different potentials. W. Evans-Wentz first came to know the occult by way of a fellowship thesis—a brilliant and charming thing on the folk-lore of the Kelts. Some years of travel and study in the East, particularly in Northern India and Tibet, convinced him that there was more in folk-lore and the like than met the eye —that in fact, this was merely the surface of a reality of great importance for the spiritual life of mankind. Hence the works of his maturity, the *Tibetan Book of the Dead, The Life of the Great Yoga Milarepa,* and the rest. In each of these books Mr. Evans-Wentz, a profound and most exact scholar, reveals to the public of Europe the map of certain psychic territories which had hardly been suspected before. He promises, if there should be sufficient public demand, some further collections of recipes for Yoga training which will bid fair to let the whole " cat out of the bag."

Mr. Evans-Wentz is also a difficult writer, but for a very different reason to that stated in the case of Woodroffe. Whereas the latter is purposely provocative and elusive when it suits his book, Mr. Wentz exemplifies the more obvious difficulty of the scholar who takes his job too seriously to concede much to popular laziness and indifference. His pages are so larded with learned notes and commentaries that it is sometimes difficult to see the wood for the trees. His enormous reading is brought in by the hair of its head to enforce his points; and his temperament has a reserved and slightly sardonic quality which inhabits a different world to that of Woodroffe, so warm and radiant and whimsical.

Nevertheless Evans-Wentz's manuals are the best of their kind. They are imbued with a passionate and altogether admirable love of truth, and the intelligence behind them is of a very high calibre. If anything there is too much material in these pages: it would perhaps have been better if the author had spread his knowledge over a wider canvas and had been content to dilute his material so that a wider public could have drunk at the stream. But when these reservations have been made, we may well be grateful to a scholar who has given his life to a study so absolute and compelling, and who has added to the as yet slight *Tantric* literature translated for the delectation of Europeans the glowing and most instructive *Book of the Dead*. It is as important in true religion to die as to live well. This *Tantra* will help any genuine searcher to forestall any calamity attendant on leaving this world by the conviction that he can choose both his mode of egress and re-entrance.

One hesitates to recommend anything further. There are many more books which attempt to treat in some measure with our subject; but they are for the most part so distorted by prejudice or inexactitude that serious misconception might be set up in the mind of the reader who is looking for something more than sensation. But in all fairness something must be said of Waddell's *Buddhism of Tibet* which has for some years held the field as a text-book of Tibetan religious customs. It is a work of indisputable thoroughness and industry; its facts are informative and the themes are well-marshalled and provided with illustrations of unusual interest and appropriateness. But it must be admitted at the same time that Mr. Waddell is the most eminent of those who look on these things from afar. Search as one may, there is no evidence in these pages of the sort of sympathy which is absolutely essential for the writer who wants to " get these matters over." Indeed, this author expresses to a nicety the reactions to his subject which have been formed by many centuries of orthodox prejudice (conditioning, by the way, is not confined to the much-discussed mechanical world of the future: it is with us here and now, and has known our company for quite a long time. The academic mind is largely a conditioned mind, living as it does on a set of beliefs which have been taken for granted instead of being profoundly and exactly examined). " How different from the home-life of our dear Queen " is a good enough attitude for discussing the goings-on at the court of the Emperor Nero ; but it is of little avail when it is a question of getting to the heart of the most subtle religious consciousness in the world. The remark of a Jesuit of my acquaintance some years ago to the effect that Christianity could "learn a great deal " from a study of Tibetan principles, expresses much more the truth of the matter than all the moralisings in the world.

Certain writers of fiction, notably Mr. Talbot Munday in his *Nine Unknown* and in the magnificent aphorisms which decorate the chapter-headings of *Om,* have come pretty near to the spirit of the *Tantras,* and one should never despise this mode of approach. Nor should one neglect to examine those European writers who, without realising it, have given voice to the spirit of Tibetan Yoga. Wherever there is sublime emotion, constructive force, concentrated will and that kind of volcanic passion which grows on what it feeds, there also is Yoga and *Tantra.* The poetry of Swinburne, a lyric of Victor Hugo, the greatest music of Wagner, such statuary as the "Balzac " of Rodin, the paintings of van Gogh and Goya—all these to name only a few—are inspired and illuminated by the grace and glory of a religious spirit that conquers time.

Apart from literature there are one or two instruction-centres in Europe where the principles and practice of the higher Yoga can be studied under adequate supervision. One of the most interesting of these was the school set up at Fontainebleu by that remarkable man, Gurdjieff, who united to great hypnotic powers a very real comprehension of Eastern techniques. Some very distinguished personalities, including such names as Orage the journalist and Ouspensky the well-known writer on scientific mysticism, foregathered at this resort and learned to correlate the activities of mind and body. In India itself there was a flourishing community at Tirrikesh which put into practice the teachings of the Tibetan sages regarding mind and will control. The present writer has also managed to interest a number of people in the pressing problems of mental and emotional economy and development and is happy to say that some remarkable advances have been made by the students.

But all the study in the world can do no good unless the heart is prepared for the message. It may be asked by the sceptic, " What is wrong? Why should we try to practise this rigid control? Surely the old way of trial and error was better?" There is something in the argument. The world is full of freak sects and feckless communities, the only excuse for whose existence is that they keep people from "doing worse." The normal man may well flatter himself that he is on the right path much more by avoiding than by subscribing to the tenets of these dubious fraternities.

But underneath the posing and the humbug, the misty speculation and the emotional ditheration, there is visible a very real and genuine striving for law and order in human thought and feeling. It is felt by all intelligent observers that there has been far too much waste in the human story, and further, that this same waste has been more often than not the direct result of the inability of the average man and woman to gauge their powers and husband their resources. It is averred, with no attempt to startle, but with a deep conviction of the truth of the statement, that the civilisation of the future will know much more than most people at present about the hidden capacities within each one of us. Slowly the wheel will come full circle, and a world of gleaming efficiency and admirable sanitation will find its deeper soul in the musings of mystics who flourished before time, in the historical sense, had hardly begun. There is nothing contradictory in this statement. There is nothing inimical to the spirit in a well-graced exterior; the soul loses no whit of its intensity by being granted the ability to spread its wings in an earthly as well as heavenly paradise: a sane and proper comfort is no bar to the intricacies of a powerful spiritual development.

It is because we owe the debt of a better world to our children that it behoves us to prepare for it in the best of all places—that is, within ourselves. We shall have to face the fact that, in the large sense, most of us have failed. We were put on this earth to learn, endure and expand,—and all that most of us can show for the experience are numbed nerves and a worn and jaded heart. This is not the way of triumph ; nor is it much preparation for the further summits we shall have to scale when this particular life is done. We must think more nobly of the soul. Above all we must learn to exult.

This can only be done when there is something to exult about. And it is needless to point out that we have not as yet succeeded in turning this universe into anything approaching a land fit for spiritual heroes to live in. A happy humanity can only be produced by a sane and unwasteful morality, a constant yea-saying to the variegated spectacle around us.

This is where Tibetan Yoga can help. For it denies nothing that we have come to respect and love ; and it amplifies and fulfils whole uncharted areas in that mystery we call the personality. Its practice, if faithfully executed and diligently revered, can import into all our veins the strength not of ten, but of ten thousand because we have learned to see where virtue is and to garner it accordingly. What are the main preparations necessary for this training for the expansion and deliverance of the powers of the soul?

First, it is obviously incumbent on the student to get the body into as fit a condition as possible. Fortunately, the apotheosis of physical fitness is no stranger to our general thinking at the present day, although some of us may cavil at the means sought to ensure it. Contrary to a sentimental current opinion, the developed adept is the last person in the world to decry physical health. Of course, we all know of great spiritual leaders who are mere bags of bones to look at, and others whose physical reactions are, to put it mildly, spasmodic and uncertain. But these geniuses are, in actual fact, no exception to the general rule that a clear blood-stream and an unfaltering sense of economy in physical habits are indispensable for realistic swift thinking. It is not bulk or even appearance that counts so much in this matter as a due adjustment of effort to endowment. The late Anatole France had an abnormally small brain ; but he was able to get more out of it than most of his critics out of theirs.

Our civilisation, which is largely a civilisation of fidgets, has erred in its training of the body as well as in many other respects. The forced passion for games, whether one happens to like these frequently idiotic methods of wasting one's time or not, the insistence on "activity" as opposed to meditation, the setting up of ideals which involve a frank advocacy of the more insane modes of self-sacrifice, have done much harm to bodily stability. There are very few people nowadays who are not oppressed with some form of nervousness, even if they are able to conceal the fact with a show of blunt brutality which is no necessary concomitant of health. The psycho-analysts have shown us that the apparently bluff and insensitive are very often the most timorous and undecided of mortals. This is not a real sanity, even of the physical kind.

It is surprising how health improves when we learn to rest instead of fritter away our energies in pointless action. A certain portion of each day, even if it can only be five minutes, should be set apart for complete relaxation. This means that the body should be allowed to "flop out" and the mind as far as possible made a blank. The results of this elementary manoeuvre are far more efficacious than any amount of "exercise" given to a tired frame. Also, the student will be astonished to find how his endurance and resilience increases after this quite unspectacular recuperation. He will also find his discriminative and intellectual faculties generally grow in strength, and he will, above all, know something of that rare and most desirable experience which we call, lamely enough, "peace of mind."

When the ground has been thus prepared for this degree of nervous control, some effort must be made at that self-analysis which is the only preparation for a constructive detachment. The reader may be startled to hear that very few human beings ever attempt to work out a rational basis for their thoughts and actions. Indeed, when they say "I think" or "such is my belief" they actually mean that they have been doped by their newspapers or their political bosses into an automatic acquiescence in things which the powers that be consider it desirable for them to uphold. The man who can think for himself, without prejudice or fear, is among the salt of the earth ; but he is not likely to find many companions. But although his bills will be heavy, he will have the infinite satisfaction of knowing that it is people like himself who justify the continuance of the species on this planet. Also he will be preparing for a strong psycho-spiritual development within himself.

The Buddha was most insistent on this point. He continually exhorted his followers to analyse the reasons for their thoughts and actions ; for only by this means could they develop the critical faculty requisite for true spiritual knowledge. Here Gautama reveals his deep wisdom. A real religion is no flight from reality, but an ability to extend its frontiers and increase its volume and density. This can only be achieved when one has learned to discriminate the true from the false by an intellectual as well as an intuitive process.

The immediate result of a first experiment in this exercise may not be particularly happy. To minds enwrapped in the cotton-wool of illusion the first glimpse of truth may cause a feeling of arid despair such as is felt by a lonely stranger on his first entrance into a foreign land. But persistence will modify and at last dispel the pain ; and the student will come to rejoice in his freedom from limitation and fear.

Take for example a common æsthetic reaction. We visit friends in the country and they of course invite us to share with them the " beauty " of some celebrated view. We acquiesce ; and, unless we are bored, we gaze on the scene with an emotion worthy of the most relentless collector of picture-postcards and snapshots. No harm is done ; but we have learned very little. What we have seen (the " Nature red in tooth and claw " of Tennyson's poem) is a horrible battlefield full of the internecine strife of animals desperately preying on each other to the point of extinction. What an opportunity for reflection! A pessimistic view, it may be said? But it happens to be a true one ; and until this truth is acknowledged we shall make little progress in our understanding of life. The real enjoyment of the view will come when it is seen as an aspect of cosmic development in which the beauty resides in lessons learned rather than in blood shed, and the exhilaration of seeing things " as they are " will more than compensate for the lack of any superficial pleasure in the phenomena.

To see things as they are! That is one of the earliest lessons the would-be yogic adept must master. If one can do this, many temptations will forthwith pass away; for it is axiomatic that when the flimsy nature of a coveted prize is realised, it ceases to have any attraction. Also, any asceticism worth the name must be founded on this insight into the hollowness of the rewards of the flesh. It is in the last resort impossible to " give up " anything which the subconscious mind still desires. Otherwise, sooner or later (usually sooner) the habit or obsession will be renewed with an added fervour.

This is by no means the same thing as saying that one becomes cold or indifferent to human concerns. On the other hand, the student who honestly seeks to rid himself of illusion finds himself developing a stronger sympathy with his fellow men. He sees now that they err and suffer, not because they are bad but because they are blind. He henceforth ceases to ask too much of people crowded together around false ideals in a desperate attempt at self-preservation, and recognises that he can do little to help others unless he shows them that the virtue he advocates is beneficial even to their earthly interests.

Detachment is not a popular quality—that is, if it is advertised in the shape and form of aloofness. No one likes to feel that he or she is being treated like a botanical specimen ; and too many advocates of the quality forget to remember that, for detachment to be a virtue, it must be a means and not an end.

No one could accuse Gandhi of being hoodwinked by the usual fallacies attendant on the life of the materialist ; but, at the same time, no one would dare to say that he was indifferent to the suffering of his fellow-creatures.

Detachment of the wrong sort is something like a malignant disease : it renders the mortal who has cultivated it not only indifferent but, more serious still, impermeable to the multifarious contacts life can offer. He misses more than half the fun by refusing to range the heights and depths of experience. The sort of detachment which Tibetan Yoga offers is of a very different nature. Instead of coldness it produces an abundant warmth, because it is based upon the Buddhist idea that the only worthy life is the life of service. A service which subscribes to two codes of behaviour: the negative one, that condemnation should be sedulously avoided and a positive, which insists on a utilitarian effort to contribute as far as in one's power lies to the progress and amelioration of the world. Every sensible citizen knows that the best happiness comes from thinking more of others than of oneself. The adept carries this conviction many stages further, because he has learned to know of what the real happiness of others consists. He is trained in all the tricks and twists of human selfishness and makes it his lifelong task to hold before the eyes and minds of his fellows a happier adherence, a more satisfying goal.

The word "power" has been used a great many times in these pages; and the writer is fully aware of the unpleasant associations which have gathered around the concept, particularly in recent times. Too often it recalls to the mind an unprincipled rapacity and cunning which knows no god but itself, a justification of the rule of the "strong" over the weak. This conception has no relation to the meaning attached to the word by the Tibetan sage.

There is not the least need to be frightened of the word as used in a yogic context. It implies simply the collecting and concentrating of one's capacities so that there is no waste in the working of the machine, and so that a vast reserve of psychic force can be always kept in readiness for any emergency that may arise. There are always emergencies in human affairs—the collapse of systems of government and morals, the dire distress of the weak and helpless who have fallen on evil days of their own making. It is the duty and privilege of the psychically strong to uplift their lesser brethren from the mire of defeat and defeatism and reset a weak and restless generation on a pair of new-found feet.

There is nothing at all fanatical in this claim. In very truth groups and individuals trained in the right use of their psychic energies can do an infinite amount of good in and to the world by sending out shafts of radiant and inescapable volitional energy which, although we cannot see it with the naked eye, is the standby and safeguard of the only true liberty, that of the cleansed and constructive will. Monks praying in their monasteries, solitary adepts all over the world, the humbly and persistently virtuous of all nations—these are the masons and the architects of progress. It is not by abandoning the spirit that advancement, personal and social comes, although this doctrine is widely held among masses of men at the present day. It is, on the other hand, only by the cultivation of the spirit that the health of body and will can function to its fullest capacity. In a word, it is the spirit that makes us happy; and unless we are masters of happiness we have in some sort failed to live our life.

The man who has trained himself to look on all things with a critical yet tolerant and unjaundiced eye, who has learned to live alone and, at the same time, has given much attention to the conservation and reinforcement of the secret capabilities of the bundle of forces within him, is in very sooth the master of the world. Nothing can depress or hamper him further. One well-directed thought of his can upset schemes and propel forces. With an effectiveness unobserved and infinitely subtle he can make his beneficent contribution to tangled, inchoate human affairs.

How much more a group trained in a wise and calculated austerity! It is obviously difficult to create such a body for the reason that it is difficult to bring voltages into line. Human nature is often intractable and perverse ; and the strong man or woman who can at the same time work harmoniously with other people is hard to find. This is why Tibetan Yoga insists on election and a due discipline in team-work as well as an independence. It behoves the applicant for adeptship to "join himself up" as early as he can with some communion of saints which will help to form strong currents for the distribution and recharging of what he has learned to collect.

By this is meant an affiliation to minds on a similar wave-length to his own. No physical contiguity is needed, although it is better that he visit at times the scenes which give him power. Once he has "cleared his mind of cant," in Dr. Johnson's famous phrase, he is free to plant it with seeds which in due course will bring forth much fruit. These seeds are set by an intensive effort at visualisation and retention. The student is exhorted to remember that by the use of imagination he can actually create the weapons to his hand. When he has *thought*, he has accomplished his own soul-armoury, which is much more durable and reliable than that of the material world. All over his mentally constituted universe he can set up his own martello-towers, places of fortification and succour which are a never-failing help in times of trouble. Interconnected by cables and wires of which he alone knows the secret, these strongholds of the spirit will be peopled by the missionaries and guides he holds most dear.

For example, most of us have a particular fondness for some inspirational voice of the past, some personality whose echo comes down to us along the avenues of time to uplift and sustain. What better practice than to contact this silent friend in his own haunts? It is not particularly difficult to see the Buddha under the bo tree or Ignatius Loyola wrestling with his soul at Manresa. This is a far more satisfying indulgence than that of "meeting one's favourite authors after death"; for it is just possible that our favourite authors were not particularly quick in the psychic uptake; and this is the only form of "uptake" which is likely to profit the spirit in the long run.

We can, then, if we will, make friends with the great psychic figures and scenes of the past. And we shall realise at the same time that, in the world of the spirit, there is no absolute past, present, nor future but one glorious sustaining Now. This is why help is so ready to our hands when we take the trouble to ask for it from "mythical" personages we have come to venerate: we are conferring with forces so near to us that they can be said to be at our very ear.

The point may seem a difficult one for the novice in psychic research, but it is all-important for an understanding of psychic issues. It brings us at once to the question of time-dimensions, a subject which has been so well analysed in our times by such writers as Arthur Hinton and J. W. Dunne. It is a commonplace of philosophical statement that we can only reckon time by the computation of a number of consecutive happenings in space. In no satisfactory sense can we speak of time as something we can measure and grasp. And indeed, to regard it as we commonly do, is to commit a breach of the higher reason. For a complete investigation into the subject seems to prove beyond all reasonable shadow of doubt that there is no division in the structure of the mode of apperception we call "time," but that all our pilgrimage is here already, the future as well as the past, the present cheek by jowl with the final arrival. To appreciate this reasoning we must regard human history as a kind of palimpsest. Scroll is piled upon scroll, record upon record, until an illusion is set up which deceives all but the mystics, who by the nature of their gift are able to pierce through the shows of things to the reality beneath. Many clairvoyants wander, albeit unwittingly, through all dimensions of the course, viewing the scenes on the shifting planes as a hypnotised spectator. It is for the scientist of the future to concentrate on the intricacies of this problem until, by mathematics or logic, psychology or ecstatic experience, they can make obvious to the multitude what is now only suspected by the scholars.

Tibetan Yoga grants the gifts of comprehending and envisaging all the permutations and combinations of time. One of the commonest manifestations of this endowment is the ease with which the fully developed adept can see his own past and future incarnations. Looking before and after, he gathers strength and resolution because he realises the inner necessity of the multitudinous experiences which make up his destined path. Also, at any moment of his course he can reinvigorate himself with subtle energies drawn from any one of these stages along which he must pass.

With this gift goes another—that of seership in any or all of its many forms. In these days there is no disputing the fact that such a faculty exists, no matter how bound up it may be with fake and fraud. It is unfortunate that it has came to be associated with the fair-ground and the palmist's parlour ; for it is worthy of a more respectful attention than that given to it by the usual frequenter of the haunts. The Buddha promised to the spiritually advanced the *siddhis* or supernatural knowledge and power. It is most instructive to note that this superb religious teacher regarded clairvoyant perception as a direct outcome of the developed intelligence, and not as a freakish excrescence of the mystical consciousness. Voltaire admired the Chinese because, as he put it, "they are so rational." If he had cast his eyes a little further afield, he would have praised the Tibetans even more for their transcending of the Confucian "reasonableness" and entering a realm where the reason becomes merged in a vision which is based on an enlargement of intellectual laws.

It is probable that the great early civilisation enjoyed this faculty on a very large scale. Brought up as they were to regard a rational religion as the main essential in life,.they did not throw. dust in their own eyes by setting up apparent logic on a pedestal for which it has no real claim. Consequently, some of the bright progressive souls of later epochs represent no atavism but a return to a clarity which is indispensable for a full enjoyment of life. The man and woman equipped with the clairvoyant faculty should find their pleasures enhanced a hundredfold because they can extend enjoyable experience into its subtilised planes and repair the ravages of exultation with the vigour culled from furthest space.

Every competent Yogi has the gift of foreknowledge, even if he does not employ any of the recognised methods of divination. It is not to be imagined that the large amount of time devoted to static attitudes by wise men in Eastern lands is consecrated to a mere *emptying* of the powers of the mind : rather is a considerable proportion of it spent in reviewing the long and fascinating procession of human achievement, the contemplation of wonders and marvels to come. This is an attitude very different from the superficial one which sees life as a colourful spectacle ; for in the former case one enjoys a subtle participation which can only be tapped by the initiated.

It is remarkable how widespread is the passion and ability for divination among all classes in Tibet. Take, for instance, the subject of astrology. In the land of snows there is no hesitation in trusting to the guidance of a good astrologer ; for it is recognised that this ancient science is founded on principles too verifiable to encourage scepticism. Every large monastery has its professional astrologer. He it is who draws up charts and gives advice on the crucial questions concerning birth, marriage and death, the key-points of individual destiny.

The Tibetan system of reckoning time is different from ours. It is based on a twelve-year and sixty-year cycle. In the former case the particular year bears the name of one to twelve animals ; namely Mouse, Ox, Tiger, Hare, Dragon, Serpent, Horse, Sheep, Monkey, Bird, Hog, Dog. In the sixth-year cycle the names of these animals are combined with the five elements—Wood, Fire, Earth, Iron and Water. The year commences in February with the rise of the New Moon ; and the days of the week are correlated with their appropriate elements. Friday and Saturday

correspond to Earth ; Thursday to Air ; Sunday and Tuesday
belong to Fire and Monday and Wednesday to Water. Each hour
of the day and week is mapped out into its "lucky" or
" unlucky " connotations, and a whole host of spirits take it in
turns to dominate the forces of these separate occasions.

The Tibetan astrologers are largely concerned with the
placating or harnessing of these spirits. If an entity cannot be
"managed " it is held that its malevolence must be circumvented
by the appropriate means. Here we are reminded of the beliefs
of sects such as the Druses who held that the good principle,
in the nature of the case, can work nothing but good, and therefore is not a particularly dangerous proposition ; but the hosts of
evil, by constitution sly and undependable, have to be "regarded
as aggressors " and a weather eye kept on them accordingly.
Students of folk-lore will be able to put two and two together when
they hear of such symbolic figures as "the black dog," the
"monster with the dragon's tail " and "the man on horseback."

The Lamaistic experts each possess an almanack (corresponding to our ephemerides) and a board on which they work out the
intricate calculations of the stars. It is hardly necessary to say
that this aid is sought by all members of the community and
implicitly followed. But besides the occult counsel of these priests,
the people have their own individual methods of prognostication
which can be practised alone. Perhaps the most popular of these
are card-packs and rosaries.

The former is a simple enough medium and the packs are to be
found in every Tibetan home, from peasant's cot to nobleman's
palace. They are small oblong strips of cardboard, each representing "lucky" or "unlucky" diagrams or pictures. After a short
invocation to the Goddess Tara, the packet is held in the left hand
on a level with the face, and, the eyes being closed, the card is
pulled at random out of the pack ; the best of a selection of three
cards is held to decide the fortune of the undertaking on which
the questioner seeks to embark.

The rosary is used in a similar manner. Taken into the palms
of the hands it is rolled between the two palms, and the hands
clapped three times. The eyes are closed, and a portion of the
rosary is seized between the finger and thumb of each hand. On
opening the eyes the intervening beads are counted. On this
numerological computation the "reading" depends. The invocations attached to these modes of fortune-telling are picturesque and

evocative. Herewith one of the most popular : "I bow before the kind, merciful and noble Lama, the Three Holy Ones, the tutelary deities, and before all the hosts of Dakins, religious protectors, and guardians of the Magic Circle. I beg that you will cause the truth to descend on this lot. I also beg you, O revered one, Brahma, Indra, the Serpent Kings, the sun, the eight planets, the twenty-eight constellations of stars, the twelve great chiefs of the Injurers, to let the true light descend on my lot, and let truth and reality appear in it."

"To let the true light descend" . . . a barbarous superstition, the sceptical will remark ! But the sceptic will be exceeding his province. There is no particular mystery in the very real value of any or all of these aids to clairvoyance if the spirit which prompts them is fully understood. Of course, the medium itself is of comparatively no account, except in so far as it has been connected for several hundred years with the association which it is desired to set up; and the habit is a great attractor of associations. The thread which runs through all these apparently varied modes of divination is continuous, and is spun from the same source. By concentration and reverent contact with the forces of other dimensions we bridge gaps in space and time, and allow streams of vision to pour through our expanded psychic veins. And when the mind and will are set in an attitude of disciplined belief ; when, too, the practice of asceticism clears away illusion and deception from the path ; then, meditating upon one fixed point, be it rosary, astrological chart or cards, the seer enters into a world in which scrying is a reality because all compromise with temporal limitations has gone by the board and everything is transposed to a firm enduring plane.

These then are some of the gifts promised to the diligent student of soul-training which has reached its loftiest expression in the heights Tibetan Yoga. It should be stressed that to keep on the wave-length necessary for the psychic agility here suggested, certain precautions should be taken. The chief of these is a regular systematic daily round of recollection and devotion which feeds the psychic nerves in the same way as the body is sustained by a regular succession of meals.

This is not so hard as it may sound, once the habit is acquired. Indeed, habits, good or bad, are notoriously easy to cultivate once the rhythm is learned, and a regular psychic meditation is so productive of powerful results, so stimulating to the entire organism, that it becomes a sheer delight to practise. A gifted woman of my acquaintance has confessed that she has never known a day's illness since she began to fortify herself with these bastions; nor has she had any need to worry about the ravages of time, for she finds herself growing daily more goodly to look upon and more sure of her every muscular and nervous reaction. Also, she has enough self-observation to note that she has developed a very strong degree of personal magnetism, since she has relied on the inner forces to give her strength. This she tests by the impressions she makes on other people: formerly she possessed her fair share of individuality and no more; but now she has produced some exciting "something" within herself which makes her the cynosure of all eyes wherever she goes.

This is only one of the more obvious results of the kind of co-ordination we have described. There are other and further grades of power which await the thoroughly accomplished master of himself. It would bewilder the reader to work out all the results of these metamorphoses even in the worldly spheres. Enough to say that there is an infinite promise ahead of all who are prepared to take their emotions and intelligence in hand, and discipline these forces for a larger harvest than is the common lot at present.

An excellent habit to acquire is the noting down of all thoughts or visualisations which the student has found to be productive of feelings of genuine elation. As far as possible, these episodes should be united into a consistent scheme which will afford meditations for the whole day. Seclusion, although preferable is not essential for these silent bird's-eye views of the magnetic powers of the spirit. They can be carried out in office, warehouse and school. They can even hold their own against a background of noise, confusion and apparent absorption in the business of the market-place; for they belong to a realm of realities which is not lightly set aside.

The present writer has in hand a compilation of the nature suggested. Meanwhile, any reader who is convinced of the necessity for a course of constructive " prayer " cannot do better than study what is perhaps up to the present the major work of this kind in Europe, the *Spiritual Exercises* of Ignatius Loyola. Whatever his religious opinions may be, he will be forced to admit that here is a psychological masterpiece of great efficacy for the training of the higher senses. It has an admirable concrete quality which is the birthright of the Spanish genius at its best, and the episodes are knit together and contrasted in a manner worthy of a great tactician in the sphere of mental and emotional mechanics. Another manual of less excellence but nevertheless of marked psychological value, is the *Meditations* of Molinos, another Spaniard very cultivated in devotional mysticism. It is hardly necessary to mention *The Imitation of Christ*, of Thomas à Kempis, a well-known recipe-book for the cultivation of moral serenity.

The Hour-Books of the Church are also rich in hints for a systematic cleansing of the mind in the waters of exaltation. It is obvious, from what has been said before in the course of this book, that a religion which gives prominence to the figure of a Mother is enormously superior to one which wilfully neglects the source of its justification. The Mother principle is the principle of those creative forces which lift up the little barques of our safety to the crests of an ecstasy which in hours of sorrow or of joy never fails to grant a tremendously heightened vigour to our senses. To reach a state in which " every sensation counts double, and every act of the mind is a lover's embrace "—this is one of the chief functions of the yogic discipline.

In Tibet there are many breviaries of the type discussed; but as these have never been translated into any European language it would be idle to recommend them for Western consumption. But some idea of the general lay-out of this type of literature may be conveyed by a short description of a mental " service of recollection " corresponding in some sort to a Mass. The severe formalism of the " imaginings " should be closely noted. There is nothing woolly or spasmodic in this psychic architecture; all is marshalled in a decorous progression, and there is climax and anticlimax in the right place and time. The best known of these is that devoted to the goddress Tara; and, as this divinity stands for all that is sweet and desirable in human aspiration, it will not be out of place to close this study of a rational religion with strains whose interpretation cannot be misunderstood.

Great benefit is said to come from this office. By reciting it with the correct attitude of mind, all realisable wealth and good fortune will be one's lot in this earth; all faults will be straightway blotted out, and a beneficent power will fall into one's hands so that one can dispense good cheer on all who come into one's life. Evil spirits can be subdued by its performance, and furthermore, " the souls in Purgatory," the old unhappy ghosts who wander disconsolate about the purlieus of the underworld, can be redeemed from their fate and reborn again in the heavens by one whose aim is diligently set on this act of mercy.

All these handsome promises may not be fulfilled immediately; nevertheless there is no harm in trying; and there is enough æsthetic and spiritual beauty in the worship of Tara to fill a month of Sundays.

There are, generally speaking, seven stages in these sacrificial rites. They are as follows: Invocation, Invitation to the Deity to be seated, Presentation of Offerings, such as water, flowers, incense, lamps, music, rice and ceremonial cakes; Hymns of Praise and Jubilation; Repetition of certain set *mantras* (Words of Power); Prayers for Benefits past and to come, and, finally a Benediction which is a sort of coda to the whole celebration.

The worship of the Mother of the Tathagatas is written for the most part in a verse-measure consisting of eight-syllabled lines, and prefaced by a prose passage of extreme beauty. Here is a literal translation. " If we worship this sublime and pure-souled goddess when we retire in the dusk or arise in the morning, then all our fears and worldly anxieties will disappear, and our errors be seen. She—the conqueror of myriad hosts—will strengthen us. She will do more than this! She will convey us directly to the end of our transmigration—to Buddha and Nirvana.

" She will expel the direst poison and relieve us from all anxiety as to food and drink and all our wants will be fulfilled; all devils and plagues will be annihilated utterly. The burden of all animals will be lightened. If you chant her hymn two or three or six or seven times your desire for a son will be satisfied. Should you wish wealth you will obtain it; all other wishes will be gratified and every sort of demon will be wholly overcome."

The Invocation is, as the word implies, a call on the goddess to make herself manifest to men. It should be remembered that the Tibetans believe that there is a special kind of intonation which causes deities, whether disposed or not, to appear when required. The technique of this subtle form of chanting is one of the most closely guarded secrets of the priesthood. But the student need not bother about these niceties: it is enough that he endeavour to absorb into his system the saving strains of the devotion behind the devotion:

" Hail, O happy Tara
The Saviour of all Beings,
Descend, we pray thee, from thy Heavenly dwelling at
Potala. . . . "

And, after She has graciously consented to reveal Herself to Her suppliants, comes the Presentation of Offerings:

" We hail Thee, O revered and peerless Tara
  Who art adored by all the Kings and Princes
  Of the Ten Directions, and of the present, past and future.
  We pray Thee to accept from us these offerings
  Of precious food, the music of cymbals.
  On confessing to Thee knowledge of their sins
  The most sinful hearts, yea! even the indulgers of the
  Ten vices and the three boundless sins
  Will obtain forgiveness, and reach
  Perfection of mind—through Thee! "

The resemblance between Yogic ceremonies and those to which some of us are more accustomed will be clearly seen if we look for a moment at the *Eucharist* of the Lamas which is as endemic among Tibetans as the sacrifice of the Mass among Catholics. But there are also marked divergencies. The chief of these is the concentration on the symbols of Life rather than on those of Death, and the more spacious canvas involved.

This elaborate ceremony is consecrated to Amitayus—" The God of Infinite Life." It consists, like other invocative rites, of a series of graded observances each of which is bound inseparably to that which precedes and that which follows it. We are taken through Introit, Kyrie, Canon, Sanctus and Dismissal after the manner of the European ceremony; but the emotional colouring and the mental outlook are very different. Here it is immediate profit which is insisted upon—the present as well as eternal benefits which will accrue from the participation in the Service. As Swinburne might have put it in his more Bacchanalian moods, it is the God of Life who figures so largely in this worship, not the God of Death.

The climax of the scheme, the Invoking of the Principle of Life which occurs in the middle of the service, is symptomatic of the spirit which illuminates the whole. " Pagan," it may be said; but a paganism which recognises that we are put on this earth to realise our lives as well as to mortify them.

The priest who officiates at the *Eucharist* must take his honour very seriously. For twenty-four hours before its commencement he fasts from all food and drink and cultivates his soul in solitude. His equipment includes many kinds of elaborate vestments which are assumed and changed with no mere æsthetic purpose, but to signify the subtle fluctuations of religious emotion and the swirlings of various kinds of psychic force. Too often it is forgotten by dabblers in ecclesiastical liturgy that any gorgeousness and brilliance that may be attached to these interests is no adventitious decoration but an integral part of the design. We need another Gabriel Fortescue, with even more industry and devotion than that most accomplished scholar, to lead us through the mazes of the " properties " of a ceremony unequalled for drama and dignity.

Apart from the officiating priest and his assistants, there are other important protagonists in the drama of the *Eucharist*. These are the communicants who kneel at the rails to receive the sacred pills which are the means by which the deity bestows the gift of his body and blood to the faithful. Having partaken of the same, they go away fully assured that they will enjoy better health and longer life. And, as in this world the things we devoutly hope and believe come true, it is highly probable that their wishes are in fact gratified. What is religion in the last resort but the aspiration to a fuller, richer and happier life ?

On this note we will conclude our account of the actualities of Tibetan worship; and in case the reader should still harbour doubts as to the purpose of all that has gone before we will clear up a few points and restate a few propositions.

Again and again we have employed similes from the electrical sciences to designate spiritual realities. This has not been done out of any desire to startle, but from a profound conviction that spiritual problems are best envisaged and interpreted by recourse to facts we can see and know.

To the fair-minded inquiring scientist nothing is more evident in this year of grace and enlightenment than the extension of consciousness, experienced, and perhaps communicated, by the mystics. This is being verified in an ever-more definite manner by what may be called the methods of an enlightened rule of thumb. There has been much excuse for the materialistic scepticism of scientists in the past. They have rightly been dubious about the claims of alleged " mystics " who have had little to recommend them except the originality of their personalities and the colourful individuality of their lives. But the men who, fifty years ago, would have shrugged their shoulders and passed on, are now avidly searching for " more light."

The real turn of the tide came perhaps with the discovery of the electrical constituents of matter. When it is recognised that the world we all inhabit in made up, not of units which are as dead as the raisins in last year's Christmas pudding, but of units of energy which can combine and recombine in as many forms as the most spacious imagination can figure, the road is opened up to an outlook on the principles of religion which is at once "reactionary" (in the sense that it goes back to possibly despised ceremonial conventions and sees that there is much virtue in them after all), and infinitely experimental and progressive. There is certainly no reason to assume that our ancestors were completely fools because they did not fully realise the logical basis for what they accepted on the grounds of faith. There is nothing hostile to development, personal or social, in the fact that we make use of the best in the past as well as take all possible measures to ensure the sanity of the future.

It may strike some reader as odd that we have had to go to the wilds of Tibet to find instances of truths which this century is gradually coming to regard as self-evident. But things happen this way. With all our worldly wisdom we have not taken sufficient precautions to ensure that our perception of ultimate truth should be as trustworthy as our sense of the lower kinds of self-preservation. In the East they have entered farther into the strongholds of the spirit, mainly because they have taken the trouble to observe where the intellect begins and the emotions leave off. There is no objection to the free use of the emotions; they are the sweeteners of life and the civilisers of human existence. But they must not be mingled indiscriminately with the processes of the mind after the manner of a badly mixed cocktail; they must be viewed as ingredients in the summoning of a recreative power. For the enduring of the religious sense at its loftiest and most intense nothing is more essential than control. And the beginnings of this control must be founded in a wise virtue which has learned to cultivate a healthy scepticism, and to pass beyond this scepticism to a realisation of the nature of that radiant energy which promises an incalculable number of inner worlds, each with its own ultimately observable laws and inter-reactions.

In that excellent novel *Lost Horizon* Mr. James Hilton has suggested that when our Western world is shattered, there will still be a haven of refuge for the cultured and the sensitive in the gardens of the monastery of Shrangrilar. We may be permitted to hope that circumstances will not compel us to pack our bags and betake us in our harassed physical forms to a region so far from everything that savours of our harmless comforts and necessary joys. There *could* be worse fates; but we will not insist on this extremity !

Nevertheless we would remind the reader that the astral travelling so beloved of Victorian occultists is always possible; and cheaper, in more ways than one, for those who have the intelligence to realise what food and drink are necessary for the full realisation of their natures. Magnanimity in conjecture, as in politics, is not seldom the best policy, and this book will not have failed of its purpose if it has drawn some attention to the fountain-head of all that men in their best moments think and feel. *Faire rêver quelques nobles âmes*, in Flaubert's fine phrase may be to light a lamp which all the dreary wiles of the cynics and the nay-sayers will find it impossible wholly to extinguish. Never has it been more necessary to recall man to his own nobility than in this age which dins with the cries of false prophets loudly proclaiming the efficacy of false nostrums. The best protection against the danger of giving too ready an ear to these dangerous guides is the realisation that the essence of the good life is not agitation, but peace and the joy that comes from peace.

INDEX